UNNATURAL NARRATOLOGY

THEORY AND INTERPRETATION OF NARRATIVE
James Phelan, Peter J. Rabinowitz, and Katra Byram, Series Editors

UNNATURAL NARRATOLOGY

EXTENSIONS, REVISIONS, AND CHALLENGES

EDITED BY

Jan Alber

AND

Brian Richardson

THE OHIO STATE UNIVERSITY PRESS
COLUMBUS

Names: Alber, Jan, 1973– editor. | Richardson, Brian, 1953– editor.
Title: Unnatural narratology : extensions, revisions, and challenges / edited by Jan Alber and Brian Richardson.
Other titles: Theory and interpretation of narrative series.
Description: Columbus : The Ohio State University Press, [2020] | Series: Theory and interpretation of narrative | Includes bibliographical references and index. | Summary: "Puts unnatural narratology into dialogue with feminism, affect theory, cultural studies, postcolonialism, and graphic and performed narratives, and offers both extensions and revisions of the movement"—Provided by publisher.
Identifiers: LCCN 2019034783 | ISBN 9780814214190 (hardcover) | ISBN 0814214193 (hardcover) | ISBN 9780814277539 (ebook) | ISBN 0814277535 (ebook)
Subjects: LCSH: Narration (Rhetoric) | Fiction—History and criticism—Theory, etc. | Literature—History and criticism—Theory, etc. | Feminism and literature. | Postcolonialism in literature.
Classification: LCC PN212 .U66 2020 | DDC 808/.036—dc23
LC record available at https://lccn.loc.gov/2019034783

Other identifiers: ISBN 9780814255643 (paper) | ISBN 0814255647 (paper)

Cover design by Laurence J. Nozik
Text design by Juliet Williams
Type set in Adobe Minion Pro

CONTENTS

List of Illustrations   vii

Acknowledgments   ix

INTRODUCTION
     JAN ALBER AND BRIAN RICHARDSON   1

CHAPTER 1   (Un)Natural Connections: Feminist Experimentation and Unnatural Narration in *Nights at the Circus*
     CATHERINE ROMAGNOLO   13

CHAPTER 2   *Anima* by Wajdi Mouawad: Unnatural or Naturalized?
     SYLVIE PATRON   31

CHAPTER 3   Unnatural Narrative in a Postcolonial Context: Impossibilities in Aboriginal Australian Fiction
     DOROTHEE KLEIN   53

CHAPTER 4   Empathy the Long Way 'Round: Unnatural Autographic Narration
     CHRISTOPHER D. KILGORE   69

CHAPTER 5	Metalepsis and Emotion in Unnatural Stories	
	DANIEL PUNDAY	99
CHAPTER 6	The (Un)Natural Response: Reading Walter Abish's *Alphabetical Africa*	
	ROY SOMMER	115
CHAPTER 7	Transcending Humanistic and Cognitive Models: Unnatural Characters in Fiction, Drama, and Popular Culture	
	BRIAN RICHARDSON	135
CHAPTER 8	(Un)Natural Temporalities in Graphic Narratives	
	RAPHAËL BARONI	165
CHAPTER 9	The Unnatural Conventions of the Interactive Gamebook	
	PAUL WAKE	189
AFTERWORD		
	JAN ALBER AND BRIAN RICHARDSON	209
Contributors		221
Index		225

ILLUSTRATIONS

FIGURE 4.1	Mouse-people (Spiegelman 1: 5)	74
FIGURE 4.2	A panel from "Prisoner on the Hell Planet!" (Spiegelman 1: 102)	76
FIGURE 4.3	"Art" as a mouse-masked human (Spiegelman 2: 41)	78
FIGURE 4.4	Narrative levels in *Maus*	78
FIGURE 4.5	First mention of Bruce's death (Bechdel, *Fun Home* 23)	82
FIGURE 4.6	The first scene illustrating Bruce's death (Bechdel, *Fun Home* 28)	83
FIGURE 4.7	Scene depicting a counterfactual event (Bechdel, *Fun Home* 59)	84
FIGURE 4.8	Third scene depicting Bruce's death (Bechdel, *Fun Home* 89)	84
FIGURE 4.9	Fourth scene depicting Bruce's death (Bechdel, *Fun Home* 116)	85
FIGURE 4.10	Helen Bechdel declining to kiss Alison good-night (Bechdel, *AYMM* 136)	88
FIGURE 4.11	Realization of parallel events (Bechdel, *AYMM* 144)	89
FIGURE 4.12	Alison and the (real) telephone (Bechdel, *AYMM* 229)	91

FIGURE 4.13	Alison and the (reconstruction) telephone (Bechdel, *AYMM* 233)	92
FIGURE 8.1	Pascal Jousselin (2014). © Pascal Jousselin. Reproduced with kind permission of the author.	168
FIGURE 8.2	Hergé, *On a marché sur la lune* (1954). © Hergé/Moulinsart 2019.	169
FIGURE 8.3	Winsor McCay, *Little Nemo in Slumberland* (October 29, 1905)	171
FIGURE 8.4	Marc-Antoine Mathieu, *L'origine* (1990). © Delcourt, 1990.	174
FIGURE 8.5	Alan Moore and Dave Gibbon, *Watchmen* (1986). © DC Comics, courtesy of DC Comics.	180

ACKNOWLEDGMENTS

THE EDITORS would like to thank James Phelan, Peter Rabinowitz, and the anonymous reader for their extensive and perceptive comments on the manuscript. Our gratitude also extends to Ana Maria Jimenez-Moreno for expertly guiding this collection to the finish line. Finally, we would like to thank Jessica Jumpertz, Jacqueline Nellißen, Karoline Rauschen, and Wiebke Tary for editorial assistance and help with the proofreading.

INTRODUCTION

JAN ALBER AND BRIAN RICHARDSON

OVER THE LAST DECADE, unnatural narratology has developed into an important and productive new paradigm in narrative theory. By focusing on antimimetic narratives and techniques and identifying antirealistic and impossible features of fictional narration, it has brought into narrative studies a new world of texts and created a number of novel analytical categories to describe both their workings and potential ways of approaching them, such as new models of narrators, characters, temporalities, and spatial settings; a fresh perspective on blends; and a number of innovative reading strategies.[1] It has also provided a new way of looking at more familiar narratives, such as omniscient narration or other texts that use zero focalization (see Alber, "Pre-Postmodernist"; Nielsen), and is now being used in relation to an ever-increasing number of genres and narrative media.

A brief history of the areas examined by unnatural narratology will help clarify this evolution. For the most part, unnatural narrative theory began as a set of concepts that were necessary to circumscribe the achievements of postmodern fiction. Early on, it became clear that certain Shandean narratives and many hyperfictions were cases that benefitted substantially from

---

1. On aspects and elements of narrative, see Richardson, *Unnatural Narrative*; Alber, *Unnatural Narrative*; and Alber et al. On unnatural (or impossible) blends, see Alber, *Unnatural Narrative* 48–49. On reading strategies, see Alber, *Unnatural Narrative* 47–57; Richardson, *Unnatural Narrative* 44–47; Mäkelä; and Nielsen.

analyses that drew on the unnatural model. The publication of Brian Richardson's *Unnatural Narrative: Theory, History, and Practice* (2015) and Jan Alber's *Unnatural Narrative: Impossible Worlds in Fiction and Drama* (2016) brought new areas into unnatural studies, especially drama, the historical avant garde, and several periods of literary history extending back to medieval (Alber) and classical Greek and Sanskrit (Richardson) narratives.

Unnatural narrative theory is now widely employed by younger scholars for investigations into unusual forms of narration and for postmodernist fiction (see, for example, Wiese). Other applications are also growing. As evidenced by several of the essays in this volume, original work is emerging that examines the unnatural in new areas and in a wide range of genres and media. Among recent developments, there is a strong interest in the application of the theory to feminist and queer texts as well as postcolonial narratives. Comics and graphic fiction have proven to be especially rich for unnatural analyses; the same is true of film, television, and digital studies. Dialogues with other critical approaches (such as reception theory and empathy studies) are appearing, and investigations into cognitive studies are animating both cognitive and unnatural approaches to narratology.[2] The essays collected here are designed to expand, clarify, revise, and assess the current state of unnatural narratology. The contributions are followed by an afterword in which Alber and Richardson respond to the individual issues raised by the authors.

As a new poetics, it should go without saying that unnatural narratology is a dynamic model that is still being created and refined. It never was a perfectly homogenous movement where all the scholars involved did the same thing; unnatural narratology never desired or attempted to be a rigorously unified approach. We all define our terms in slightly different ways and the terrain each covers varies somewhat. Generally speaking, we are quite content with this state of things, knowing that, in the end, the most effective conceptions will win out. We will now move on to identify some of these definitions. In the following section, we define unnatural narratives, examine possible responses to the unnatural and unnatural narratology, and we will also respond to points of criticism that have so far been leveled.

There is in fact substantial agreement among theorists of the unnatural concerning which texts include unnatural elements; different individuals,

---

2. Three recent journal special issues testify to the spread of unnatural narrative theory. The Winter 2016 issue of *Storyworlds* (8.2) has four essays on feminist fiction and unnatural narratology; the March–June 2018 issue of *Poetics Today* (39.1–2) is devoted to dialogues between unnatural and cognitive narratology; and the Spring 2018 issue of *Frontiers of Narrative Studies* (4.1) focuses on unnatural narrative theory and contains articles on extreme forms of narration by women and minority authors and studies of film, games, and practical narratology from an unnatural perspective (see Richardson, "Recent Work").

however, prefer to articulate the subject in differing formulations. For Alber, for instance, the term *unnatural* denotes "physically, logically, or humanly impossible scenarios and events" (*Unnatural Narrative* 25; see also "Gaping"), regardless of whether they have already been conventionalized in the context of generic conventions or not. From this perspective, speaking animals in beast fables or flying magicians in fantasy narratives are as unnatural as the many striking impossibilities of postmodernism (such as dead narrators, characters that transform into different ones, retrogressive timelines, and settings that change their shapes).

Richardson, for his part, states that events, characters, settings, or frames are unnatural insofar as they are antimimetic, that is, representations that contravene the presuppositions of nonfictional narratives and violate the practices of realism (*Unnatural Narrative* 3–5). Richardson distinguishes between what he calls the *antimimetic* (i.e., the properly unnatural), the *nonmimetic* (or conventional nonrealist), and the *mimetic* (or realist), thus basing his definition of the unnatural on the transgressive features of works that parody mimetic practices. Thus, a fictional world with a similar canon of probability to the actual world is mimetic in this aspect, a supernatural world based on familiar notions of destiny or providence is nonmimetic, and a world in which past events can be altered or erased is antimimetic or unnatural.

It should be pointed out that Richardson no longer insists that unnatural narrative elements must also defy the conventions and expectations of existing, established genres; such an effect is a feature of reception, not the storyworld. We may usefully compare this to the practice of parody: A parody does not cease to be a parody just because it is repeated, conventionalized, or even clichéd—it remains a parody, albeit a stale one. Unnatural elements are the same; thus, they do not lose their unnaturalness—antinomic temporal progressions in which a character moves forward into the past and causality is inverted will always be obviously impossible and therefore unnatural. Such events can even partially constitute their own conventions. Something like this has happened to the theater of the absurd and is happening with postmodern fiction. This revised position also constitutes another divergence with Alber's conception of the unnatural and aligns itself instead with Stefan Iversen's call for an account of "permanent defamiliarization."

Many texts, especially postmodernist ones, flaunt their unnatural features and thereby signal the appropriateness of an unnatural analysis. There are numerous other texts, however, that present themselves as substantially mimetic but, when examined more closely, reveal key passages that violate the preconditions of mimeticism. This is abundantly present in *Don Quixote* and common in *Tom Jones,* a work that is frequently thought of as a foundational text in the realist tradition of the English novel (pace Ian Watt) but is riddled with asides in which the narrator discloses the many ways in which he could have altered the events he is depicting. An unnatural analysis of Fielding shows him to be much closer to Sterne than traditional conceptions normally imagine, and links him up with radical Continental experimenters like Denis Diderot and Jean Paul. An unnatural analysis will appreciate the antimimetic authorial commentaries in the work of Trollope that so annoyed Henry James and will also locate them in other ostensibly realist writers like Austen, Dickens, Thackeray, and Eliot (see Richardson, *Unnatural Narrative* 110–20).[3] Unnatural analyses routinely turn up more antimimetic material than is generally acknowledged by more mimetic-oriented sensibilities.

Other conceptual definitions we will be employing are as follows: For Richardson, a narrative is a representation of a causally related series of events. For Alber, it is a cultural phenomenon that evokes a world that is populated by characters who undergo certain experiences. Furthermore, these experiences are related to events (or event sequences) so that there is also a sense of moving through time. The question of "what it is like" to experience this storyworld-in-flux, finally, takes center stage. Alber believes that a definition in terms of multiple features is advantageous because it allows one to establish different degrees of narrativity. An interesting question in this context is how much unnaturalness a cultural phenomenon may display to still qualify as a narrative. Alber argues that unnatural narratives typically play around with one or two of these features, while the other features conform to realist expectations.

Moreover, we employ the term *realism* as a loose synonym for the mimetic, and define the mimetic in a flexible manner as a set of representational practices that are intended to be perceived as congruent with lived experience. We see nineteenth-century realism as a species of mimetic representation, as are late seventeenth- and eighteenth-century verisimilar (*La Princess de Cleves* [1678]) and pseudo-autobiographical (*Robinson Crusoe* [1719]) narratives. A key criterion for us is whether a work can be reasonably critiqued for being unrealistic: It makes no sense to criticize the fairy tale "Jack and the Beanstalk" (1734, 1807) or Angela Carter's postmodernist *The Infernal Desire Machines of Dr. Hoffman* (1972) for lacking in verisimilitude, since they make

---

3. This is not to deny that the vast majority of the characters, events, and settings of these novels remain mimetic; instead, it is to identify the additional presence of the antimimetic. Likewise, when an author like George Eliot comments on the narrative she is writing, there is no antimimetic rupture: It is only when authors like Fielding or, at times, Trollope indicate that the world they depict is fictional and can be altered if they choose that the mimetic illusion is violated and we have an antimimetic scene in the narrative.

no pretensions to realism. On the other hand, if we were to find characters, events, or settings that cannot exist in the actual world, such as a twenty-foot-tall man or contradictory temporalities in Hardy's Wessex, we would register a failure to adhere to the mimetic canon of probability that governs the work—unless, of course, it is signaled that the novel has in fact a very different, nonmimetic or antimimetic orientation. We may note parenthetically that it is the relative lateness of just this kind of transformation in the novel that so upset many readers of John Fowles's *The French Lieutenant's Woman* (1969) (see also Phelan 83–106).

As far as making sense of the unnatural is concerned, unnatural theorists often employ (and occasionally modify) approaches that build on readers' cognitive architecture. Thus, Alber explains that recipients process unnatural scenarios and events on the basis of cognitive frames, scripts, and principles that are derived from real-world experiences. However, when they are confronted with unnatural scenarios or events, they are invited to conduct seemingly impossible mapping operations to orient themselves within storyworlds that refuse to be organized exclusively by real-world parameters. In such cases, they are urged to blend preexisting frames or scripts and create what Mark Turner calls "impossible blend[s]" (60) to adequately reconstruct the unnatural elements. The unnatural invites recipients to create cognitive frames or scripts that transcend their real-world knowledge (such as that of the talking breast, the dead character, the retrogressive temporality, or the shapeshifting house). Alber argues that once readers have reconstructed the unnatural by creating new frames or scripts, they try to interpret the unnatural element as, say, an exemplification of a specific theme; as part of an allegory that says something about the human condition (as opposed to particular individuals); as a satire that mocks psychological predispositions or states of affairs; as part of a transcendental setting; or as an invitation to create one's own story. Furthermore, his analyses of the unnatural operate on the basis of a double vision involving these reading strategies and what Alber calls "the Zen way of reading," which presupposes a stoic reader who accepts the potentially disconcerting emotional reactions that the unnatural evokes in her or him (Alber, *Unnatural Narrative* 47–57).

Richardson is in substantial agreement with many of these points, and further insists on thematic connections and motivations for unnatural elements in particular works, such as the deformed temporality on the night of the regicide in *Macbeth* (1606) that is, as one of the characters asserts, "unnatural, / Even like the deed that's done" (2.4.10–11; see Richardson, *Unnatural Narrative* 104–10). But Richardson also stresses that he is "content to appreciate unnatural elements on their own terms, simply as violations of mimetic conventions" and observes that "the antimimetic provides its own pleasures" ("Unnatural Narrative Theory" 401). He cautions that the complexity of the unnatural can easily elude "any single or combined set of interpretive frameworks" ("Rejoinders" 507) and cautions against critical reductionism.

It is worth noting here that Henrik Skov Nielsen offers what he calls "unnaturalizing reading strategies." He writes that in unnatural narratives, the reader "can trust as authoritative and reliable what would in real life be impossible, implausible or, at the very least, subject to doubt" (92). For him, the unnatural "cue[s] the reader to interpret in ways that differ from the interpretation of real-world acts of narration and of conversational storytelling" (91). Maria Mäkelä has also produced important insights into the differences between classical and unnatural reading practices in her account of interpreting Robbe-Grillet's *La Jalousie* (1957). The area of reception is a dynamic one that continues to attract new formulations.[4]

Unnatural narratology is, then, the systematic study of unnatural elements in narratives and, at its most capacious, offers new and revised categories of narrative analysis and an expanded model of narrative representation in fiction. Thus, we see as needlessly limiting theories of narration that only acknowledge the mimetic possibilities of first- and third-person or heterodiegetic and homodiegetic narration, since other distinctly fictional forms that cannot be contained within such a framework require a more expansive theoretical formulation. We similarly reject simple, mimetically grounded approaches to possible worlds and to the *fabula/syuzhet* distinction which then cannot encompass the impossible fictional worlds of Beckett, Borges, Calvino, and others or the circular, multiple, contradictory, or denarrated *fabulas* of contemporary fiction (see Alber, *Unnatural Narrative* 29–34; Richardson, *Unnatural Narrative* 28–46).

Our narratological conception posits a dual, interactive model of mimesis and antimimesis: Without the latter, we have a seriously incomplete, primarily mimetic theory. By definition, a purely mimetic model cannot comprehend antimimetic works that violate the rules of mimetic representation. To comprehend unnatural narratives, we need a second, additional poetics. We do not offer an alternative paradigm so much as an additional, complementary one; thus, we are interested in supplementing existing models rather than replacing them. We work toward a binocular vision and a dialectical poetics, one that is able to address fiction as fiction, as well as pretended nonfiction. Above all, we strive for a more comprehensive poetics.

---

4. Kang Mengni from Nanyang Technological University (Singapore) is currently working on a PhD thesis (partly supervised by Alber) in which she develops a reading model that takes Nielsen's unnaturalizing reading strategies as its starting point.

Not surprisingly, unnatural narrative theory has been critiqued by scholars from a number of perspectives. Some are skeptical of its innovativeness or the underlying understanding of mimesis. Tobias Klauk and Tilmann Köppe, for instance, have expressed doubts that unnatural narratology constitutes a new type of narratology. They claim that unnatural narratologists "do not name a single concrete narratological concept that is allegedly [sic] challenged" (94). By contrast, we argue that we have provided several, including numerous types of unnatural narrators (Richardson, *Unnatural Voices*; Alber, *Unnatural Narrative* 61–103), unnatural characters (Alber, *Unnatural Narrative* 104–48), impossible sequences of events, and contradictory settings (Alber, *Unnatural Narrative* 149–214; see also Richardson, *Unnatural Narrative* 51–66 and *A Poetics of Plot*). We also examine the frames and scripts that we need to conceptualize these phenomena, and we note how they affect our understanding of what a narrator, a character, a temporality, or a setting in a fictional narrative is or can be. Unless we are very much mistaken, these phenomena have not been discussed in such a systematic manner before.

The case of temporality is particularly illuminating in this context. Richardson has identified six types of temporal construction that are impossible in the real world and are not discussed in conventional narratology that limits itself to structuralist categories of order, duration, and frequency. He has gone on to construct an unnatural model to articulate these impossible kinds of temporality (Richardson, "Beyond Story and Discourse"; *A Poetics of Plot* 99–119; see also his *A Poetics of Plot* 99–125 for a revised version of this essay). The paradigm shift that we call for focuses on both extending the kinds of texts we theorize and constructing new or emended models to embrace them. We also freely grant that unnatural narratology is not entirely unprecedented because it is inspired by and builds on the important studies of theorists such as Viktor Shklovsky, Mikhail Bakhtin, Christine Brooke-Rose, Monika Fludernik, Brian McHale, James Phelan, and Werner Wolf (among many others).

Other commentators raise different issues. Bo Pettersson and Monika Fludernik ("How Natural") feel that unnatural narratology needs to clarify its relationship to mimesis and the mimetic. It might be helpful to briefly relate the unnatural to the two conceptions of mimesis as they were developed by Plato and Aristotle. In Book X of Plato's *Republic*, Socrates equates mimetic art with "the art of imitation" (Plato 431, 595A; see also 439, 600C and 443, 601B). According to Socrates, art merely reproduces empirical reality as we know it and is illusory because it does not take us to the transcendental World of Ideas, where we can grasp the essence of all entities. By contrast, in his *Poetics*, Aristotle equates mimesis with the process of representation, projection, or simulation (Aristotle 33–37, 1448a-b). For him, "mimesis coincides with artistic representation as such: epic poetry, drama, the art of dithyrambs, of flute and lyre, painting, choreography, and religious poetry are all mimetic" (Schaeffer and Vultur 309).[5] The unnatural is of course only antimimetic in Plato's sense because it does not try to imitate or reproduce the world as we know it. However, the unnatural is quite obviously mimetic in the sense of Aristotle because impossibilities can be represented in the world of fiction.[6]

For Alber, the term *unnatural* comprises two types of impossibilities. More specifically, the term denotes physically, logically, or humanly impossible phenomena that have not yet been conventionalized—that is, turned into a basic cognitive category—and therefore still strike us as odd, strange, and disconcerting. Second, the term also refers to physical, logical, or human impossibilities that have already been conventionalized and have thus become familiar conventions for narrative representation. Most of the unnatural elements of postmodernism fall into the first category: They have not yet been conventionalized and are still defamiliarizing, or perhaps we are currently in the process of conventionalizing them (see below). Examples of unnatural elements that have become literary conventions include the speaking animals in beast fables and children's stories, the magic in romances and fantasy narratives, the speaking objects in eighteenth-century circulation novels, the omniscient narrator, the impossible renderings of character interiority in modernist fiction, and the impossibilities in science fiction. Such instances of the unnatural do not strike us as being defamiliarizing; rather, we see them as elements of the overall aesthetic illusion tied to a specific genre.[7] In comparison with earlier narratives, postmodernist texts acquire their specificity through the concentration and radicalization of unnaturalness. However, it is worth noting that

---

5. Aristotle also argues that the poet needs to follow the laws of probability and necessity; if a poet introduces an impossibility, he or she is guilty of an error. Nevertheless, it is fair to say that compared to Plato, Aristotle foregrounds the world-creating (rather than the world-reflecting) dimensions of mimesis.

6. The unnatural is also mimetic in the sense of Kendall L. Walton's game of make-believe. As he puts it, fictional worlds make certain propositions fictional. For example, "it is fictional that there is a society of six-inch-tall people called Lilliputians [in Swift's *Gulliver's Travels* (1726, 1735)], and also that a certain Gregor Samsa was transformed into an insect [in Kafka's "Metamorphosis" (1915)]" (Walton 35). Walton here illustrates nicely that the propositions that are made fictional may also move beyond real-world possibilities and thus involve the unnatural.

7. In these cases, we can account for the unnatural element by identifying it as belonging to a literary genre, that is, a suitable discourse context within which the anomaly (or impossibility) can be embedded. For a discussion of how earlier (medieval and eighteenth-century) readers dealt with magic, see Alber, *Unnatural Narrative* 40–41.

the unnatural scenarios and events of postmodernism are not brand-new phenomena, and also that we are currently in the process of conventionalizing postmodernism. Sooner or later, readers will be familiar with the unnatural games of postmodernist narratives.

Another important issue that has arisen is the question of cultural relativity. If we define the unnatural as the representation of physically or logically impossible events, who is to determine what is possible and impossible, since these terms change over time and across cultures? Many things that we in the West no longer believe to be possible are widely affirmed to be possible by other cultures. Why should we assume that scientific standards are the only arbiters of the possible? Richardson's response is that when he refers to an action or event as unnatural, he generally means it is impossible according to the laws of physics or the axioms of logic. The fundamental laws of physics do not change over time, and they are the same all over the world. That's why they are laws of physics. If it is objected that our knowledge of the laws of physics changes over time, we agree but point out that the kinds of violations of those laws that we call unnatural are not borderline cases but almost always operate at a level that is obvious. A strong wind cannot blow a ship to the moon, as it does in Lucian's *A True Story,* nor can a dung beetle, even a large one, carry a man to heaven, as it does in Aristophanes's *The Peace*. It doesn't matter whether one draws on Einsteinian, Newtonian, or Aristotelian conceptions of gravity—these events will be impossible in every case. The axioms of logic are similarly universal: The law of the excluded middle similarly does not—and cannot—change over time or across cultures. A man cannot die once and for all in 1967 and die again in 2018.

Alber, for his part, posits a historically constant notion of the unnatural that contradicts the known laws governing the physical world, accepted principles of logic (such as the principle of noncontradiction), or standard human limitations of knowledge and ability. In other words, he assumes that, say, speaking breasts, talking corpses, retrogressive temporalities, or flying islands are impossible all over the world and across time. The only presupposition for the identification of the unnatural is that the recipient believes in these laws, principles, and limitations. Alber therefore emphasizes that in his readings, he assumes

> the position of a contemporary and neurotypical reader who has a rationalist-scientific and empirically minded worldview. From the perspective of such a reader, it makes perfect sense to measure the fictional narratives of different literary periods against the foil of our real-world knowledge and

to address the question of why literary texts so frequently disregard or transcend it. (*Unnatural Narrative* 38)

Others have expressed disapproval of the idea of impossible fictional worlds. David Herman, for instance, claims that many unnatural narratives are "purposefully designed to thwart the worldmaking process" (Herman et al. 233). We agree that unnatural texts often involve lower degrees of narrativity than more prototypical narratives, but we would also like to highlight that for us, impossible worlds are clearly present in fiction: They can of course be represented. Martin Amis's *Time's Arrow* (1991) would be an example (because in the represented world, time moves backward), or *The Infernal Desire Machines of Doctor Hoffman* (because the setting continuously transforms itself). In this respect, we follow the possible-worlds theorist Marie-Laure Ryan, who has recently explored and clarified several aspects of this subject in her article, "Impossible Worlds."

Various commentators have responded to the term *unnatural narratology*. Some admire it, some object to it, a few misunderstand it, and others, like Catherine Romagnolo in chapter 1, tease out and braid together popular and technical senses of the term. We can affirm that we agreed upon the provocative term with varying degrees of enthusiasm, and we use it to refer to the systematic analysis of "antimimetic" or "physically, logically, or humanly impossible" phenomena in fictional narratives. We assert that our usage of the term *unnatural* has no connection to any practices regarded as deviant or perverse by any society. We also wish to clarify that an unnatural narrative is not diametrically opposed to a natural narrative. The opposite of a natural (i.e., spontaneously occurring oral) narrative in the sense of Labov is a carefully composed and written story. The opposite of an unnatural narrative is a mimetic (or realist) one (such as, say, Defoe's *Robinson Crusoe*).[8]

This volume is intended to complement and extend the work done in our earlier anthology, *A Poetics of Unnatural Narrative* (2013, co-edited with Henrik Skov Nielsen). It covers hitherto unexplored territory and explores different subjects, some of which were made possible—if not, in fact, inescapable—by the earlier work in the field. This is particularly evident in the development of feminist and postcolonial poetics, which now seem essential aspects of unnatural narrative studies. The same may be said of non-Western literature and popular culture. Specifically, the essays collected here put unnat-

---

8. Thus, unnatural narratives are opposed to conversational (natural) narratives only insofar as they resemble nonfiction, but an antimimetic "tall tale" or nonsense rhyme is, by our definitions, unnatural. See also the discussions in Richardson (*Unnatural Narrative* 22–23) and Alber (*Unnatural Narrative* 16).

ural narratology into dialogue with feminism, affect studies, cultural difference, postcolonialism, empathy, the affordances of graphic narratives, and those of the game book. Unnatural narratives are everywhere, waiting to be investigated from this expansive theoretical perspective.

In addition to exploring the unnatural's relation to these various issues and to other critical approaches, each contributor engages in a dialogue with previous work in unnatural narratology. Those dialogues lead to a range of proposals for revising, extending, or challenging that previous work. In light of those engagements with previous theory, we have decided to deviate from the standard format of offering summaries of each contribution in this introduction. Instead, we will let the contributors make their cases and then respond in an afterword that continues the dialogue with each contributor, beginning with our summary of that contributor's project.

WORKS CITED

Alber, Jan. "Gaping before Monumental Unnatural Inscriptions? The Necessity of a Cognitive Approach." *Style*, vol. 50, no. 4, 2016, pp. 434–41.

——. "Pre-Postmodernist Manifestations of the Unnatural: Instances of Expanded Consciousness in 'Omniscient' Narration and Reflector-Mode Narratives." *Zeitschrift für Anglistik und Amerikanistik*, vol. 61, no. 2, 2013, pp. 137–53.

——. *Unnatural Narrative: Impossible Worlds in Fiction and Drama*. U of Nebraska P, 2016.

Alber, Jan, et al. "Unnatural Narratives, Unnatural Narratology: Beyond Mimetic Models." *Narrative*, vol. 18, no. 2, 2010, pp. 113–36.

Aristotle. *Poetics*. Edited and translated by Stephen Halliwell, Harvard UP, 1995.

Fludernik, Monika. "How Natural Is 'Unnatural Narratology'; or, What Is Unnatural about Unnatural Narratology?" *Narrative*, vol. 20, no. 3, 2012, pp. 357–70.

Herman, David, et al. *Narrative Theory: Core Concepts and Critical Debates*. The Ohio State UP, 2012.

Iversen, Stefan. "Permanent Defamiliarization as Rhetorical Device; or, How to Let Puppymonkeybaby into Unnatural Narratology." *Style*, vol. 50, no. 4, 2016, pp. 455–62.

Klauk, Tobias, and Tilmann Köppe. "Reassessing Unnatural Narratology: Problems and Prospects." *Storyworlds*, vol. 5, 2013, pp. 77–100.

Mäkelä, Maria. "Navigating—Making Sense—Interpreting (The Reader behind *La Jalousie*)." *Narrative Interrupted: The Plotless, the Disturbing and the Trivial in Literature*, edited by Markku Lahtimäki et al., De Gruyter, 2012, pp. 139–52.

Nielsen, Henrik Skov. "Naturalizing and Unnaturalizing Reading Strategies: Focalization Revisited." *A Poetics of Unnatural Narrative*, edited by Jan Alber et al., The Ohio State UP, 2013, pp. 67–93.

Pettersson, Bo. "Beyond Anti-Mimetic Models: A Critique of Unnatural Narratology." *Rethinking Mimesis: Concepts and Practices of Literary Representation*, edited by S. Isomaa et al., Cambridge Scholars Publishing, 2012, pp. 73–92.

Phelan, James. *Reading People, Reading Plots: Character, Progression, and the Interpretation of Narrative*. U of Chicago P, 1989.

Plato. *Plato in Twelve Volumes: The Republic II Books VI–X*. Edited and translated by Paul Shorey, Harvard UP, 1970.

Richardson, Brian. "Beyond Story and Discourse: Narrative Time in Postmodern and Nonmimetic Fiction." *Narrative Dynamics: Essays on Time, Plot, Closure, and Frames*, edited by Brian Richardson, The Ohio State UP, 2002, pp. 47–63.

———. *A Poetics of Plot for the Twenty-first Century: Theorizing Unruly Narratives*, The Ohio State UP, 2019.

———. "Recent Work in Unnatural Narrative Studies," *Word and Text*, forthcoming.

———. "Rejoinders to the Respondents." *Style*, vol. 50, no. 4, 2016, pp. 492–513.

———. "Unnatural Narrative Theory." *Style*, vol. 50, no. 4, 2016, pp. 385–405.

———. *Unnatural Narrative: Theory, History, and Practice*. The Ohio State UP, 2015.

———. *Unnatural Voices: Extreme Narration in Modern and Contemporary Fiction*. The Ohio State UP, 2006.

Ryan, Marie-Laure. "Impossible Worlds." *The Routledge Companion to Experimental Literature*, edited by Joe Bray et al., Routledge, 2012, pp. 368–79.

Schaeffer, Jean-Marie, and Ioana Vultur. "Mimesis." *Routledge Encyclopedia of Narrative Theory*, edited by David Herman et al., Routledge, 2005, pp. 309–10.

Shakespeare, William. *The Complete Works of Shakespeare*. 5th ed., edited by David Bevington, Pearson Longman, 2004.

Turner, Mark. *The Literary Mind*. Oxford UP, 1996.

Walton, Kendall L. *Mimesis as Make-Believe: On the Foundations of the Representational Arts*. Harvard UP, 1990.

Wiese, Annjeanette. "Who Says? Problematic Narration in Paul Auster's *City of Glass*." *Frontiers of Narrative Studies*, vol. 3, no. 2, 2017, pp. 304–18.

CHAPTER 1

(Un)Natural Connections

Feminist Experimentation and Unnatural Narration in Nights at the Circus

CATHERINE ROMAGNOLO

TWENTIETH-CENTURY FEMINIST WRITERS often made use of experimental formal strategies to tell their stories and perform their ethical and cultural work. Through fragmented chronologies, unusual perspectives, hybrid genres, and unstable causalities, texts by writers such as Toni Morrison, Margaret Atwood, Maxine Hong Kingston, and Angela Carter posed challenges to conventional narrative strategies and hegemonic constructions of subjectivity. Over the last several decades, critics have debated the theoretical implications of using the language of postmodernism to describe and analyze the complex signification of narrative form in novels such as these. Often objections to the postmodern lens are based on the problematic relationship between feminist thought and postmodern philosophical positions. As Seyla Benhabib points out, despite the

> "elective affinity" between feminism and postmodernism . . . the postmodernist position(s) thought through to their conclusions may eliminate not only the specificity of feminist theory but place in question the very emancipatory ideals of the women's movements altogether. (20)

Similarly, Jacqui Alexander and Chandra Mohanty suggest that "postmodernist theory . . . has generated a series of epistemological confusions regarding the interconnections between location identity, and the construction of knowledge" (xvii). Sue Kim extends these assertions, defining what she calls "otherness postmodernism," which "often lead[s] to the underconsideration of the various actual historical contexts that impact a writer and his/her texts" (3). These reservations have been extended to literary and narratological criticism by theorists such as Linda Hutcheon and Beth Boehm, who have expressed concern that the postmodern critical model often falls short of accounting for ideological valence in texts crossing gender, cultural, national, generic, and formal boundaries.[1] Hutcheon puts this as follows:

> I happen to think that postmodernism is political, but not in a way that is of much use, in the long run, to feminisms: it does challenge dominant discourses (usually through self-consciousness and parody), but it also re-instates those very discourses in the act of challenging them. To put it another way, postmodernism does deconstruct, but doesn't really reconstruct. No feminist is happy with that kind of potential quietism, even if she (or he) approves of the deconstructing impulse: you simply can't stop there. (qtd. in O'Grady 20)

Building on this idea, Boehm asserts that reading through the lens of postmodern metafiction primes us as readers not to expect a particular text to "help us understand or protest the ideological structures of our culture, but rather to simply entertain us with a virtuoso performance" (37). Several alternative heuristics for the analysis of these texts have emerged at the intersections of narrative theory and transnational, intersectional feminisms, a development that suggests an important embracing of multivalent nonhierarchical ways of reading narrative form. I want to argue that the recent turn in narrative theory toward examining the "unnatural" represents a provocative framework for the analysis of contemporary experimental feminist narratives—one that may circumvent the masculinist and apolitical associations of the postmodern.

In the *Dictionary of Unnatural Narratology*, Jan Alber, Henrik Skov Nielsen, Brian Richardson, and Stefan Iversen explain that "unnatural narrative theory analyzes and theorizes the aspects of fictional narratives that transcend or violate the boundaries of conventional realism." This definition seems to suggest an affinity between the unnatural in narrative theory and the established interest of many feminist critics in narrative techniques that challenge convention and undermine hegemonic ideologies. Examining experimental feminist narratives for their ability to subvert established norms, many femi-

---

1. See Hutcheon; Boehm.

nist theorists have critiqued conventional mimetic forms. Some have gone so far as to claim that these forms are irredeemably tainted by masculinist, even misogynist associations. As Richardson has noted, these critics see virtually "any anti-realist poetics [as] essentially progressive or emancipatory" (692).

Many other theorists, however, have rejected this proposition, asserting that narrative form is "potentially polyvocal and polymorphous" (Friedman 180). Although they often critique mimetic forms, they push back against the conception that certain narrative forms are essentially or inherently linked to particular ideological stances. In alignment with these critics, I maintain that narrative form attains its value from the social uses to which it is put.[2] As writers such as Margaret Homans and Robyn Warhol have argued, narrative is flexible, possessing the ability to reify cultural norms as well as to undermine them. I posit that the unnatural lens has the potential to reach beyond the ideological boundaries that have historically adhered to the language of postmodernism as well as essentialism. This potential contributes to the utility of unnatural narrative theory as a tool for exploring the complexity of experimental feminist narrative strategies.

According to its primary theorists, unnatural narratology is not defined by time, history, or literary movements. As Alber et al. suggest, the unnatural is present and of importance in narratives from "antiquity to postmodernism," in texts as varied as Aristophanes's *Peace,* Poe's "The Telltale Heart" (1843), and Alice Sebold's *The Lovely Bones* (2002) ("What Is Unnatural" 380). This assertion suggests that unnatural narrative theory is malleable, useful for analyzing varied experimental strategies from a range of historical moments. However, in its unintentional evocation of the ideologically unnatural—that is, disobedient subjects who break/transcend/disrupt the boundaries of naturalized gender and sexuality—unnatural narratology is de facto occupying a space within the history of the naturalization of normative gender and sexuality (as well as other subjectivities). Perhaps one might argue that this unintentional positioning makes its critical use-value questionable for transnational feminism's work of *de*naturalizing national, cultural, racial, and gendered subjectivities. I would suggest, instead, that we engage the challenge that a his-

---

2. I wish to avoid any position that tends to essentialize narrative form by implying that narratives utilizing particular techniques (linearity, sequentiality) are inherently either hegemonic or counterhegemonic. These essentializing theories posit a monolithic view of narrative, which occludes the many writers who strategically utilize so-called conventional, or mimetic, forms to disrupt hegemonic effects. Moreover, as Molly Hite has argued, this view also has a tendency to elide the "distinction between the woman writer's deliberate attempts to create innovative and disruptive narrative structures or styles—to write other-wise—and the otherness that a masculine culture posits and expects" of women (14).

toricized feminist perspective might pose, a challenge to fully consider the implications of these historical inflections.

As of yet, theorists have not embraced this challenge. Understandably, they have disavowed what they describe as the conservative ideological inflection of the term *unnatural*. Monika Fludernik, in her appraisal of unnatural narratology, highlights the fact that the terms *natural* and *unnatural* are not intended to evoke ideological conceptions such as "naturalization":

> The term itself, with its unfortunate associations of perversity, the denatured or deviant, actually has no such loaded meanings. In fact it is equivalent to a variety of meanings that include the fabulous, the magical, and the supernatural besides the logically or cognitively impossible. (362)

Indeed, Alber et al. explicitly steer clear of the historical uses of the term as an "ideological tool." In response to this claim, they state the following:

> Unfortunately, the term "unnatural" carries a large amount of cultural baggage, which has nothing to do with our narratological investigations. Unnatural narratology has no position on the nature/culture debate and does not designate any social practices or behavior as natural or unnatural. ("What Is Unnatural" 380)

I ask, however, whether it is possible to extricate these terms from their historical inflections. And I suggest that the lingering impulse to divorce the field from these evocations indicates that it is not possible.[3] What, then, if we consciously return these terms to their connotations and ask: What are the implications for our readings of the unnatural in actually doing so?

Perhaps instead of disavowing these connections, we can take our lead from experimental fiction writers like Angela Carter. Her novel *Nights at the Circus* (1984) suggests that gendered associations with the ideologically unnatural cannot be denied or ignored but must be subverted. *Nights at the Circus* takes ideological paradigms that have historically been used to oppress women—the deployment of the concept of "nature" to naturalize submission, subjugation, and objectification—and upends them. Similarly, I argue that what Alber et al. in "What Is Unnatural about Unnatural Narratology" view as the accidental historical associations of unnatural narratology could be felici-

---

3. Alber et al. state that "the provocative term 'unnatural' . . . will inevitably cause a certain amount of confusion among the uninformed, but since the name is now fairly well established, we are prepared to live with its natural (and unnatural) consequences" ("What Is Unnatural" 374).

tous, helping to illuminate the complex ideological purposes with which the formally unnatural is sometimes aligned.

Although space is too limited here to thoroughly tackle such a large claim, I hope my reading will suggest that in certain feminist fictions the connection between antimimetic, experimental, that is, *unnatural* narrative forms, and the narrative representation of alternative, so-called *unnatural,* gendered subjectivity, is not incidental. Instead, I would argue that the example of *Nights at the Circus* suggests Carter's strategic/deliberate linking of what we have identified as "unnatural" narrative techniques and the representation of gendered subjectivities historically deemed unnatural. Conventional, mimetic narrative forms have often served as the scaffolding for the construction of naturalized hegemonic conceptions of gender, prompting many female writers to revise, reconfigure, and undermine these forms. As theorists such as Kim, Homans, and Marianne Hirsch have asserted, realist forms can carry with them a history of usurping female agency.[4] They contend that many female writers have viewed "linear narrative as a continuation of a destructive past" (Homans 12).[5] Carter exploits these historically acquired valences for cultural, political, and ideological purposes. As a writer who seeks to undermine naturalized notions of gender, Carter utilizes unnatural narrative techniques to further support the work performed by the content of her narrative.

Alber et al. assert that unnatural narratology can elucidate "the ways in which strange and innovative narratives challenge mimetic understandings of narrative" ("Unnatural Narratives" 115). Their call to "preserve the oddity of the strange and illogical" (115) provocatively echoes Carter's treatment of the ideologically unnatural. As readers of *Nights at the Circus,* we come to see the marginal, the freakish, and the outlandish as liberatory and central. This demarginalization performed by Carter's novel actually mirrors the work that unnatural narratologists say they are doing—their stated purpose being to illuminate "the consequences that the existence of [unnatural] narratives may have for the general conception of what a narrative is and what it can do" (Alber et al., "Unnatural Narratives" 115). What is illuminated, then, by looking at feminist texts through this lens? How does this affect the way we read a narrative and what it can do—politically and ideologically?

The unnatural in *Nights at the Circus* comes to represent freedom from conventional, naturalized, ideological structures. Indeed, Carter's novel

---

4. See Kim; Homans; and Hirsch.

5. This does not imply for these critics that *all* realist narratives reinforce patriarchal structures. Nor does it imply that realist structures cannot be used to undermine gendered norms. As Rita Felski argues, "those who drew on such plots could also question them or present them in an ironic light, smuggling in subversive messages" (106).

includes among these structures narrative patterns historically associated with restrictive notions of female subjectivity, such as the fairy tale and the romance. The novel sets up fairy-tale expectations only to thwart them. The consequences of the fairy-tale ending are clear to the central protagonist, and she intends to find a way out of them: "I assure you, I did *not* await the kiss of a magic prince, sir! With my two eyes, I nightly saw how such a kiss would seal me up in my *appearance* for ever!" (39). Carter evokes romantic conventions throughout the novel, often referencing the legend of "Sleeping Beauty," and at times having the heroine, Fevvers, wish for a prince to save her. (For example, when she feels she is in danger she tells her companion, Lizzie, that her "young man will come and save us" [241].) Many reviewers seemed unsure of what to do with the evocation of these conventions, criticizing *Nights at the Circus* for its sentimental reliance on romance (see, for instance, See). However, as Boehm asserts, this misreading results from an inability or unwillingness on the reviewers' parts to acknowledge the novel's explicit feminist critique of the conventions it invokes:

> [By] employing interpretive strategies appropriate to the romantic quest, See completely overlooks the parodic, metafictional, *and* feminist conclusion of *Nights at the Circus,* a conclusion that revises the masculine bias of the heroic quest. (41)

Indeed, if we read more carefully, we must acknowledge that Fevvers categorically dismisses her own romantic longings, claiming: "We shall set boldly forth and rescue *ourselves*" (244; emphasis added).

The experimental elements of Carter's novel are definitively political, explicitly feminist, and undeniably unnatural. Through the use of unnatural narration and an unnatural storyworld, Carter's narrative techniques denaturalize historically restrictive notions of female voice and subjectivity. According to Alber et al., an unnatural storyworld is characterized by "physical or logical impossibilities" ("Unnatural Narratives" 116). In *Nights at the Circus,* much happens that is physically, spatially, and temporally impossible. Published in 1984, the novel tells the story of a brash, blond bird-woman, who takes on the name Fevvers because at a young age she spontaneously sprouted wings: "I had taken off my little white nightgown . . . when there was a great ripping in the hind-quarters of my chemise and, all unwilled by me, uncalled for, involuntarily, suddenly there broke forth my peculiar inheritance—these wings of mine!" (24). Fittingly, she has settled into a career as a trapeze artist—indeed, the most famous "aerialiste" of 1899. The text opens with Fevvers giving an exclusive interview to a skeptical US reporter named Jack Walser.

In this interview, we learn that "just like Helen of Troy," she was hatched from an egg:

> When I was a baby, you could have distinguished me in a crowd of foundlings only by just this little bit of down, of yellow fluff, on my back, on top of both my shoulder blades. Just like the fluff on a chick, it was. . . . [They found] me in the laundry basket in which *persons unknown* left me, a little babe most lovingly packed up in new straw sweetly sleeping among a litter of broken eggshells. (12)

Raised to young adulthood in a brothel run by a one-eyed madam named Nelson, she is forced by economic circumstances to move on from her childhood home, finding herself a prisoner in Madame Schreck's house of freaks, from which she finally escapes through the use of her wings. When we meet her, she has become an international sensation, just back from a European tour and about to embark on a "Grand Imperial Tour" to Russia and Japan, then on to a "Democratic Tour of the United States of America":

> On that European tour of hers, Parisians shot themselves in droves for her sake; not just Lautrec but *all* the post-impressionists vied to paint her; Willy gave her supper and she gave Colette some good advice. Alfred Jarry proposed marriage. When she arrived at the railway station in Cologne, a cheering bevy of students unhitched her horses and pulled her carriage to the hotel themselves. . . . In Vienna, she deformed the dreams of that entire generation who would immediately commit themselves wholeheartedly to psychoanalysis. Everywhere she went, rivers parted for her, wars were threatened, suns eclipsed, showers of frogs and footwear were reported in the press. (11)

Fevvers's narrative, told to the reporter in quoted text, clearly paints an unnatural, mythical storyworld, one that is presided over by a winged protagonist, who taught herself to fly by watching the sparrows outside of her window. Walser, we are told, intends to expose her as one of the "Great Humbugs of the World," but Fevvers relishes the skepticism over her ontological status, herself coining the tagline, "Is she fact or fiction?" "If she isn't suspect," the narrator tells us, "where's the controversy? What's the news?" (11–12).

Despite the fact that the opening of the narrative encourages doubt and speculation about Fevvers's wings, it becomes clear by the end of part 1 that we, the narrative audience, are to believe that Fevvers is indeed what she claims to be. Her authoritative voice and powerful narrative convince us, even if they have not yet quite convinced Walser. If, however, the question of Fevvers's fictive status is settled early in the text, her status in relation to "nature" is not. Do we as readers view Fevvers as an "unnatural freak" who has thwarted the natural rules of the universe, or is she merely a natural woman with an unusual deformity? Or perhaps, as Lizzie states,

> we've entertained an angel unawares! . . . I think you must be the pure child of the century that just now is waiting in the wings, the New Age in which no women will be bound down to the ground. (25)

As this quotation suggests, the reader is encouraged to see Fevvers's status vis-à-vis nature as standing in for her status as a woman at the turn of the twentieth century. As Anne Fernihough suggests, "*Nights at the Circus* lures us, then, into a search for the origins of Fevvers's identity and sexuality, metonymically represented by her wings" (96). Fevvers's powerful, wealthy, independent, immodest, dominating presence certainly challenges the boundaries of proper womanhood. Among other things, she controls her own wealth and career, is unabashed about her body (she even farts in Walser's presence), and has an insatiable appetite for food and drink (11, 17, 22). The text, however, refuses to resolve the question of her naturalness, and instead works to deconstruct the concept itself:

> Through the extraordinary figure of Fevvers, the winged *aerialiste* in *Nights at the Circus*, . . . Carter literalizes the metaphor of the performing trajectory, the lifelong impersonation of womanhood. . . . She demonstrates the "groundlessness" of that womanhood. (Fernihough 89)

At times in *Nights at the Circus*, Fevvers appears to reject the notion of her unnaturalness altogether:

> It was those fine gentlemen who paid down their sovereigns to poke and pry at us who were the unnatural ones, not we. For what is "natural" and "unnatural," sir? The mould in which the human form is cast is exceedingly fragile. Give it the slightest tap with your fingers and it breaks. (61)

And at other times, she appears to embrace it, even as it is a burden: "I knew I was not yet ready to bear on my back the great burden of my unnaturalness" (30). The "unnaturalness" of Carter's protagonist, then, is not merely a fictional conceit; it forms the ideological center of Carter's text. As Fernihough puts it, Fevvers "actually destabilizes the distinction [between fact and fiction], and as a bird-woman, a hybrid species, she confuses categories at the most basic level of all" (99). Deconstructing essentialist notions of femininity at the same time as it insists on the materiality of Fevvers's gendered existence, the unnaturalness of Carter's storyworld undermines gendered notions of authority and voice.[6]

The unnaturalness of the protagonist in *Nights at the Circus* primes us to notice other unnatural elements of the narrative, beginning with the narration. As Alber et al. tell us, "we miss out on a great deal . . . if we insist on reading [a] novel's presentation of consciousness as we would in the case of natural or real-world minds" ("Unnatural Narratives" 124). Indeed, in this case, if we apply an exclusively mimetic lens, we do not merely miss out on Carter's metafictional commentary, but we miss the complexity of her feminist critique.

Glossing over the narration in parts 1 and 2 of the novel, many critics seem to see only a conventional heterodiegetic narrator, focalizing the events through Walser, who appears to be mediating Fevvers's story as he scribbles his perceptions in his notebook:[7]

> First impression: physical ungainliness. Such a lump it seems! But, soon, quite soon, an acquired grace asserts itself, probably the result of strenuous exercise. (Check if she trained as a dancer.) (16)

As this quotation suggests, at first, we seem to be limited to Walser's perspective on the strangeness of the scene before him. The narration reads as a barely filtered representation of the commentary he is jotting down in his notebook, as in this passage where the narrator describes the end of Fevvers's performance:

> Bouquets pelt the stage. Since there is no second-hand market for flowers, she takes no notice of them. Her face, thickly coated with rouge and powder so that you can see how beautiful she is from the back row of the gallery, is

---

6. When she discusses her role as a cupid for the brothel in which she was raised, she emphasizes the lack of essence underlying her representation: "And for seven long years, sir, I was nought but the painted, gilded *sign* of love, and you might say, that so it was I served my apprenticeship in *being looked at*—at being the object of the eye of the beholder" (23). The self-awareness of Fevvers's voice overcomes the confusion of Walser's voice. Walser appears to be limited by his belief in master narratives of truth and reason.

7. See Michael and Boehm as notable exceptions—critics who carefully note the unusual use of perspective in *Nights at the Circus*.

> wreathed in triumphant smiles; her white teeth are big and carnivorous as those of Red Riding Hood's grandmother. (18)

The sarcasm evident in this description clearly represents Walser's point of view, as does the description of Fevvers as a strange, beautiful, and carnivorous beast. As Walser's interview proceeds, however, Fevvers's quoted narrative proliferates and eventually seems to overwhelm Walser's perspective with its capaciousness and power. Several times, Walser attempts to regain control of the narrative, and the reader is privy once again to his bemused view of Fevvers:

> She fixed Walser with a piercing, judging regard, as if to ascertain just how far she could go with him. Her face, in its Brobdingnagian symmetry, might have been hacked from wood and brightly painted up by those artists who build carnival ladies for fairgrounds or figureheads for sailing ships. (33)

But, the strength of Fevvers's voice becomes increasingly evident as she "lassoed him with her narrative and dragged him along with her before he'd had the chance to ask" (60).

Critics tend to read this narrational coup as Carter's model of strong female agency and voice, a voice that speaks so authoritatively that it strips the conventionally authorized voice of its masculine authority. As Michael suggests, "Fevvers defies Walser's attempt to prove her a fake . . . by taking command of her own self-definition as she tells him her story and thus assumes a position of authority" (497). Fevvers's voice is one that wrests control of her would-be objectification and insists upon herself as subject.

This reading certainly captures Fevvers's power, but it is incomplete and even problematic. That is, if we read the text in this way, despite the force of Fevvers's voice, we must read her agency as mediated through Walser's pen. Is this not merely another case of masculine representation of female subjectivity? Indeed, Walser's perspective is quite sexist, describing Fevvers as "more like a dray mare than an angel," noting during her act: "My, how her bodice strains! You'd think her tits were going to pop right out. What a sensation *that* would cause; wonder she hasn't thought of incorporating it in her act" (17).

If, however, we look closely at the unnatural features of the narration, this reading is dislodged, the perspective of the novel complicated. Narrational conventions and natural models of narrative do not fully apply here. While the text does begin with Walser's point of view, other perspectives quickly and often intrude into his consciousness. The narrator is not omniscient, and the text does not seem to fit into the shifting-perspective category occupied by writers like Toni Morrison and William Faulkner. Some passages, such as the following, appear to be focalized through Walser:

> Her lumps, big as if she bore a bosom fore and aft, her conspicuous deformity, the twin hills of the growth she had put away for those hours she must spend in daylight or lamplight, out of the spotlight. So, on the street, at the soiree, at lunch in expensive restaurants with dukes, princes, captains of industry and punters of like kidney, she was always the cripple, even if she always drew the eye and people stood on chairs to see. (19)

But later, another unidentified perspective bubbles to the surface in a description of the reporter:

> Walser had not experienced his experience *as* experience; sandpaper his outsides as experience might, his inwardness had been left untouched. In all his young life, he had not felt so much as one single quiver of introspection. If he was afraid of nothing, it was not because he was brave; like the boy in the fairy story who does not know how to shiver, Walser did not know *how* to be afraid. So his habitual disengagement was involuntary; it was not the result of judgment, since judgment involves the positives and negatives of belief. (10)

This perspective indicates a deep understanding of Walser's inner workings, so it cannot be Fevvers, and it is clearly not Walser himself, because the narrator here and elsewhere indicates Walser's ignorance concerning his own motives.

The narration seems to fracture here, and we are unable to identify all the pieces. This fragmentation, then, signifies not, as most critics have argued, a masculine authority that has been taken over by another stronger feminine authority, but authority as always already fragmented, difficult to locate. Agency does not reside entirely in the voice of Walser, but neither does it reside entirely with Fevvers. Rather than signifying the inversion of a binary structure of masculine authority and feminine subjection, the text performs a more radical break with gendered structures, refusing to uphold conventional notions of authority, voice, and authorship.

If we look carefully at the narration in parts 1 and 2, we will also notice that although they are primarily in third person, there appears to be an unidentifiable "I" who is, at least at times, narrating. The following is that narrator's description of Walser:

> Yet there remained something a little unfinished about him, still. He was like a handsome house that has been let, furnished. There were scarcely any of those little, what you might call *personal* touches to his personality, as if his habit of suspending belief extended even unto his own being. I say he had a propensity for "finding himself in the right place at the right time"; yet it was almost as if he himself were an *objet trouvé*, for, subjectively, *himself* he never found, since it was not his *self* which he sought. (10)

Who, then, is this *I*? Clearly it is neither Walser nor Fevvers. Conventional models of narration would have us looking to the other characters in the text, or perhaps to an intrusion of an authorial narrator. But, the lens of the unnatural allows us to consider even more interesting possibilities. As Richardson notes, in such fiction, "one narration is collapsed into another, and one consciousness bleeds into a second one, or a foreign text inscribes itself on a mind" (12). As the narrative progresses, we come to understand that Carter's storyworld, while based on our natural world, does not follow the same rules of space and time that we follow. In this world, time stands still, speeds up, and moves at different speeds depending upon who is experiencing it:

> During the less-than-a-blink of time it took the last chime to die there came a vertiginous sensation, as if Walser and his companions and the very dressing room itself were all at once precipitated down a vast chute. It took his breath away. As if the room that had, in some way, without his knowledge, been plucked out of its everyday, temporal continuum, had been held for a while above the spinning world and was now—dropped back into place. (87)

In this world, a notably larger-than-life bird-woman can escape from a would-be rapist and kidnapper in a toy model of the Trans-Siberian Express, and when that train derails, the circus tigers who were her co-passengers do not die, but are somehow transmogrified into fragmented images in a mirror:

> Then amongst the ruins of the "wagon salon," I beheld a great wonder. For the tigers were all gone into the mirrors . . . [and] of those lovely creatures, not a trace of blood or sinew, nothing. Only pile upon pile of broken shards of mirror, that segmented the blazing night around us in a thousand jagged dissociations. (205)

I would argue that in a world like this, it is well within reason to consider some explicitly unnatural possibilities for the narrator of this first section.

Well into part 1 of the narrative, we are told that Walser no longer feels himself to be in control of the story: "He felt more and more like a kitten tangling up in a ball of wool it had never intended to unravel in the first place" (78). He thinks: "The hand that followed their dictations across the page obediently as a little dog no longer felt as if it belonged to him" (78). Could it be that Walser's disembodied hand is narrating this part of the story? Or, perhaps, this is a case of some type of ventriloquism by a future version of Fevvers, one who looks back and comments upon the present Fevvers and Walser? In fact, in the end of the text, Fevvers indicates that she will use Walser in just this way. She tells Lizzie the following:

> Think of him, not as a lover, but as a scribe, as an amanuensis. . . . And not of my trajectory, alone, but of yours, too, Lizzie; of your long history of exile and cunning which you've scarcely hinted to him, which will fill up ten times more of his notebooks than *my* story ever did. Think of him as the amanuensis of all those whose tales we've yet to tell him, the histories of those women who would otherwise go down nameless and forgotten. (285)

Perhaps Walser's voice has been appropriated just as his hand has. The narrator suggests a model of narration that supports this kind of unnatural ventriloquism:

> Her voice. It was as if Walser had become a prisoner of her voice, her cavernous, somber voice. . . . Her dark, rusty, dipping, swooping voice, imperious as a siren's. . . . Yet such a voice could almost have had its source, not within her throat but in some ingenious mechanism or other behind the canvas screen, the voice of a fake medium at a séance. (43)

Reading through the lens of the unnatural allows us to consider these narrational possibilities, but more importantly to my mind, it illuminates ideological possibilities. Although the majority of critics read *Nights at the Circus* as an inversion of gendered power structures, an unnatural reading shows that the text does not simply reverse the masculine and feminine positions. The narrative voice is instead polyvocal, at turns masculine and feminine, at turns indistinguishable and genderless. Carter unquestionably deconstructs masculine authority, the masculine subject, and female objectification, but she does not replace them with a centralized authoritative, natural female subject. Moreover, the possibility that this narration represents a kind of temporal merging of present-day Fevvers and Walser and future Fevvers and Walser suggests a complex understanding of history, memory, and storytelling. Carter makes space for an antimimetic, polyvocal, counter-hegemonic construction of history, one more akin to the fractured mirror in which the tigers reside. To reiterate this significant description: "pile upon pile of broken shards of mirror, that segmented the blazing night around us in a thousand jagged dissociations" (205).

The polyvalent narration in *Nights at the Circus* extends even to Fevvers's quoted narrative. The notion that Fevvers wrests control of her narrative from Walser is a common reading, but a close examination of the text reveals that even her voice is not singular. Indeed, we are told that Fevvers and Lizzie "unfolded the convolutions of their joint stories together" (40). Creating a seamless dialogic story, Fevvers's and Lizzie's narration suggests a more communal notion of voice and authority—a type of narrative perspective akin to what Susan Lanser calls "sequential communal narration" (21). Walser is spellbound, describing the joint storytellers as "not one but two Scheherezades, both intent on impacting a thousand stories into the single night" (40). Lizzie, the narrator tells us, "fixed Walser with her glittering eye and seized the narrative between her teeth" (30). What is important here, however, is not simply that Lizzie and Fevvers seize the masculine power of narrativizing, but that this power is reconfigured, disrupting a conventional notion of authority, subjectivity, and authorship, and replacing it with a contingent communal construction.[8]

As the narrative comes to a close in part 3, the narration becomes less and less conventional, more and more fragmented. Beginning in true first person (narrated by Fevvers) and then switching without warning to a heterodiegetic narrator, the unnaturalness of this section affirms and explicitly draws attention to Alber et al.'s. claim that

> the sentences of first-person narratives approximate the condition of third-person narratives. Both third- and first-person narratives are thus characterized by not having a narrator who speaks about something, but rather a narrative world created by the reference. ("Unnatural Narratives" 125)

The alternation between what appears to be an omniscient narrator (who is distinct from the narrator of the first and second sections) and Fevvers draws attention to the constructedness of all narratives but in particular narratives of the gendered self. Narrating events she has "no proper recollection of" and

---

8. Boehm asserts that Carter "gives voice to eccentrics, those who exist on the margins of dominant culture and dominant literary structures. The elaborately detailed and embedded narrative centers these characters, and the authorial reader, like Jack Walser, must step across the threshold to the unknown" (44).

speaking directly to the reader, the dialogue that Fevvers enters into with the other narrator denaturalizes narrative conventions, drawing the reader's attention to its artifice:

> Then, as she clipped away at her toenails, just as the train had stopped for no reason, so, for no reason, she began to grizzle. How can I tell why I began to blubber away like that? Who hasn't cried since Ma Nelson died. But to think of Ma Nelson's funeral only made me bellow more, as if the enormous anguish that I felt, this anguish of the solitude of our abandoned state in this world that is perfectly sufficient to itself without us—as if my sudden and irrational despair hooked itself on to a rational grief and clung there for dear life. (200)

As the novel draws to a close, Fevvers seems ready to naturalize all of the unnatural elements of her narrative, both for the reader as well as for Walser. Explaining that Lizzie possesses "household Magic," Fevvers admits, "We played a trick on you with the aid of Nelson's clock the first night we met, in the Alhambra, London; but the clock is gone and I'll play tricks on you no more" (292). The last passages of the novel cast doubt on the entire narrative. Walser asks Fevvers: "Why did you go to such lengths, once upon a time, to convince me you were the 'only fully-feathered intacta in the history of the world'?" Her response is uncontrollable, gleeful laughter: "'To think I really fooled you!' she marveled. 'It just goes to show there's nothing like confidence'" (295).

This ending leaves the reader completely off-balance. At first it seems to evoke Fevvers's wings and her ability to fly, but on closer reading, the passage reveals itself to be impossible to untangle. Did she fool us into thinking she could fly? Did she fool us into thinking she was a virgin? Or did she fool us into thinking she was a natural woman? Just as the magic of Carter's unnatural narrative cannot be fully contained by this ending, neither can the notion of femininity and womanhood be naturalized. The untied threads of Carter's ending leave open multiple narrative and gendered possibilities.

The use of the unnatural lens to analyze *Nights at the Circus* provides us with a tool to illuminate the ideological valence of Carter's formal strategies, drawing links between the ways in which she denaturalizes conventional forms in order to denaturalize conventionally gendered notions of authority, voice, and authorship. Transcending the debate over the political implications of postmodernism, unnatural narratology is eminently useful for the examination of experimental feminist narratives. Fevvers's story is revealed to be definitively unnatural, embodying the paradox of being both true and untrue, magical and real, masculine and feminine. Fevvers's last statement—"There's nothing like confidence"—does not expose her story as untrue, so much as it is paradigmatic of the power and importance of all narrative (285). Indeed, Fevvers tells Lizzie her story will "help to give the world a little turn into the new era that begins tomorrow" (285). Perhaps the unnaturalness of Carter's narrative strives to do the same.

WORKS CITED

Alber, Jan, et al. *Dictionary of Unnatural Narratology*. Aarhus University, http://nordisk.au.dk/forskning/forskningscentre/nrl/undictionary/.

———. "Unnatural Narratives, Unnatural Narratology: Beyond Mimetic Models." *Narrative*, vol. 18, no. 2, 2010, pp. 114–36.

———. "What Is Unnatural about Unnatural Narratology? A Response to Monika Fludernik." *Narrative*, vol. 20, no. 3, 2012, pp. 372–82.

Alexander, M. Jacqui, and Chandra Talpade Mohanty. *Feminist Genealogies, Colonial Legacies, Democratic Futures*. Routledge, 1995.

Benhabib, Seyla. "Feminism and Postmodernism: An Uneasy Alliance." *Feminist Contentions: A Philosophical Exchange*, edited by Nancy Fraser, Routledge, 1995, pp. 17–24.

Boehm, Beth A. "Feminist Metafiction and Androcentric Reading Strategies: Angela Carter's Reconstructed Reader in *Nights at the Circus*." *Critique*, vol. 37, no. 1, 1995, pp. 35–49.

Carter, Angela. *Nights at the Circus*. Penguin Books, 1985.

Felski, Rita. *Literature after Feminism*. U of Chicago P, 2003.

Fernihough, Anne. "'Is she fact or is she fiction?': Angela Carter and the Enigma of Woman." *Textual Practice*, vol. 11, no. 1, 1997, pp. 89–107.

Fludernik, Monika. "How Natural Is 'Unnatural Narratology'; or What Is Unnatural about Unnatural Narratology?" *Narrative*, vol. 20, no. 3, 2012, pp. 357–70.

Friedman, Susan Stanford. "Lyric Subversion of Narrative in Women's Writing: Virginia Woolf and the Tyranny of Plot." *Reading Narrative: Form, Ethics, Ideology*, edited by James Phelan, The Ohio State UP, 1989, pp. 162–85.

Hirsch, Marianne. *The Mother/Daughter Plot: Narrative, Psychoanalysis, Feminism*. Indiana UP, 1989.

Hite, Molly. *The Other Side of the Story: Structures and Strategies of Contemporary Feminist Narratives*. Cornell UP, 1989.

Homans, Margaret. "Feminist Fictions and Feminist Theories of Narrative." *Narrative*, vol. 2, no. 1, 1994, pp. 3–16.

Hutcheon, Linda. "The Politics of Postmodernism: Parody and History." *Cultural Critique*, no. 5, 1986-1987, pp. 179–207.

Kim, Sue. *Critiquing Postmodernism in Contemporary Discourses of Race*. Palgrave, 2009.

Lanser, Susan S. *The Narrative Act: Point of View in Prose Fiction*. Princeton UP, 1981.

Michael, Magali Cornier. "Angela Carter's 'Nights at the Circus:' An Engaged Feminism via Subversive Postmodern Strategies." *Contemporary Literature*, vol. 35, no. 3, 1994, pp. 492–521.

O'Grady, Kathleen. "Theorizing—Feminism and Postmodernism: A Conversation with Linda Hutcheon." *Rampike,* vol. 9, no. 2, 1998, pp. 20–22.

Richardson, Brian. *Unnatural Voices: Extreme Narration in Modern and Contemporary Fiction.* The Ohio State UP, 2006.

See, Carolyn. "Come on in and See the Winged Lady." Review of *Nights at the Circus. The New York Times Book Review,* 24 Feb. 1985, 7.

Warhol, Robyn. *Gendered Interventions: Narrative Discourse in the Victorian Novel.* The Ohio State UP, 1989.

CHAPTER 2

Anima by Wajdi Mouawad

Unnatural or Naturalized?

SYLVIE PATRON
TRANSLATED BY MELISSA MCMAHON

INTRODUCTION

This chapter is offered as a study of the modes of narration in *Anima*, inspired by current "unnatural narratology" research, and as an attempt to reevaluate certain aspects of unnatural narratology in the light of the study of Wajdi Mouawad's novel.[1] It focuses on the problem that the notion of naturalization, understood as a reading way or strategy,[2] can pose when we try to apply it to Mouawad's novel.

Unnatural narratology is the systematic study of narratives that are unnatural or considered as such (or narratives that are the opposite of narratives

---

1. A French version of this article was published in Badiou-Monferran and Denooz 41–62. I thank Claire Badiou-Monferran and Laurence Denooz for their gracious authorization to publish a new version of it in translation, and Jan Alber, Brian Richardson, and the three anonymous readers for their useful comments and suggestions for improving this version. *Anima* was published by Talonbooks in November 2017, in a translation by Linda Gaboriau. Here I use the original French version. The quotations are translated by Melissa McMahon.

2. The term used in particular by Jan Alber and Henrik Skov Nielsen is "naturalizing" or "unnaturalizing reading strategies." Alber, "Impossible Storyworlds" 81; Alber and Heinze 10; Alber et al., "What Is" 376, 377, 381, "What Really" 109, and *Poetics* 8; Alber, "Unnatural Narratology" 451–52 and "Unnatural Spaces" 49; Nielsen, "Naturalizing" 67–68 and "The Unnatural" 239–40; Alber, "Postmodernist Impossibilities" 261–62.

considered to be natural by certain theorists).[3] It calls for an approach that combines classical narratology, postclassical narratology, and interpretive criticism. While it has become increasingly popular since the end of the 2000s, it is not without a certain number of problems and may be seen as "work in progress," as much on the theoretical level as the analytic and interpretive level.[4] For Brian Richardson, an unnatural narrative is defined as

> one that conspicuously violates conventions of standard narrative forms, in particular, conventions of nonfictional narratives, oral or written, and fictional modes like realism that model themselves on nonfictional narratives. Unnatural narratives furthermore follow fluid, changing conventions and create new narratological patterns in each work. In a phrase, unnatural narratives produce a defamiliarization of the basic elements of narrative. ("What Is" 34; Richardson, "Unnatural Narratology" 97; Alber et al., "What Is" 372)

Richardson takes care to differentiate between what he calls the nonmimetic or nonrealistic poetics that govern traditional nonrealistic works such as fairy tales and ghost stories, and the antimimetic work of an author like Beckett that defies the principles of realism. His conception of unnatural narratives clearly privileges antimimetic narratives or other types of antimimetic text.

Jan Alber, for his part, understands the term *unnatural* as referring to "impossible scenarios and events, that is, impossible by the known laws governing the physical world, as well as logically impossible ones, that is, impossible by accepted principles of logic" ("Impossible Storyworlds" 80, qtd in Alber and Heinze 4–5), or else humanly impossible, which is to say impossible in relation to the limits of human abilities, in particular cognitive abilities (Alber et al., "What Is" 373; Richardson, "Unnatural Narratology" 98; Alber, *Unnatural Narrative* 3–4). Henrik Skov Nielsen puts more emphasis on the question of interpretation. For him, unnatural narratives are fictional narratives that "cue the reader to employ interpretational strategies that are different from those she employs in non-fictionalized, conversational storytelling situations" ("Fictional Voices" 59; Alber et al., "What Is" 373).

---

3. See Fludernik, *Towards*. See also the debate between Fludernik ("How Natural") and Alber et al. ("What Is").

4. Among the main works on unnatural narratology, we can cite Richardson, *Unnatural Voices*; Alber, "Impossible Storyworlds"; Alber et al., "Unnatural Narratives"; Alber and Heinze; Hansen et al.; Alber et al., *Poetics*; Alber and Hansen; Richardson's contributions to Herman et al.; Richardson, *Unnatural Narrative*; and Alber, *Unnatural Narrative*, which has just been published and which I could not use extensively in this article. See also the Unnatural Narratology website: http://projects.au.dk/narrativeresearchlab/unnatural/. Among the debates raised by unnatural narratology, see above n. 3, and Klauk and Köppe and Alber et al., "What Really".

Anima seems to lend itself particularly well to an unnatural narratological approach. In three of the four parts of the novel, the narration is taken over by animals: those owned by the protagonist (the cat of the first and sixth chapters) and those, much more numerous and varied, that he meets on the different stages of his journey. Narratives taken over by animals could be invoked to illustrate all of the definitions of unnatural narrative. They violate conventions of standard narratives, in particular those of nonfictional narratives, oral or written; they present scenarios that are impossible in the real world, empirically and logically (from the point of view of the distinguishing criteria between human and animal); and they cue the reader to employ interpretational strategies that are different from those employed in standard situations of narration. Such narratives are moreover mentioned in all the works of unnatural narratology.[5] Unnatural narratologists generally trace the origins of narration taken over by animals to Tolstoy's *Kholstomer* (literally "the land surveyor," the name of a horse) and also often refer to *Sweet William: A Memoir of Old Horse* by John Hawkes. Richardson effectively differentiates traditional nonrealist works such as fables, and, we could add, certain children's stories, from the narrative experiments of a Tolstoy or a Hawkes, which take place within a realist context and in particular within one of psychological realism ("What Is" 34; *Unnatural Narrative* 4). Alber speaks in the first case of unnatural scenarios that have been conventionalized, and he also reserves the defamiliarizing effect for the second category ("Impossible Storyworlds" 94 n. 4; Alber and Heinze 13; Alber, *Unnatural Narrative* 20, 42–43, 225).

However, because of the way it embeds the first three parts of the novel inside the "manuscript" evoked in the fourth part, *Anima* calls on unnatural narratologists to address the question of the naturalization of unnatural elements. On the one hand, Mouawad's novel provides another example of Alber's attempt to itemize the strategies used or usable by readers when they are confronted with unnatural elements (strategies that Alber initially sees as "naturalization strategies"). The first strategy is: "Some impossible elements can simply be explained as dreams, fantasies, or hallucinations ('reading events as internal states')" ("Impossible Storyworlds" 82).[6] This first strategy

---

5. See Richardson, *Unnatural Voices* x, 3; Alber, "Impossible Storyworlds" 82, 89, 93–94; Alber et al., "Unnatural Narratives" 116, 131; Alber and Heinze 7; Richardson, "What Is" 34; Alber, "The Diachronic" 41, 49–50; Richardson, "Antimimetic" 23; Alber, "Interview" 13, 14 n. 4, "Unnatural Narratology" 450, 452, 456, and "Unnatural Narrative" 10; Alber et al. Poetics 2; Alber and Hansen 4; Alber, "Postmodernist Impossibilities" 274 n. 17, 18; Richardson, *Unnatural Narrative* 4, 33; and Alber, *Unnatural Narrative* 62–71. See also Bernaerts et al., which takes a critical distance from the unnatural narratology approach.

6. The other strategies are (2) "foregrounding the thematic," (3) "reading allegorically," (4) "blending scripts," and (5) "frame enrichment" (Alber, "Impossible Storyworlds" 82–83;

becomes the third in Alber et al., but the description remains the same: "We can explain some impossibilities by attributing them to the *interiority* of the narrator or one of the characters; in this case, the natural is *naturalized* insofar as it turns out to be something entirely natural (namely somebody's hallucination)" ("What Is" 377). A note in the same article specifies that the term *naturalization* should be reserved for this third reading strategy, "while all the other navigational tools are perhaps better described as explanatory mechanisms or as ways of coming to terms with the unnatural" (381; see also Alber, *Unnatural Narrative* 51, 237 n. 14).

Mouawad's novel adds to explanations by reference to dreams, fantasies, or hallucinations, in short by reference to the internal states of the narrator, the explanation by way of fictionality—which is to say, the fictionality inside the fiction. The manuscript received by the coroner, the narrator of the fourth part of the novel, is in fact described as a "work of fiction that recounts the facts" (388). It is presented as having been written by the protagonist, Wahhch Debch, who wanted to tell his story by entrusting the task of narration to animals. On the other hand, the manuscript is only brought up in the fourth part of the novel and nothing in the writing of the first three parts hints at their embedded status (and change of ontological level: a fiction inside the fiction). If we consider only the first three parts of the novel, *Anima* occupies an interesting place in the debate between Alber and Nielsen.[7]

Whereas Alber identifies reading strategies based on the experiential frames of the real world, Nielsen argues for the legitimacy of an unnaturalizing reading of unnatural narratives, resisting the application of real-world limitations to all narratives and refraining from limiting interpretations to what is possible in literal communicative acts and representational models. He even posits an incompatibility between Alber's third reading strategy, and perhaps the other strategies, and the unnatural narratological approach:

> An unnatural approach . . . allows the reader to construct such situations as authoritative, reliable or matter-of-fact renderings of the fictional universe. This also goes to show that if the reader constructs something strange within

---

Alber and Heinze 10; Alber, "Interview" 12–13). See also Alber ("Unnatural Spaces" 48–49) for a slightly different list, and Alber (*Unnatural Narrative* 47–48) for a singularly expanded one. I will briefly evoke the last strategy in the most recent list, "the Zen way of reading," at the end of this article.

7. This also includes Stefan Iversen and Brian Richardson. See Alber et al., "Unnatural Narratives" 129–30; Alber and Heinze 9–11; Richardson, "Unnatural Narratology" 101–2; Alber et al., "What Is" 376–78; Alber et al., Poetics 7–9; Iversen 95; Alber, "Unnatural Narrative"; Richardson, *Unnatural Narrative* 19–20; and Alber, *Unnatural Narrative* 17–19.

the fictional universe as, say, a dream or a hallucination then, for me, that would not count as unnatural which in turn goes to show that naturalization or familiarization, for me, annihilates the unnatural. ("The Unnatural" 241)

In opposition to his unnaturalizing reading, Nielsen calls "naturalization" the process of normalizing the unnatural emblematized by Alber's project.[8]

In the rest of this essay, I will turn my attention first to the unnatural elements, or those considered to be such by unnatural narratologists, in the first three parts of *Anima*. Then I will address the question of the naturalization by fictionality that takes place in the fourth part of the novel, in order to finish with the possible effects of this naturalization on a second reading of the novel.

THE UNNATURAL ELEMENTS IN *ANIMA*

As unnatural narratologists recognize, unnatural elements are always in a dialectical relationship with other natural or mimetic elements of the narrative (see Richardson, "What Is" 33; Alber, *Unnatural Narrative* 4). An examination of Mouawad's novel also shows that some elements can be considered to simultaneously accentuate the unnatural character of the narrative and to naturalize or render more plausible elements inside the unnatural situation created by the text of the novel. In the following sections, I will discuss the narrators, the narrative situation, epistemic consistency, and other unnatural elements on macro- and micro-textual levels.

The Narrators

The term *narrator* comes from Mouawad himself, in the "Notice" that is given as an appendix to the novel: "Writing *Anima* required, given the nature of the multiple narrators and the geography covered by the character of Wahhch, a certain amount of research" (393). The story of how the novel came about that appears on the website of publisher Actes Sud also contains synonyms of or comments on this term: "a voice," "a voice that says I" (an "I" who is not co-referential with the "I" of the author: "It wasn't me"), "an animal voice," "a

---

8. Alber, for his part, warns against the risk of monumentalizing the unnatural, which results, according to him, from Nielsen's position (see Alber et al., "Unnatural Voices" 365; Alber, "Unnatural Narratology" 455; Alber, "Unnatural Narrative").

cat, their cat, their pet, tells the story of the macabre discovery and the man fainting," and "in the second chapter, the birds at the window of his hospital room take up the story."[9] In the novel, the narrators are identified in the chapter titles by their scientific name (genus, species, sometimes subspecies)—*Felis sylvestris catus carthusianorum, Passer domesticus, Canis lupus familiaris inauratus investigator,* and so on—and by certain indicators generally linked to their behavior (e.g., in the case of the cat: "I ate the tuna that was in the bag and drank the water in the toilets" [14]).[10] The "I" sometimes becomes a "we"—from the second chapter: "Did he get up when night came . . . ? Our nature, linked to the diurnal movement of existence, prevents us from saying so with any certainty despite the attention our whole group paid to him" (15). In some short chapters, the "I" is completely effaced: "He's sleeping. A man comes in. A giant. The cat sits up" (85).

The nature and multiplicity of the narrators has as its corollary a specific lexicon, made up of numerous references to "the man" or "humans" or else to Wahhch's "fellow human beings," and a set of stylistic choices that are supposed to correspond to the characteristics of the species in question. I will just give one example:

The yapping of the dog decided everything.
   Yes.
   Together, obeying the voice of prudence, we slid over the partitions of the present to leave the statues and crevices of the clock tower where we nest.
   Spreading our wings, we launched our bodies into the void.
   Yes. ("Columba livia" 19)[11]

The first three parts of the novel also contain typical passages of what the Russian Formalists called "defamiliarization": the defamiliarization of certain gestures (the sign of the cross, 30); certain objects (the telephone, on several occasions, 35, 41, 42, 56, 57, 122, 322, 344); certain foods, especially beverages (beer, 51, 181, 307); and even human language (54, 291–92). The discourse of the chimpanzee on the misuse of possessive pronouns in human discourse—

---

   9. See http://www.actes-sud.fr/catalogue/litterature/anima. Accessed 21 Sep. 2014.

   10. We can observe a certain nominalism in the choice of gender of the animal narrators: Thus, the skunk (Lat. *mephitis,* Fr. *la mouffette,* feminine noun) is a female skunk, and the spider (Lat. *tegenaria domestica,* Fr. *l'araignée,* feminine noun) is a female spider; on the other hand, the fox (Fr. *le renard,* masculine noun) is male, as is the butterfly (Fr. *le papillon,* masculine noun) (Mouawad 48, 50, 58, 141). A counterexample would be the female raccoon (Fr. *le raton-laveur,* masculine noun) (140).

   11. The translation focuses on the signified, to the detriment of the signifier. In French, the repetition of "Oui" ("Yes") is supposed to imitate the cooing of the pigeon.

"The humans say My, my, my. For example, Coach says My monkey, pointing to me" (102)—seems to be taken directly from Tolstoy's "Kholstomer" (1863).

The result of this narratorial choice is that the character of Wahhch is always described from the outside (no internal monologue, no representation of his thoughts in free indirect style, no authoritative presentation of his thoughts in general, barring a few exceptions I will return to). On the other hand, he is described with an unusual precision and type of detail that is linked to what could be called "animal experientiality." Here is a typical example:

> We dogs perceive the colored emanations that living bodies produce when they are in the grip of a violent emotion. Often humans have the aura of the green of fear or the yellow of grief and sometimes still more rare shades: the saffron of happiness and the turquoise of ecstasy. This man, tired, worn out, engulfed by the opaline opacity of the journey, gives off a jet black from the center of his back, the color of drifting and sinking, the signature of natures unable to leave behind their memory and their past. ("Canis lupus familiaris" 216–17)

The Narrative Situation

The term *narrative situation* refers to the situation of the narrator at the moment he or she tells the story. It is part of the fiction. It can be oral or written (or thought, in the case of an interior monologue, though there is the question of whether it is appropriate in this case to use the notion of the narrative situation, which is based on the model of natural narrative situations). It may or may not imply someone who is addressed by the narrator and located in the same fictional world. It includes the motivation the narrator may have for telling the story.

In *Anima,* the situation of the narrators is neither oral nor written, and it is only by default that it can be called thought (few narratives, in fact, deserve to be called interior monologues). The text does not suggest that the narrative act involves any sort of medium. On the contrary, it thematizes the fact that the narrators are not able to speak, and a fortiori write, on several occasions (105, 270, 295, 330). Nor does the text suggest that the narrators are telling the story to an addressee, or that they have motivation for their narration, or even that they are aware of being engaged in the act of narrating. On the contrary, it thematizes the fact that they are alone, or that they are the only ones of their species, facing humans for example, on several occasions (20, 33, 42–43, 49).

Most narratives are told in the past tense, indicating that the moment of narration comes after the narrated story. But some are told in the present tense. Here is an example:

> They sit down. She pours a dark liquid into the cups placed in front of them. I sing. I move from one trapeze to another then from the trapeze to the rock and from the rock to the trapeze. I sing. He looks at me. I sing. I leave the trapeze, hang on to the cage with my feet, wear down my beak on the metal, turn myself around, head upside down, I sing. She gets up, opens the window of my house, holds out her finger. I sing. I climb onto her hand. She turns around and sits down. She places me on her shoulder. He looks at me. I sing. ("Serinus canaria" 33)

This is neither a case of the historical present nor the present tense used in an internal monologue, but rather what Dorrit Cohn has called the "fictional present" (106) to highlight the fact that it is specific to fiction.[12] The absence of an oral or written narrative situation is further emphasized here by the impossibility of distinguishing between the moment of the narration and the moment of the experience, the narrating self, and the experiencing self.

Epistemic Consistency

I have taken the expression "epistemic consistency" from Richardson ("What Is" 23–24 and *Unnatural Narrative* 39–40). This is his shorthand for the fact that it is impossible for a character based on the model of a real-world person to know in any detail the contents of the mind of another character.[13] We find several (more or less) clear-cut violations of this principle in *Anima*. See, for example, the following three passages:

---

12. See also Richardson, "Beyond" 53; Nielsen, "The Impersonal Voice" 141; Hansen, "First Person" 319; Alber et al., "Unnatural Narratives" 130; Nielsen, "Natural Authors" 290 and "Fictional Voices?" 60; Richardson, *Unnatural Narrative* 26.

13. The violation of this principle or commitment is referred to as "paralepsis" in Genette 195. See also Nielsen, "The Impersonal Voice" 144; Heinze 280–81; Alber et al., "Unnatural Narratives" 130; Richardson, "What Is" 26–28; Nielsen, "Unnatural Narratology" 75–77 and "Fictional Voices" 55, 67–68; Hansen, "Backmasked Messages" 164, 167; Alber et al., Poetics 3; Richardson, *Unnatural Narrative* 26, 39; Alber, *Unnatural Narrative* 80–84. James Phelan, for his part, refers to "implausibly knowledgeable narration" ("Implausibilities" 168–69).

Get the soil off my head, he wanted to scream, like the day when some men had buried him alive. I mustn't cry, he repeated to himself, if I cry, if I cry out, they will start again, take me out, kill me and put me back inside. And there again, standing in the middle of the entrance hallway, losing all notion of time, he did not move, did not breathe, for fear of it starting again, of her dying again, which was in the end absurd since she was obviously dead, her hands clutching the blade, a bunch of flowers on her broken belly. ("Felis sylvestris catus carthusianorum" 13)

This man, if it were up to him, would have preferred to give his mind over to insanity than be judged in his sorrow as he was. ("Corvus corax" 30)

If he had found the strength to save his dog, he would find the strength to save her [Winona]. Hearing him speak, in the hut, she knew we were her only chance of being saved. She could not be wrong. (The dog of the third section, 317–18)

However, some narrators deny having any knowledge of Wahhch's thoughts: "I can't say what thought crossed his mind, nor what abyss opened up beneath his feet, nor what he fell towards" ("Felis sylvestris catus" 91). Others engage in conjectures or inferences on the subject of these thoughts, in a way that is not fundamentally different from what people in the real world do.

Richardson notes that violations of epistemic consistency frequently occur in "we" narrations (*Unnatural Voices* 40–43, "What Is" 27–28, and *Unnatural Narrative* 34). This is also true in *Anima*, but it seems to me that we should see this more as an element of naturalization inside the fiction. It always concerns social animals, who live in colonies (or are gathered together by man, in the case of the rabbits who are used as food for the boa constrictor):

There were, it is true, a lot of us, and we found it very hard to stay calm, so maddening was the smell of the cadaver. We were coming out of winter and we were starving, crazed with the need to feast on a rotting corpse. ("Corvus corax" 29)

We all believed in his fall, but he did not show the least hesitation. ("Larus delawarensis" 39)

The box opened. Terrified, we lifted our heads to try to understand where we were and what had to be done to regain a comforting sense of security.

> Everything was hostile: smells, perceptions, lights, sounds and the face of the man. ("Oryctolagus cuniculus" 77)

Other Unnatural Elements

Here I should mention the often very long passages of dialogue presented as direct speech, in French or other languages.[14] I have already mentioned that the text does not suggest that the narrative act involves any kind of medium. Similarly, it does not suggest that the dialogues are communicated in the same medium as the rest of the narrative. The text sometimes makes a point of the fact that the words exchanged during these dialogues are understood by the narrators (68, 76, 102–3, 105, 163) and, more rarely, the fact that they are not (159, 302). But most often it says nothing about the abilities of the narrators to understand when they are confronted with human language.

On the microtextual level of certain chapters or passages of chapters, we can identify other unnatural elements that have often been noted in the works of unnatural narratologists. There is first the case of narratives where the narrator narrates his or her own death.[15]

> I move away. I flit about. I don't see the danger come. I don't see it. I am hardly aware of the rustle of wings. I don't know that I'm lost. I am lost. ("Papilio polyxenes asterius" 141)

> I step back on the large joist to return to the shadows, but, lost, scared, losing my bearings, I take one step too many and tumble into the void. ("Mus musculus" 240–41)

In these two examples, the narrative of the prey is immediately followed by that of the predator (the crow, the cat), which confirms the event of their

---

14. On dialogues, see Nielsen, "Natural Authors" 290; Alber et al., "What Really" 110; Nielsen, "The Unnatural" 241–42.

15. Narratives that are taken over by a cadaver or dead person are mentioned in all works of unnatural narratology. See Richardson, *Unnatural Voices* x, 3, 100; Heinze 288–89; Alber, "Impossible Storyworlds" 82, 89–90; Alber et al., "Unnatural Narratives" 116; Alber and Heinze 7; Alber, "The Diachronic" 41; Richardson, "Antimimetic" 23; Alber, "Interview" 13; Alber et al., "What Is" 376; Alber et al., "What Really" 109, 116 n. 11 and Poetics 2; Alber, "Unnatural Narratology" 452 and "Unnatural Narrative" online; Alber and Hansen 4; Alber, "Postmodernist Impossibilities" 261–62; Richardson, *Unnatural Narrative* 18, 33, 43. See also Nielsen, "Natural Authors" 291, 297 on passages that narrate that the narrator is falling asleep.

death. The mare also narrates her own death in the cattle truck full of horses destined for the abattoir:

> Fatigue overcomes me, sadness, I collapse. In the animal faeces, I collapse. I won't get up, I won't get up. I am losing consciousness. I am slipping away. Finally, finally. (209)

There is also this narrative in the future tense (where we can see another kind of violation of the principle of epistemic consistency):[16]

> The persistence of the fireflies will color the valleys, just as the dog will save the fainted man. He will be his shadow and the man, his light. He will make him his master and the man will make him his dog. Nothing will be able to separate them. One, guardian of the other, one, in the footsteps of the other, they will go, binding their destinies together, to the edge of the ends of the earth and will have no more fear of the fear of death. ("Lampyris noctiluca" 262)

We can also cite the internal monologue of the chimpanzee, containing ironic references to human speech, which indicates a knowledge that the chimpanzee simultaneously has and does not have:[17]

> They were flabbergasted. Naturally. A "monkey" eats bananas and scratches its armpits going Oooh! Oooh! It doesn't roll cigarettes! It's an animal, a "monkey," it doesn't know that it is inhabited by an immortal soul! It's true. I admit it. I don't know that my soul is immortal. So? What's the difference, because watching these men the way I watch them, I sometimes wonder if they know it any more than me. (104)

On the other hand, *Anima* does not contain any narratives of facts or episodes that the narrators have not witnessed (this point is even made explicit in the sparrow's narrative; 15, 17). Nor does it contain any "denarrated" narratives, which is to say narratives that deny facts previously posited as existing in the

---

16. See Richardson, *Unnatural Voices* 29, 68, 144 n. 5; Heinze 280, 291–92; Alber, "Impossible Storyworlds" 90.

17. On certain passages of narratives that narrate something that the narrator does not notice or know, see Nielsen, "The Impersonal Voice" 140–41.

fictional world.[18] It never gives contradictory versions of the same events (at most, these events are sometimes perceived differently by the different narrators according to their nature and experientiality[19]).

This list of unnatural elements is, however, not without its problems. In particular, it places fictional elements proper, which is to say ones posited as existing in the fictional world created by the text (the animal narrators, their knowledge or not of Wahhch's thoughts, for example) on the same level as elements that are just the result of using certain narrative techniques (such as narration in the present tense, for example). Unnatural narratologists very often amalgamate the two, even if some of them sometimes show a certain awareness of the problem. For example, Nielsen takes a stand against Phelan about narratives in the fictional present tense: "Right, there is 'no occasion of narration' . . . , but to describe this as the narrator 'doing the impossible—living and telling at the same time' runs the risk of placing the paradox and the impossibility at the story world level as if this was a story about a character capable of the impossible" ("Fictional Voices" 65).

Sometimes unnatural narratologists even amalgamate fictional elements proper and elements that are just the result of certain habits of language created by the theory: For example, the "omniscient narrator" to describe narrative modes for presenting the internal life of characters in third-person fictional narratives.[20] This can be explained by the dependence of unnatural narratologists on classical narratology as well as on forms of postclassical narratology they claim to be opposed to: natural narratology and rhetorical narratology.[21] They do not have any well-developed conception of the status of fiction and its relationship to different domains of reality. In particular, they do not have at their disposal the concept of "representational correspondence,"

---

18. On denarration, see Richardson, "Denarration" and *Unnatural Voices* 87–94. See also Richardson in Herman et al. 79.

19. I could go so far as to speak of unreliable narration for the narrative of the fish (20–24) or for the nightmare of the dog (125–26). But here again, it is a case of an element of naturalization inside the fiction (see, moreover. this information contained in the narrative of the coroner: "Have, I too, a memory of less than seven seconds" [377]).

20. See, for example, Richardson, *Unnatural Voices* 42, 60; Alber, "Impossible Storyworlds" 94 n. 4; Alber et al., "Unnatural Narratives" 120, 124, 131; Alber, "The Diachronic" 56, 58 and "Interview" 14 n. 4; Alber et al., "Unnatural Voices" 352; Alber, "Unnatural Narratology" 452, "Pre-Postmodernist," "Postmodernist Impossibilities" 274 n. 17, and *Unnatural Narrative* 43, 61, 87–103. Alber compares the omniscient narrator to "wizards and witches": "Like wizards and witches, the third-person narrators or voices in these types of fiction are capable of omnimentality" (*Unnatural Narrative* 103).

21. This dependency has already been noted by Skalin 103–4 and Patron 31. See also Klauk and Köppe 98 n. 10 on the relationship between unnatural narratologists and alternative theories to classical and postclassical narratology.

nor its corollary, the "limitation of representational correspondence" (Currie 58–64, 78–79), which allows us to conceptualize the fact that in representational works, only certain features of the representation serve to represent features of the things represented.

For example, there is representational correspondence between the words uttered by the actor and the words uttered by the character of Othello in Shakespeare's play, but while the words uttered by the actor constitute great poetry, they are not represented as constituting great poetry in the mouth of Othello (Currie 59–60; this example is taken from Walton 181–82). Jan-Noël Thon provides other examples of the limitation of representational correspondence: "Even though the English language is used for representing character speech, the characters in Louis Leterrier's blockbuster film *Clash of the Titans*, Frank Miller's graphic novel *300*, or SCE's action-adventure *God of War* are not represented as 'actually' speaking English" (86), since the events narrated in all these narrative works are supposed to take place in Ancient Greece. Further, "Michel Hazanavicius's *The Artist* uses black-and-white pictures for the most part, but there are no good reasons for spectators to imagine the film's storyworld to be black and white"—this assumption being further reinforced "since none of the characters thematizes what would certainly be a striking lack of color in a world otherwise appearing to largely conform to our (historicized) real world expectations" (Thon 87).

In the same way, in *Anima*, there is a representational correspondence between the words we read (in French or English translation) and the narratives of the animal narrators; however, the words we read are not represented as belonging to language (be it French, English, or any other language) or as being expressed orally or in writing. Nor are they represented, in the case of the present-tense narratives, as being expressed at the same moment that their animal narrators are living the experiences they narrate. These assumptions are further reinforced since none of the narrators thematizes what would certainly be striking contradictions in a world otherwise appearing to largely conform to our (historicized) real-world expectations.

NATURALIZATION THROUGH THE WRITING OF A FICTIONAL NARRATIVE

The fourth part of *Anima* begins in the following way: "The events I am going to try to relate occurred more than a year ago, not very long after my wife's death, but well before I received, in a posted parcel, the manuscript of the preceding text" (373). The manuscript itself is described a few pages later, with its "three distinct parts."²² Its content is also summarized by the coroner in a passage that amounts to a recapitulation of the characters and events of the first three parts. Here the coroner takes on the traditional role of the fictional editor, with the difference that the manuscript in question is that of a novel, or more specifically a *faction*—a "work of fiction that recounts the facts" (388)—and not that of a factual narrative.

The revelation of the existence of the manuscript comes as a surprise to the reader. Like all narrative surprises, it leads the reader to reconsider an earlier part of the text—in this case, the first three parts—and to reevaluate the way it has been actualized. This reevaluation precisely concerns the unnatural elements listed above, or at least some of them. As Alber et al. write, "the unnatural is *naturalized* insofar as it turns out to be something entirely natural" ("What Is" 377)—which is to say, the product of someone's creative imagination.

The choice of the animal narrators is attributed to Wahhch inside the fiction and is explained by what he experienced at the moment of the massacre of Sabra and Chatila: "I remember the muteness, the muteness of all of these beasts who had just been subjected to this appalling thing that nevertheless had nothing to do with them, I remember trying speak for them, putting my words in their mouths" (335–36). It is part of a process to develop resilience, a dynamic, constant process, from Wahhch's childhood to his age at the moment of writing his story.

There is a narrative situation, in the sense of the situation of writing a story (once again, inside the fiction). It does not imply an addressee intended by the author of the narrative, but the virtual addressee who is the addressee par excellence of the literary text. As for the time of the narration, we know that at least part of the manuscript was written on the road; this part or version of the manuscript was already readable in "Cairo, Illinois" (270).

As it concerns a fictional narrative, even if it is recounting actual facts, we can speak of the infallibility of the epistemic source.²³ It explains the narrations or other modes of presentation of thoughts, for example, Winona's, and the future-tense narrative of the firefly. The dialogues are invented by Wahhch based on his memory of actual conversations he has had and are represented

---

22. Curiously, they are called "Animae verae," "Animae fabulosae," and "Canis lupus lupus," whereas the two first parts, as they appear in the novel and in the table of contents, are called "Bestiae verae" and "Bestiae fabulosae" (11, 117, 387, 397). The text does not offer any explanation of this. We can see in it a voluntary or involuntary limitation of the representational correspondence between the text of Wahhch's manuscript and that of Mouawad's novel.

23. One can speak of a case of "illusory paralepsis" in Heinze's sense: "Paralepsis seems present but delayed discourse reveals that there are natural, realistic sources of the character narrator's unusual knowledge" (285).

in writing in the form of direct speech. There is thus nothing unnatural in their length, or in the fact that we, as readers, have access to them. We can nevertheless wonder, in the case of the dialogues in English, why Wahhch did not translate them into French.

The revelation of the existence of the manuscript also provides an explanation, within the fiction, of the compositional elements and other features of a written text: the division into chapters; the titles; the transitions or links between the chapters; the textual echoes between different chapters, sometimes very far apart, whether literal echoes (e.g., place names) or thematic ones (e.g., the theme of the monster or monstrosity). It also explains why the "disclosure functions" often override the "narrator functions," to use Phelan's terminology (see *Living* 12–13), and why the revelation of certain facts happens both within each chapter and through the effect of their interaction. The strong teleology of Wahhch's overall narrative is stressed by the coroner— "everything pointed to the scavengers of Tank Mountain" (388)—even if the essential function of this passage is to authenticate the narrated facts.

THE FICTIONAL NATURALIZATION AND THE SECOND READING OF *ANIMA*

Given the fictional naturalization that takes place in the fourth part, we might think that it is necessary to change the logic of the first reading in any second reading of the novel. This would assume the blanket application of a naturalizing reading strategy to the unnatural elements of the first three parts. My hypothesis goes precisely in the opposite direction, based on considerations of a cognitive (memorial) and also of an emotional nature, in order to posit the possibility and perhaps even the necessity of an unnaturalizing second reading, which is to say the opposite of the reading prescribed by the text of the fourth part.

First, I will quote a reflection by Mary Galbraith on the narrator in fictional narratives. She argues that "even the creation of an overt narrator does not necessarily mean that this narrator exists for the reader behind those parts of the narrative that do not evoke his presence," adding that "if the narrator is not continually activated by signs in the text, and if his or her presence is not of importance to the overall meaning of the work, then it is hypothesized . . . that his or her telling of the story will decay and eventually drop from the reader's construction" (48). In the same way, I would tend to think that even the creation of a fictional author at the end of *Anima* does not necessarily mean that this fictional author exists for the reader on a second reading.

More specifically, he may exist during the first pages but, as I already said, nothing in the writing of the first three parts hints at their embedded status and change of ontological level (a fiction inside the fiction), and then we can make the same hypothesis as Galbraith: His writing of the story will decay and eventually drop from the reader's construction.

I will turn to the second point. Like the first reading, the second reading requires the reader's investment, based on empathy and identification with the character of Wahhch. It seems to me, however, that an empathetic connection with Wahhch is jeopardized by a naturalizing reading of the first three parts. I am thinking in particular of all of the passages that establish Wahhch's singular ability to relate to animals. Here are just a few examples:

> I think he must have sensed my panic because, without making any sudden movement, he sat back down on the rock and started to watch me with a sort of fatigue. He could have crushed me at any moment, but did not do so. His eyes, a clear green, filled with tears.
>
> He carefully brought his hand flat down on the ground. He waited for me to return to solid ground. ("Lasius niger" 42–43)

> He looked at me. He smiled at me. I held out my hand to him. Without playing games or showing off, or even expressing delight, he held out his. He placed his palm on my palm. He was not familiar in his manner towards me at any time. If he had been alone, he would have spoken to me the way people speak to those with ears. But without saying anything, he let me contemplate him and revealed the distress of his soul to me in the faltering of his glazed eyes. I loved him from that moment. ("Pan troglodytes" 110)

> He crouched down, he watched me, I watched him, I whined, he held out his hand towards me and said Me too! Me too! under the ground, under the ground, and alone! and he burst out sobbing. Moved by his friendship, by his deep affection, free and generous, I could offer him nothing in return. How could I match such a gift that allowed me to glimpse what is sublime in the gesture of holding out a hand to one's fellow creature? ("Ratus norvegicus" 134)

The effect of these passages is completely changed if they are read on the presupposition that they were written by Wahhch. They become expressions of self-satisfaction, self-complacency, smugness even.

Another argument will no doubt appear stronger than the first due to the greater number of passages involved. It seems to me that the trust in the reliability of the narration is also jeopardized by a naturalizing reading of the first three parts. Here is one example among many others:

> He screams. He screams again and sits straight up, without waking. His arms sweep the air. No! No! He says words, makes sounds that I can't quite understand. I become frightened. He wants to get up, but barely does he put any weight on his sore leg than he collapses at the foot of his bed. He wakes up. He stays there, dazed, gradually reorienting his thoughts. We, the animals, hear him crying. He calms down. He says Léonie . . . Léonie . . . and falls back asleep right there on the floor, fists clenched, pressed against his face, grinding his teeth. ("Equus asinus" 159)

Reading a passage like this, the reader may be tempted to ask: Why does Wahhch narrate this, and how can he narrate this, so long after the event? What is fact and what is fiction, or reconstruction, in what he narrates? Or, in relation to other passages: What is observation and what is anthropomorphic projection in the narratives he attributes to the animal narrators? There is also this passage that narrates events Wahhch did not witness:

> The door closed again. The old man was alone again. He returned to his chanting, louder than usual, as if he was trying to accompany the person who had just left him:
>   *And if a man lie with a beast, he shall surely be put to death; and ye shall slay the beast. And if a woman approach unto any beast, and lie down thereto, thou shalt kill the woman, and the beast; they shall surely be put to death; their blood shall be upon them.* ("Boa constrictor" 81)

Here again, the effect of this passage is completely changed if it is read on the presupposition that it was written by Wahhch; it becomes a pure product of his imagination, with, in addition, a quote from Leviticus that is difficult to interpret from his position. Even more generally, the effect of the first three parts is completely changed, or at least the text is rendered difficult or even impossible to interpret, if it is read on the presupposition that all the "he"s referring to Wahhch, or all the circumlocutions describing him, are "actually" (i.e., fictionally) hidden "I."

Against the hypothesis of a second naturalizing reading, I think we can posit the possibility and even the necessity of a second unnaturalizing reading, setting aside the fictional naturalization that takes place in the fourth part of the novel. Such a reading is perfectly captured in the terms used by Nielsen to describe the unnaturalizing reading that he defends as a general rule: "The reader has the option to try to maximize relevance by applying a qualitatively different set of interpretational rules. For example, the reader can strategically assume that it actually makes sense to trust narrative details which the first-person narrator cannot possibly know" ("Fictional Voices" 79). Nielsen also argues that "an unnatural approach . . . allows the reader to construct such situations as authoritative, reliable or matter-of-fact renderings of the fictional universe," and that "an unnaturalizing reading is an interpretational choice that, unlike naturalizing readings, does not assume that real world conditions and limitations have to apply to all fictional narratives when it comes to logic, physics, time, enunciation, framing, etc." ("The Unnatural" 241).[24]

It seems to me, for example, that even on the second reading of the novel, the reader can and perhaps even must consider that it makes sense to believe that animal narrators take over the narration. He or she can and no doubt even must represent the narrated facts to him- or herself as corresponding to recognized facts in the fictional world, including when it is a case of the thoughts of characters that in principle the narrators should not be able to know.

I also think that even on the second reading of the novel, the reader can and perhaps must consider that it makes sense to accept the narrative in which the mare narrates her own death, the future-tense narration of the firefly, the interior monologue of the chimpanzee that reveals a knowledge that the chimpanzee simultaneously has and does not have, and the narrative of the boa constrictor that recounts events that Wahhch did not witness, as reliable and authoritative narratives, recounting recognized facts in the fictional world.

Regarding the dialogues, I think these statements of Alber et al. can also be applied to them:

> We make a legitimate but naturalizing choice if we interpret the words in a dialogue novel told by a character-narrator, or the rendering of a dialogue that took place fifty years ago, as only *appearing* to be verbatim accounts. If we believe instead that such speech exchanges are part of the invented act of narration, we can also treat these dialogues as literally verbatim accounts and thus base interpretations on the claim that the characters are saying some words rather than others. (Alber et al., "What Really" 110; Nielsen, "The Unnatural" 241)

---

24. Alber, "Unnatural Narratology" 454–55 establishes a link between Nielsen's unnaturalizing reading and his last reading strategy, "the Zen way of reading." But it seems to me that Nielsen's unnaturalizing reading is active and Alber's Zen way of reading more passive. Moreover, the idea of a Zen way of reading fits very poorly with the reading of *Anima*, which contains passages of unbearable violence.

On the other hand, and even on the second reading of the novel, there are certain specifically textual phenomena that the reader can only explain by referring to the author, by which I mean not the fictional author (Wahhch), but the real author of the novel (Mouawad). These phenomena include the compositional elements and other features of a written text (the division into chapters, the titles, etc.); the fact that the "disclosure functions" often override the "narrator functions" and that the revelation of a certain number of fictional facts occurs both inside each chapter and through the effect of their interaction; and the refusal to translate the dialogues in English. The reader does not need to assume a representational correspondence between these external phenomena and the facts posited as existing in the fictional world.

CONCLUSIONS

We have seen that the examination of unnatural elements in *Anima* invites us to reevaluate the key concept of unnatural narratology, i.e. the concept of the unnatural itself, and in particular to distinguish between the unnatural elements that properly belong to the fiction and elements that are only the result of certain narrative techniques, or even certain habits of language created to account for these techniques.[25] Insofar as the novel contains a process of fictional naturalization in its fourth part, it also invites us to reflect on the nature of a possible second reading of the first three parts. This reflection seems to support Nielsen against Alber when the first asserts the legitimacy of an unnaturalizing reading of unnatural narratives.[26] In the case of *Anima*, not only does an unnaturalizing reading seem "a more appropriate choice than applying the principles of naturalization and familiarization" (Nielsen, "Naturalizing" 67), I could go so far as to say that the naturalizing reading, which follows logically from the fictional naturalization that takes place in the fourth part, blocks the second reading of the novel as it is designed to be read.

---

25. This observation seems to agree with that of Klauk and Köppe 81–82 concerning the necessity of defining unnatural narratives as narratives containing an impossible storyworld in the strong sense of the term. They do not, however, specify how they understand "strong sense."

26. Or Alber, when he recognizes the possibility of a "Zen way of reading," even if the expression itself is misfitted. I must add that, in my opinion, the choice between a naturalizing or unnaturalizing reading of the first three parts of *Anima*, on a second reading, has no impact on the application of Alber's other strategies, in particular "foregrounding the thematic" (the animal theme and totemism, the more general theme of the relationship between human and nonhuman animals) and "reading allegorically" (the allegory or the myth of the golden age, where human and nonhuman animals were speaking the same language).

WORKS CITED

Alber, Jan. "The Diachronic Development of Unnaturalness: A New View on Genre." *Unnatural Narratives—Unnatural Narratology*, edited by Jan Alber and Rüdiger Heinze, De Gruyter, 2011, pp. 41–67.

———. "Impossible Storyworlds—and What to Do with Them." *Storyworlds*, vol. 1, 2009, pp. 79–96.

———. "[Interview with] Jan Alber." *Narrative Theories and Poetics: 5 Questions*, edited by Peer F. Bundgaard et al., Automatic Press/VIP, 2012, pp. 11–20.

———. "Postmodernist Impossibilities, the Creation of New Cognitive Frames, and Attempts at Interpretation." *Beyond Classical Narration: Transmedial and Unnatural Challenges*, edited by Jan Alber and Per Krogh Hansen, De Gruyter, 2014, pp. 261–80.

———. "Pre-Postmodernist Manifestations of the Unnatural: Instances of Expanded Consciousness in 'Omniscient' Narration and Reflector-Mode Narratives." *Zeitschrift für Anglistik und Amerikanistik*, vol. 61, no. 2, 2013, pp. 137–53.

———. "Unnatural Narrative." *The Living Handbook of Narratology*, edited by Peter Hühn et al., Hamburg University, 2013, http://www.lhn.unihamburg.de/article/unnatural-narrative. Accessed 15 Sep. 2014.

———. *Unnatural Narrative: Impossible Worlds in Fiction and Drama*. U of Nebraska P, 2016.

———. "Unnatural Narratology: The Systematic Study of Anti-Mimeticism." *Literature Compass*, vol. 10, no. 5, 2013, pp. 449–60.

———. "Unnatural Spaces and Narrative Worlds." *A Poetics of Unnatural Narrative*, edited by Jan Alber et al., The Ohio State UP, 2013, pp. 45–66.

Alber, Jan, et al., editors. *A Poetics of Unnatural Narrative*. The Ohio State UP, 2013.

———. "Unnatural Narratives, Unnatural Narratology: Beyond Mimetic Models." *Narrative*, vol. 18, no. 2, 2010, pp. 113–36.

——— "Unnatural Voices, Minds, and Narration." *The Routledge Companion of Experimental Literature*, edited by Joe Bray, Alison Gibbons, and Brian McHale, Routledge, 2012, pp. 351–67.

———. "What Is Unnatural about Unnatural Narratology? A Response to Monika Fludernik." *Narrative*, vol. 20, no. 3, 2012, pp. 371–82.

———. "What Really Is Unnatural Narratology?" *Storyworlds*, vol. 5, 2013, pp. 101–18.

Alber, Jan, and Per Krogh Hansen, editors. *Beyond Classical Narration: Transmedial and Unnatural Challenges*. De Gruyter, 2014.

Alber, Jan, and Rüdiger Heinze, editors. *Unnatural Narratives—Unnatural Narratology*. De Gruyter, 2011.

Badiou-Monferran, Claire, and Laurence Denooz, editors. *Langues d'Anima: Écriture et histoire contemporaine dans l'œuvre de Wajdi Mouawad*. Garnier, 2016.

Bernaerts, Lars, et al. "The Storied Lives of Non-Human Narrator." *Narrative*, vol. 22, no. 1, 2014, pp. 68–93.

Cohn, Dorrit. *The Distinction of Fiction*. Princeton UP, 1999.

Currie, Gregory. *Narrative and Narrators: A Philosophy of Stories*. OUP, 2010.

Fludernik, Monika. "How Natural Is 'Unnatural Narratology'; or What is Unnatural about Unnatural Narratology?" *Narrative*, vol. 20, no. 3, 2012, pp. 357–70.

———. *Towards a "Natural" Narratology*. Routledge, 1996.

Galbraith, Mary. "Deictic Shift Theory and the Poetics of Involvement in Narrative." *Deixis in Narrative: A Cognitive Science Perspective,* edited by Judith F. Duchan et al., Lawrence Erlbaum Associates, 1995, pp. 19–59.

Genette, Gérard. *Narrative Discourse: An Essay in Method.* Translated by Jane E. Lewin, Cornell UP, 1980.

Hansen, Per Krogh. "Backmasked Messages: On the *Fabula* Construction in Episodically Reversed Narratives." *Unnatural Narratives—Unnatural Narratology,* edited by Jan Alber and Rüdiger Heinze, De Gruyter, 2011, pp. 162–85.

———. "First Person, Present Tense: Authorial Presence and Unreliable Narration in Simultaneous Narration." *Narrative Unreliability in the Twentieth Century First-Person Novel,* edited by Elke d'Hoker and Gunther Martens, De Gruyter, 2008, pp. 317–38.

Hansen, Per Krogh, et al., editors. *Strange Voices in Narrative Fiction.* De Gruyter, 2011.

Heinze, Rüdiger. "Violations of Mimetic Epistemology in First-Person Narrative Fiction." *Narrative,* vol. 16, no. 3, 2008, pp. 279–97.

Herman, David, et al., editors. *Narrative Theory: Core Concepts and Critical Debates.* The Ohio State UP, 2012.

Iversen, Stefan. "Unnatural Minds." *A Poetics of Unnatural Narrative,* edited by Jan Alber et al., The Ohio State UP, 2013, pp. 94–112.

Klauk, Tobias, and Tilmann Köppe. "Reassessing Unnatural Narratology: Problems and Prospects." *Storyworlds,* vol. 5, 2013, pp. 77–100.

Mouawad, Wajdi. *Anima.* Léméac/Actes Sud, 2012.

Nielsen, Henrik Skov. "Fictional Voices? Strange Voices? Unnatural Voices?" *Strange Voices in Narrative Fiction,* edited by Per Krogh Hansen et al., De Gruyter, 2011, pp. 55–82.

———. "The Impersonal Voice in First-Person Narrative Fiction." *Narrative,* vol. 12, no. 2, 2004, pp. 133–50.

———. "Natural Authors, Unnatural Narratology." *Postclassical Narratology: Approaches and Analyses,* edited by Jan Alber and Monika Fludernik, The Ohio State UP, 2010, pp. 275–301.

———. "Naturalizing and Unnaturalizing Reading Strategies: Focalization Revisited." *Poetics of Unnatural Narrative,* edited by Jan Alber et al., The Ohio State UP, 2013, pp. 67–93.

———. "The Unnatural in E. A. Poe's 'The Oval Portrait.'" *Beyond Classical Narration: Transmedial and Unnatural Challenges,* edited by Jan Alber and Per Krogh Hansen, De Gruyter, 2014, 239–60.

———. "Unnatural Narratology, Impersonal Voices, Real Authors, and Non-Communicative Narration." *Unnatural Narratives—Unnatural Narratology,* edited by Jan Alber and Rüdiger Heinze, De Gruyter, 2011, pp. 71–88.

Patron, Sylvie. "Introduction." *Toward a Poetic Theory of Narration: Essays of S.-Y. Kuroda,* edited by Sylvie Patron, De Gruyter, 2014, pp. 1–36.

Phelan, James. "Implausibilities, Crossovers, and Impossibilities: A Rhetorical Approach to Breaks in the Code of Mimetic Character Narration." *A Poetics of Unnatural Narrative,* edited by Jan Alber et al., The Ohio State UP, 2013, pp. 167–84.

———. *Living to Tell About It: A Rhetoric and Ethics of Character Narration.* Cornell UP, 2005.

Richardson, Brian. "Antimimetic, Unnatural, and Postmodern Narrative Theory." *Narrative Theory: Core Concepts and Critical Debates,* edited by David Herman et al., The Ohio State UP, 2012, pp. 20–28.

———. "Beyond Story and Discourse: Narrative Time in Postmodern and Nonmimetic Fiction." *Narrative Dynamics: Essays on Time, Plot, Closure, and Frames,* edited by Brian Richardson, The Ohio State UP, 2002, 47–63.

———. "Denarration in Fiction: Erasing the Story in Beckett and Others." *Narrative,* vol. 9, no. 2, 2001, pp. 168–75.

———. *Unnatural Narrative: Theory, History, and Practice.* The Ohio State UP, 2015.

———. "Unnatural Narratology: Basic Concepts and Recent Work." *Diegesis,* vol. 1, no. 1, 2012, pp. 95–103. https://www.diegesis.uni-wuppertal.de/index.php/diegesis/article/view/112/119. Accessed 14 Sep. 2014.

———. *Unnatural Voices: Extreme Narration in Modern and Contemporary Fiction.* The Ohio State UP, 2006.

———. "What Is Unnatural Narrative Theory?" *Unnatural Narratives—Unnatural Narratology,* edited by Jan Alber and Rüdiger Heinze, De Gruyter, 2011, 23–40.

Skalin, Lars-Åke. "How Strange Are the 'Strange Voices' of Fiction?" *Strange Voices in Narrative Fiction,* edited by Per Krogh Hansen et al., De Gruyter, 2011, pp. 101–26.

Thon, Jan-Noël. *Transmedial Narratology and Contemporary Media Culture.* U of Nebraska P, 2016.

Walton, Kendall L. *Mimesis as Make-Believe: On the Foundation of Representational Arts.* Harvard UP, 1990.

CHAPTER 3

Unnatural Narrative in a Postcolonial Context

Impossibilities in Aboriginal Australian Fiction

DOROTHEE KLEIN

THE PAST few decades have seen a shift in Indigenous Australian writing toward more playful fiction (Alber, "Towards Resilience").[1] Many of these recent works teem with impossibilities, that is, events and scenarios that are physically, logically, or humanly impossible—to borrow from Jan Alber's definition of unnatural narrative ("Unnatural Narratology" 69). We find, for instance, rivers that decide to change their course from one day to the next, islands of rubbish that transform themselves into paradisiacal places, or humans that can hover in the air and report the thoughts and emotions of people that lived long before them.[2] In this chapter, I wish to demonstrate that in Aboriginal fiction, impossibilities play an important role as world-constructing and meaning-producing devices. In particular, I refine Alber's definition of and approach toward the unnatural by offering a modified definition of unnatural narrative that is sensitive to cultural discrepancies between the sender and the receiver, and I add a further reading strategy to the ones proposed by him ("Unnatural Narratology" 76–79) to account for the cultural particularities of these texts. The overall framework of this essay is thus to

---

1. I am grateful to the anonymous reviewers for their helpful comments on an early version of this essay.
2. See Wright, *Carpentaria* and Scott, *Benang*.

extend existing theories of unnatural narrative to make them fruitful for analyzing texts from non-Western, postcolonial societies.[3]

Reading the novel *Benang* (1999) by the Noongar author Kim Scott along the lines of these conceptual refinements, I argue that the unnatural can have two key functions in a cross-cultural context. On a general level, theorizing and analyzing unnatural narrative can possibly contribute to the difficult process of reconciliation because it may achieve what Roy Sommer identifies as the "didactic purpose" or "utopian dimension" of an intercultural narratology: "fostering and promoting intercultural understanding" (77). Specifically, with regard to Scott's novel, I seek to demonstrate that a focus on impossible events and scenarios potentially yields new interpretative insight because it allows for a detailed analysis of how the specific form of the narrative influences and reflects its politics. In this context, the projection of impossibilities has ethical and ideological ramifications in that it urges us to adopt a reading stance that is not only sympathetic to the history that Harley, the first-person narrator, wants to tell, but in fact enacts the novel's overall theme to engage with other, formerly repressed stories and perspectives.

A caveat is necessary here. My understanding of the terms *impossible* and *unnatural* is decidedly positive. It is intended neither to trivialize Aboriginal cosmologies and epistemologies nor to question the validity of the projected storyworlds. More specifically, by investigating events and scenarios whose depictions are cognitively challenging for the non-Aboriginal reader, I wish to show how Indigenous writers can use them as means to dissociate their representational practices from those of the dominant culture and thereby foster a critical engagement with the culturally contingent ideas and world views that shape our reaction to literary texts.[4]

TOWARDS A DEFINITION OF UNNATURAL NARRATIVE IN A CROSS-CULTURAL CONTEXT

Various definitions of the "unnatural" exist (see Alber et al., "What Is" 372–73), but so far, the cultural context, questions of cultural differences between authors and readers, as well as discrepancies in the sender's and the receiv-

---

3. Most Aboriginal Australian writers disagree with the use of the term *postcolonial* because they feel they are still colonized (Heiss 43–46). I understand the *post* not in its temporal implications but in the sense of an enhanced awareness of the colonial legacies.

4. As Brian Richardson has argued, "a study of unnatural narrative can foreground experimental techniques developed by oppositional writers, whether feminist, minority, or postcolonial, to carve out different representational practices from those of the dominant culture" (38).

er's notion of what counts as impossible have not been addressed in detail. Laura Buchholz, for one, uses the theoretical insights of unnatural narratology to scrutinize traditional readings of Salman Rushdie's *Midnight's Children* (1981) and suggests that "this new unnatural aspect of postclassical narrative theory might hold greater ramifications for wider postcolonial critical uses" (334). However, while acknowledging the problematic connotation of the term *unnatural* in a postcolonial context, she does not provide any modifications to consider issues of context or of the author's and the reader's cultural background. Similarly, Andrea Moll, in her essay on unnatural events in oral forms of Aboriginal storytelling, makes a compelling argument for "taking cultural differences into account when assessing the 'naturalness' or 'unnaturalness' of narratives" because "what may seem an 'unnatural' narrative element or strategy from a Western perspective may be fully 'naturalized,' that is cognitively conventionalized and internalized by members of another culture living in a different social and cultural environment" (267). However, she leaves open the question of how existing definitions can be modified to account for the fact that, as Danièle Klapproth has put it, "people socialised in two widely divergent cultures may live in very different conceptual and perceptual worlds" (310).

The discrepancy at work, then, I wish to argue, is not one between natural and unnatural narratives in general, but one between different cultural encyclopedias[5] and their inclusion or exclusion of elements that can be termed impossible, implausible, or strange from an empirically scientific and rationalist perspective. Devices that invoke concepts that are not part of our real-world or literary cognitive parameters can lead to what Viktor Shklovsky has termed "defamiliarization" (12). I therefore propose the following definition of "unnatural" texts in a cross-cultural context: An unnatural narrative is one that contains scenarios and events that are physically, logically, or humanly impossible relative to the sender's and/or the receiver's cultural encyclopedia. It may therefore be presented as strange and odd, and/or it has a defamiliarizing, disorienting, or puzzling effect on a reader from a different cultural background. In this conceptualization, the unnatural is intrinsically linked to the transgression of cognitive boundaries and the questioning of a clear-cut division between the possible and the impossible. The question we need to ask, then, is not "What is unnatural?" but "What is unnatural *for whom*?"

---

5. Fusing Lubomír Doležel's notions of actual-world and literary encyclopedias (177), I use the umbrella term *cultural encyclopedia* to refer to a person's culturally determined perception of the world and her literary knowledge about fictional worlds as the two contingent parameters that determine whether a depicted scenario or event is perceived as possible or impossible.

Before turning to Scott's novel, a narrative that plays complex games with notions of the possible and the impossible, let me first briefly provide a more straightforward example of an "unnatural" Aboriginal text to demonstrate my point. For white readers, many Aboriginal dreaming stories contain physically impossible events in that they frequently feature self-transformations of humans into animals—that is, people transform themselves rather than being transformed by magicians (Muecke 90–91). As Klapproth contends, such "transformations of story characters into animals . . . would be classified as marvel or enchantment [from an Anglo-Western point of view]," yet they have a different status in Aboriginal cultures (345). In the story "Emu and the Jabiru," for instance, two men fight over food, in the course of which they turn into a jabiru (a black-necked stork) and an emu. One of these self-transformations is described as follows: "Then Gandji started jumping around in fear of what Wurrpan might do to him. From jumping he started flying, higher and higher. As he flew he turned into a Jabiru without a beak and flew away" ("Emu and the Jabiru" n. pag.).

From an empirical-scientific perspective, this transformation constitutes a physically impossible act, similar to the transformation of a floating pile of rubbish into a paradisiacal island in Alexis Wright's novel *Carpentaria* (2006). However, as Wright maintains in an essay, "such stories could be called supernatural and fantastic, but I do not think of them in this way" ("On Writing" 88). In other words, self-transformation seems to be an accepted occurrence in Indigenous storytelling. The crucial point here is therefore not whether readers believe in such physically impossible events, but whether or not they have a defamiliarizing effect on them.

In dreaming stories, for example, self-transformation often serves a didactic purpose (Muecke 91). More specifically, the event of humans turning into animals (or rocks, rivers, trees, etc.) functions to narrate the Law, which ensures that everyone knows their interconnectedness with and responsibilities for other people, Country, and the ancestor spirits (Grieves 7). For the culturally informed reader, such a physically impossible event does not therefore have a disorienting or puzzling effect, and hence the narrative qualifies as an unnatural one only for the non-initiated reader who is unfamiliar with this cultural tradition.

The question "unnatural *for whom*," which I posit to be the central one in a cross-cultural context, is much more complicated to answer in the case of Scott's *Benang*, not least because the novel playfully undermines clear-cut divisions between the possible and the impossible. The central unnatural element in this text is Harley, who is both a character with physically impossible abilities and a first-person narrator who possesses humanly impossible knowledge. As we learn at the very beginning of the narrative, he has a tendency to float in the air:

> Eventually, I realised that my face was pressed hard against the ceiling. I pushed out my hands and shot rapidly away from it. Thus, I fell. Still groggy from the collision with the floor, and once more floating toward the ceiling, I kicked out and managed to hook my feet in the wrought-iron bedstead. (12)

Since people in the real world cannot simply hover in the air without the help of any technological devices, we are here presented with an unnatural event, but why exactly does it strike us as strange or odd? I wish to argue that besides cognitive parameters, we also need to consider textual clues indicating the naturalness or unnaturalness of the presented scenario and the way in which features from the reader's real-world and fictional encyclopedias are combined to account for the defamiliarizing effect the projected impossibility has. Thus, the first aspect to analyze is how the narrative presents the narrator's propensity for elevation.

First of all, it is striking that Harley registers surprise about his ability to float and comments on the strangeness of it:

> I wanted to be bold, but walking felt very peculiar. Had I ever known how? I held my shoulders back, placed each foot precisely and, flicking my toes and flapping my arms, desperately tried to propel myself forward. It was very difficult to maintain balance, and although perhaps it should have been laughable I was, in fact, desperate and tearful because—more than anything else—*I wished to appear as normal as possible.* (13; emphasis added)

The narrator here explicitly notes the unnaturalness of the situation because something very natural for human beings, namely walking, turns out to pose a major challenge for him. Moreover, his wish to appear normal indicates that his floating is not an accepted element of the projected storyworld.[6] In fact, the narrative problematizes the notion of having a clear-cut division between the natural and the unnatural. This becomes clear, for instance, in Harley's gradual adjustment to his "peculiar" condition. The narrator describes how at times, when sitting around a campfire with his uncles and his grandfather,

---

6. According to David Herman, storyworlds are "mental models of who did what to and with whom, when, where, why, and in what fashion in the world to which interpreters relocate . . . as they work to comprehend a narrative" (570).

he would "ease [himself] into the air, and hover like a balloon anchored by a fine line" because he "was more comfortable that way" (189). Reflecting upon this preference, he remarks: "I feared to think what it meant: that I preferred to be let drift, and that it *came so naturally* to me" (189; emphasis added). The adverb "naturally" seems to stand in stark contrast to the action it modifies, that is, the unnatural scenario of a flying human being. What seems to happen here is a blurring of the boundaries between the physically possible and impossible.

I therefore wish to argue that the defamiliarizing effect of the unnatural in *Benang* is based on a fusion of different encyclopedias. The projected storyworld (except, of course, for the first-person narrator Harley) correlates to our cognitive parameters and in particular to our knowledge of space, time, and other human beings. The narrative blends this real-world encyclopedia with our literary encyclopedia of fantastic texts, or ghost stories, by using a ghostly character, whose impossible features are problematized by the text, in the context of an otherwise perfectly realist narrative, and this fusion accounts for the defamiliarizing effect it has on the (white) reader.[7]

Besides his unnatural tendency to float in the air, Harley also possesses an impossible mind in that his mental abilities clearly deviate from our real-world understanding of human cognition. This is most notable in his ability to report and comment on events that happened before he was born and his familiarity with his ancestors' thoughts and feelings. The narrative thus features unnatural acts of narration in that it includes enunciations that are mnemonically and psychologically impossible. For instance, when hovering in the campfire smoke, Harley provides a shockingly detailed description of a massacre. What is noteworthy here is that the passage is (impossibly) rendered from the perspective of his great-great-grandfather Sandy One: "The gun metal was cold against Sandy One's skin. He touched the barrel with his tongue, still tasted its bitter tang as he pressed the rifle against his shoulder. He thought he might fire upward, into the sky" (186). It appears that Harley's ability to float in the air enables him to see the past and to convey his ancestor's thoughts and feelings. In other words, his unnatural ability to hover seems to allow for impossible knowledge and results in an unnatural narration.

Benang presents us with what Rüdiger Heinze calls "first-person paraleptic narrators" (285), a fairly common literary convention that can be found in works ranging from Laurence Sterne's *Tristram Shandy* (1759–67) to Jeffrey Eugenides's *Middlesex* (2002) and Rushdie's *Midnight's Children*. Manfred

---

7. It therefore uses a strategy often found in the unnatural narratives of postmodernism, as demonstrated by Alber, "Unnatural Narratology" 83–84.

Jahn defines *paralepsis* as an "infraction caused by saying too much; a narrator assuming a competence he/she does not properly have; typically, a first-person narrator (or a historiographer) narrating what somebody else thought . . . or what happened when s/he was not present" (N3.3.15). This is indeed the case in *Benang* and ultimately leads to "violations of mimetic epistemology" (Heinze 279). Interestingly, this not only results in a defamiliarization for (non-Indigenous) readers, but it is also presented as strange, as the other characters' reaction to Harley's story indicates. His uncles are "staring up at [him], open-mouthed," and ask, "How did you do that? How do you know that?" (187). Possessing detailed knowledge about the thoughts and feelings of one's ancestors is not a "normal" human ability in the projected storyworld.

On the other hand, Harley often complains about his "poor" (14) and "inadequate" (27) memory and makes clear that he is not sure about some aspects of his story. His narrative challenges our understanding of the human mind by simultaneously postulating two incompatible ones, an unnatural and a natural one, which appear both on the level of the story and the level of the discourse. As with Harley's unnatural ability to float in the air, the defamiliarizing effect of his narration can be attributed to a blending of two encyclopedias: our real-world knowledge of how the human mind and memory work, and thus what a first-person narrator would be able to authoritatively narrate if he or she were a "normal" human being, and our familiarity with, strictly speaking, "unnatural acts of narration in fictional third-person narratives, including reflector-mode narratives or narrative 'omniscience'" (Alber et al., "Unnatural Narratives" 124). Harley, the first-person narrator, whose (in)ability to remember is often described in terms that evoke a decidedly human mind, can move in time and space and into the thoughts of other characters; that is, he possesses an ability that is humanly impossible and usually attributed to third-person narrators. To summarize, the defamiliarizing effect of the projected impossibilities in *Benang* results from a blending of encyclopedias, and the unnatural is explicitly commented on by other characters and the narrator.

Since the central question I wish to investigate is "unnatural *for whom*," it is worth looking in more detail at the position of the narratee and the implied reader and their (un)familiarity with cultural protocols. Reader addresses are widespread in *Benang* and they are frequently explicitly inclusive, as in "I have written this story wanting to embrace all of you, and it is the best I can do in this language we share" (495). Harley addresses an Aboriginal as well as non-Aboriginal audience, while acknowledging, "Of course, there is an older tongue which also tells it [this story]" (495), hinting at a deeper level that the non-Indigenous reader is barred from. The position of the narratee is constructed as both Aboriginal and white, and the same holds true for that of the implied reader. As Kim Scott has repeatedly pointed out, he wants to reach as broad an audience as possible and "try and allow entrances in [his] work for 'noninitiated' readers" (qtd. in Wheeler 165). While he attempts to put "Noongar culture at the very centre of things" (qtd. in Brewster 12–13), he is also aware of his white readership, whom he does not want to exclude (Scott, "Interview"). It is thus not a tension between different positions on different levels of the literary communication model that may explain the function of unnatural elements in *Benang*, but the inherent multiplicity and diversity of cultural traditions and epistemologies woven into the text. This inclusiveness turns the unnatural into a particularly effective means to foster a reading stance that is sympathetic to Harley's project, as I will demonstrate below.

It should be noted, though, that other "unnatural" Aboriginal narratives are much more overtly addressed to a decidedly Aboriginal audience. Alexis Wright, for instance, integrates the Waanyi language and local stories into her narratives, while also using a narrative style that replicates the oral style of storytelling that an Aboriginal person would find familiar ("On Writing" 80). As she maintains, such features may be unfamiliar and distancing to non-Indigenous readers (89), and she explicitly notes that she "do[es] not think of other people as readers of [her] book outside of [her] own community," although she also admits that she wants "the whole world to read it" ("Politics" 19). In this case, a rhetorical approach to the unnatural may be helpful to reconstruct what different audiences believe in order to answer the question "unnatural *for whom*"—although such an approach contains a number of pitfalls and questions, for instance, how to determine the belief systems of actual audiences. With regard to *Benang*, however, such an approach is of little interpretative advantage given the inherent multiplicity of the positions of the narratee, the implied audience, and, most likely, the actual audience.

HOW TO INTERPRET THE UNNATURAL—"CULTURALIZATION"

Discussions of Aboriginal-authored fiction that contains impossible events and scenarios have frequently turned toward magical realism, or what, in the Australian context, Mudrooroo (Colin Johnson) has termed "maban reality," as an explanatory model. Frances Devlin-Glass, for instance, reads *Carpentaria* as a magical realist text that draws on Waanyi dreaming stories "to insist that mythological meanings are embedded in the mundane and everyday real" (393). According to her, reading the novel as "a new form of magical realism based in Indigenous knowledge" (392) provides insight into Indigenous knowledge systems. Alison Ravenscroft, on the other hand, is critical of such attempts to lessen the narrative's unfamiliarity and its strangeness. She maintains that magical realism is not a form of writing that has its roots in another culture but that such a reading results from Western impulses to frame the unknown in terms of the known, namely magic and realism (195). She proposes reading these narratives through a "paradigm of radical uncertainty, an *impossible* dialectic" (197). From yet another perspective, Maria Takolander argues against approaches that see "magical realism as expressive of marginalized mythological worldviews" (2) and instead points out the importance of ironic incongruity in these texts, thus substituting an ironic reading for an ethnographic one.

It seems that magical realism, as an interpretative tool, is of little help, since there is much disagreement on terminology (the implicit binary of magical or mythic and real), the ontological status of what is termed "magical," and the validity or payoff of anthropological or ethnographic readings. Using the paradigm of unnatural narratology allows for a different approach to these narratives by working up from the text, thereby allowing it the authority to negotiate the possible and the impossible. Such a bottom-up approach is better suited to capture the various interpretative challenges these narratives pose because it is more responsive to their impossible features, that is, those aspects that constitute a cognitive challenge to us readers. Focusing on narrative techniques instead of applying generic concepts such as magical realism will furthermore allow me to analyze in more detail the effects of the novel's poetics of representation in terms of its intervention into cultural and historical discourses.

How, then, are we to interpret Harley's levitation and his seemingly impossible knowledge? For one, we can read these impossibilities as a demonstration of Harley's lack of cultural roots and his insecure Aboriginal identity (Alber's reading strategy [4], "foregrounding the thematic"; "Unnatural Narratology" 77). Furthermore, we can read them as a satirical comment on the colonizers' aim to "uplift and elevate these people to [their] own plane" (Chief Protector of Aborigines A. O. Neville, qtd. in *Benang* 11) (Alber's reading strategy [6], "satirization and parody"; "Unnatural Narratology" 77–78). As an additional reading strategy, I wish to propose reading the projected impossibilities as the materialization of elements derived from culturally contingent world views into physical objects or human beings embodied in the storyworld, a strategy I refer to as "culturalization."[8] This interpretative move is similar to the one put

---

8. There are of course further ways to analyze the unnatural in *Benang*. I would like to thank Brian Richardson for pointing out that the events can be treated as a hermeneutical mystery that can be read along the lines of Todorov's fantastic (Todorov 33), that is, that they could

forward by Harry Garuba, in reference to African literature and culture, who uses the term "*animist realism* to describe this predominant cultural practice of according a physical, often animate material aspect to what others may consider an abstract idea" (274). Like Garuba, I do not understand the term *materialization* metaphorically but as connoting the physical or sensory perceptible presence of, for instance, ancestral spirits in the landscape. I am here drawing on Bill Ashcroft, Frances Devlin-Glass, and Lyn McCredden's characterization of Aboriginal cultures as a "presence culture" in which the land plays a central role in the form of "place as an embodied presence" (Ashcroft et al. 23). It should be stressed, though, that this reading strategy aims at allowing for a movement toward engaging with other world views rather than arriving at a deep understanding, and it can only ever be provisional.

'SPEAKING FROM THE HEART'—READING HARLEY'S UNNATURAL ABILITIES AS CULTURAL CONCEPTS

To date, critics have largely ignored the unnatural elements in *Benang* and instead have focused almost exclusively on the integration of oral storytelling and the appropriation of archival material to challenge and correct non-Indigenous assumptions about Aboriginal identity and to provide an alternative view on Australian history—aspects that also feature dominantly in Aboriginal life-narratives.[9] This mimetic bias, however, is ill suited to capture the multifarious and varied effects of the novel because by focusing merely on its counter-discursive quality, its message of hope and renewal remains mostly unheard. This message is intrinsically linked to Harley's impossible abilities as a representation of Indigenous cultural traditions, in particular, an intimate relation to the land.

For one, *Benang* frequently narrates a conflation of the self and the other. For instance, Harley's account of the massacre, as analyzed above, ends as follows: "The paths *we took* have disappeared and been sealed, and yet at the very least *we still skim*, humming, along the scar tissue" (187; emphasis added).

---

have either a supernatural or a naturalistic explanation, and that Harley's propensity for elevation, furthermore, can be read metaphorically, as in "he [the grandfather] said I was brightest and most useful in an uplifted state" (13). Moreover, the projected impossibilities could also be seen as a literalization of metaphors. However, I am hesitant to limit my discussion to such a focus on metaphor since, as Patricia Linton argues, "metaphor offers the Euro-American reader a comfortable 'literary' account of an otherwise unaccountable event" because when we are confronted with alien cultural concepts, "it may be easier for readers enculturated in a different worldview to read 'as if' when the text says 'is'" (32).

9. For a brief overview of the characteristics of Aboriginal life-writing, see Seal 79–80.

Here, the narrator identifies with both his ancestors and his Noongar contemporaries by presenting himself as part of the past and the present group. As Hanne Birk has convincingly demonstrated, Harley's historiographical project goes beyond individual life stories (307), and this transcending of the human lifetime is reflected in the impossible narrator whose mind transcends human cognition. More specifically, the narrative evokes a continuous consciousness that encompasses the living and the dead in that the narrator is connected with his ancestors by a collective memory that embraces the past and the present. We are thus presented with what Alan Palmer calls "intermental thought," which is "joint, group, shared, or collective" (213). According to Jan Alber, Henrik Skov Nielsen, and Brian Richardson, intermental thought is natural "if the projected minds are temporally and spatially connected and may thus interact" ("Unnatural Voices" 357) and unnatural if they are not, and the latter is indeed the case in *Benang*. But how exactly can Harley resurrect the memories of his ancestors?

Harley's unnatural narration not only conflates the living and the dead, it also merges the human being and nature, thus literally depicting how the land resonates with the voices of the ancestors. In other words, it actualizes the intrinsic quality of Aboriginal presence culture. Memory is preserved in nature, and nature's rhythm allows Harley to reconnect with his ancestors (32, 146). This notion of interconnectedness is made tangible in the unnatural acts of narration, thus enabling us to tentatively engage with this different perceptual world. One episode about his great-great-grandparents, for instance, ends with the words, "The mist hangs above the rocks where the big sea blooms. Blooms. Booms. Booms its heartbeat" (469). The visual perception of the land merges with an auditory one, a conflation that is reenacted on a phonological level through the use of assonances. The repetition further adds a steady, rhythmic quality to the passage, thereby reproducing the sound of a beating heart. We are here presented with an idea, however vague, of what it might be like to perceive of nature, time, and human beings as interrelated entities.

In his physically and humanly impossible status of hovering in the air, the narrator remarks, "Speaking from the heart, I tell you that I am part of a much older story, one of a perpetual billowing from the sea, with its rhythm of return, return, and remain" (495). It is not actually Harley, the person, who is narrating the stories of his ancestors, but his heart, which reproduces the heartbeat of the land and thereby the memories preserved in it: "Sing? Perhaps that is not the right word, because it is not really *singing*. And it is not really *me* who sings, for although I touch the earth only once in my performance . . . through me we hear the rhythm of many feet pounding the earth, and the strong pulse of countless hearts beating" (7–8). These hearts—that is, Noongar culture—are a living connection of the past, the present, and even the future, and Harley's ability to transform them into words, or rather the fact that he is transformed by them, ensures that the voices of the ancestors are still heard by their descendants. It is in this sense that the novel ends with an "affirmation of survival, cultural strength, and hope" (Fielder 7).

Harley's unnatural propensity for elevation and his unnatural acts of narration thus serve to give visible form to the central notion of an intimate interrelatedness between body and land as a source of strength and hope for the Noongar community. In other words, the unnatural here makes present the continuous relation Noongar people have with their Country. Significantly, this is not merely a past-oriented strategy to recuperate a lost culture, but more importantly a future-oriented one that seeks to substitute a focus on time, as implied in Harley's initial, historiographic project, with a turn to "the importance of continuity of place and relationships" (Brewster 16) for Noongar well-being. As the narrator states at the end, drawing on a Noongar word referring to one of his ancestors and also meaning "tomorrow," "We are still here, Benang" (495). The unnatural emphasizes the Noongar people's continuous presence in this particular place through a story that is told and originates, as the subtitle of the novel already indicates, *"from the heart."*

CONCLUSIONS—THE ETHICAL AND POLITICAL IMPLICATIONS OF ABORIGINAL UNNATURAL NARRATIVES

At the beginning of *Benang,* Harley states, "I know I make people uncomfortable" (7), an effect that is reproduced by the narrative itself in that it projects impossibilities that have a potentially disturbing, disorienting, and defamiliarizing effect on the (non-Indigenous) reader. However, this clash of different conceptions is not without benefits. More specifically, the unnatural is an effective means to incite readers to adopt a reading stance of deference and respect. In *Benang,* Harley emphasizes this point by contrasting his grandfather's reaction to his story with what he hopes his readers will display: "He snorted when he read of my ancestors floating from the pages and up, up, up among clouded peaks. I hope for more respect when I share the incident with you" (36). As Takolander convincingly argues, "Scott's narrator effectively taunts the reader to assume an ethical and active role" (8). Unnatural elements, such as Harley's elevation and his impossible narration, urge us to assume such an active yet humble role because they foreclose a simple immersion and instead make us aware of our own reading positions.

As I have argued in this chapter, cultural discrepancies between senders and receivers do not necessarily pose an impediment to interpreting unnatural narratives from a different cultural background. Instead, a critical analysis of the ways in which these texts negotiate the possible and the impossible can yield vital insights into their potential workings. In Scott's novel *Benang*, the unnatural functions to make present and tangible the importance of an interrelatedness between humans and the land. Moreover, by playing complex games with notions of the possible and impossible, the narrative form and storyworld of *Benang* reflect the significance of dialogue and openness toward other ways of being—not only in attempts to come to terms with the past and to rewrite Australian history from an Aboriginal perspective but also as a possible path for the future.

Generally speaking, then, unnatural narratives invite readers to reflect upon their reading positions and the cultural background they bring to the text and to engage with other perspectives on and conceptions of the world we live in. Since developing respect for and an appreciation of Indigenous knowledges and histories constitutes a key component of the reconciliation process in Australia, unnatural narratives by Aboriginal authors might therefore contribute to raising cultural awareness and sensitivity.

WORKS CITED

Alber, Jan. "Towards Resilience and Playfulness: The Negotiation of Indigenous Australian Identities in Twentieth-Century Aboriginal Narratives." *European Journal of English Studies*, vol. 20, no. 3, 2016, pp. 292–309.

———. "Unnatural Narratology: Developments and Perspectives." *Germanisch-Romanische Monatsschrift*, vol. 63, no. 1, 2013, pp. 69–84.

Alber, Jan, et al. "Unnatural Narratives, Unnatural Narratology: Beyond Mimetic Models." *Narrative*, vol. 18, no. 2, 2010, pp. 113–36.

———. "Unnatural Voices, Minds, and Narration." *The Routledge Companion to Experimental Literature*, edited by Joe Bray et al., Routledge, 2012, pp. 351–67.

———. "What Is Unnatural about Unnatural Narratology? A Response to Monika Fludernik." *Narrative*, vol. 20, no. 3, 2012, pp. 371–82.

Ashcroft, Bill, et al. *Intimate Horizons: The Post-Colonial Sacred in Australian Literature*. ATF P, 2009.

Birk, Hanne. *AlterNative Memories: Kulturspezifische Inszenierungen von Erinnerung in zeitgenössischen Romanen indigener AutorInnen Australiens, Kanadas und Aotearoas/Neuseelands*. WVT, 2008.

Brewster, Anne. "Kim Scott." *Giving This Country a Memory: Contemporary Aboriginal Voices of Australia*, edited by Anne Brewster, Cambria P, 2015, pp. 1–21.

Buchholz, Laura. "Unnatural Narrative in Postcolonial Contexts: Re-Reading Salman Rushdie's *Midnight's Children*." *Journal of Narrative Theory*, vol. 42, no. 3, 2012, pp. 332–51.

Devlin-Glass, Frances. "A Politics of the Dreamtime: Destructive and Regenerative Rainbows in Alexis Wright's *Carpentaria*." *Australian Literary Studies*, vol. 23, no. 4, 2008, pp. 392–407.

Doležel, Lubomír. *Heterocosmica: Fiction and Possible Worlds*. The Johns Hopkins UP, 1998.

"Emu and the Jabiru." *Dreamtime*, 2000, http://dreamtime.net.au/emu/. Accessed 6 Sep. 2017.

Fielder, John. "Country and Connections: An Overview of the Writing of Kim Scott." *Altitude*, vol. 6, 2005, pp. 1–12.

Garuba, Harry. "Explorations in Animist Materialism: Notes on Reading/Writing African Literature, Culture, and Society." *Public Culture*, vol. 15, no. 2, 2003, pp. 261–85.

Grieves, Vicki. *Aboriginal Spirituality: Aboriginal Philosophy, the Basis of Aboriginal Social and Emotional Wellbeing*. Discussion Paper No. 9, Cooperative Research Centre for Aboriginal Health, 2009.

Heinze, Rüdiger. "Violations of Mimetic Epistemology in First-Person Narrative Fiction." *Narrative*, vol. 16, no. 3, 2008, pp. 279–97.

Heiss, Anita. *Dhuuluu-Yala: To Talk Straight—Publishing Indigenous Literature*. Aboriginal Studies P, 2003.

Herman, David. "Storyworld." *Routledge Encyclopedia of Narrative Theory*, edited by David Herman et al., Routledge, 2008, pp. 569–70.

Jahn, Manfred. *Narratology: A Guide to the Theory of Narrative*. English Department, University of Cologne, http://www.uni-koeln.de/~ame02/pppn.htm. Accessed 5 Feb. 2015.

Klapproth, Danièle M. *Narrative as Social Practice: Anglo-Western and Australian Aboriginal Oral Traditions*. De Gruyter, 2004.

Linton, Patricia. "Ethical Reading and Resistant Texts." *Post-Colonial Literatures. Expanding the Canon*, edited by Deborah L. Madsen, Pluto P, 1999, pp. 29–44.

Moll, Andrea. "Natural or Unnatural? Linguistic Deep Level Structures in AbE: A Case Study of New South Wales Aboriginal English." *Unnatural Narratives—Unnatural Narratology*, edited by Jan Alber and Rüdiger Heinze, De Gruyter, 2011, pp. 246–68.

Mudrooroo (Colin Johnson). "Maban Reality and Shape-shifting the Past: Strategies to Sing the Past Our Way." *Critical Arts: A South-North Journal of Cultural & Media Studies*, vol. 10, no. 2, 1996, n. pag.

Muecke, Stephen. "Ideology Reiterated: The Uses of Aboriginal Oral Narrative." *Southern Review*, vol. 16, no. 1, 1983, pp. 86–101.

Palmer, Alan. "Social Minds in Fiction and Criticism." *Style*, vol. 45, no. 2, 2011, pp. 196–240.

Ravenscroft, Alison. "Dreaming of Others: *Carpentaria* and Its Critics." *Cultural Studies Review*, vol. 16, no. 2, 2010, pp. 194–224.

Richardson, Brian. "What Is Unnatural Narrative Theory?" *Unnatural Narratives—Unnatural Narratology*, edited by Jan Alber and Rüdiger Heinze, De Gruyter, 2011, pp. 23–40.

Scott, Kim. *Benang: From the Heart*. 1999. Fremantle P, 2011.

———. "Interview." *ATSIC*, February 2000, http://pandora.nla.gov.au/pan/41037/20050516-0000/www.atsic.gov.au/news_room/atsic_news/February_2000/what_Does_It_Mean_To_Be.html. Accessed 19 June 2019.

Seal, Graham. "Indigenous Australian Life Histories: A New Genre of Writing and Publishing?" *International Journal of the Book*, vol. 3, no. 1, 2005/2006, pp. 79–84.

Shklovsky, Viktor. "Art as Technique." 1917. *Russian Formalist Criticism: Four Essays,* edited by Lee T. Lemon and Marion J. Reis, U of Nebraska P, 1965, pp. 3–24.

Sommer, Roy. "'Contextualism' Revisited: A Survey (and Defence) of Postcolonial and Intercultural Narratologies." *Journal of Literary Theory,* vol. 1, no. 1, 2007, pp. 61–79.

Takolander, Maria. "Magical Realism and Irony's 'Edge': Rereading Magical Realism and Kim Scott's *Benang.*" *Journal of the Association for the Study of Australian Literature,* vol. 14, no. 5, 2014, pp. 1–11.

Todorov, Tzvetan. *The Fantastic: A Structural Approach to a Literary Genre.* Translated by Richard Howard. Foreword by Robert Scholes, Cornell UP, 1975.

Wheeler, Belinda. "An Interview with Kim Scott." *A Companion to the Works of Kim Scott,* edited by Belinda Wheeler, Camden House, 2016, pp. 158–69.

Wright, Alexis. *Carpentaria: A Novel.* 2006. Atria Books, 2009.

——. "On Writing *Carpentaria.*" *Heat Magazine,* vol. 13, 2007, pp. 79–95.

——. "Politics of Writing." *Southerly,* vol. 62, no. 2, 2002, pp. 10–20.

CHAPTER 4

Empathy the Long Way 'Round

Unnatural Autographic Narration

CHRISTOPHER D. KILGORE

AS AN APPROACH to literary texts, the "unnatural narrative" model has offered a powerful alternative to mimetic models, from normative realism to the conception of the cognitive "prototype," but its application to nonfictional narrative remains problematic: If unnatural narratives are taken to be those that deviate from the author and reader's real world (as Alber and others suggest), or if they are taken to be those that deviate from the conventions of mimetic realism (as Richardson argues in *Unnatural Voices* and *Unnatural Narrative*), then nonfiction texts might seem to be excluded a priori. In this chapter, I use three graphic novels—Art Spiegelman's *Maus* (1980–91), Alison Bechdel's *Fun Home* (2006), and *Are You My Mother?* (2012)—to propose that even if being considered nonfiction makes it difficult to call the *texts* unnatural, some nonfictional narratives do use "unnatural" narrative techniques, for the purpose of cultivating an unusual type of empathy between reader and autographic narrator. In recognition of the more straightforward empathy outlined in Suzanne Keen's article on "fast tracks to narrative empathy" in graphic narrative, I will call the present texts' gambit "empathy the long way 'round."

By understanding features of these narratives as "unnatural," the present study advances two related purposes. First, for the purpose of textual interpretation, it calls attention to the ongoing negotiations required to make sense of these complex texts. Ironically, the labels "self-reflexivity," "ambiguity," or "ambivalence," so often associated with texts identified as postmodernist (as these often are), tend to arrest the interpretive process. These texts' maneuvers allow readers to empathize with identity formations and subject positions sometimes understood as "unnatural" in a pejorative sense; in so doing, the texts enact recuperative processes that Judith Butler or Jean-François Lyotard might recognize, carrying forward a connection with the reader that is anything but merely ambiguous. Second, for the purpose of "unnatural poetics" and narrative theory, the present analysis offers an important alternative suggestion to common theories of nonfiction reading, suggesting that putative nonfictionality operates as a "top-down" cognitive frame, rather than an all-pervading mode or reading practice.

For some (including Alber, Heinze, and sometimes Richardson and Iversen), "unnatural" narratives feature a storyworld that does not match the consensus conception of reality. For those who adhere *rigidly* to this definition, "unnatural nonfiction" simply will not do—it must be an empty category, a contradiction in terms. But even if analysts do not rule out unnatural nonfiction a priori, critics using Alber's definition, and focusing on the existents and events within the storyworld, would usually render unnatural nonfiction unlikely.[1]

Other theorists turn to the realm so often underappreciated in conversations about the structuralist distinction between story (the "what") and discourse (the "how"): the story's instantiation through the cognitive processes of reading itself. As even Seymour Chatman suggests, storyworlds are in important ways "virtual," that is, not really present "in" the text, but rather present only when the text is activated, traversed, and recognized as narrative by the reader (27). For Mäkelä, Nielsen ("Naturalizing"), and others, *unnaturalizing* is a reading process, not a property of texts. To read "unnaturally," we have to de-tune our recognizing wetware, reading across the grain of the conventional, like the protagonist in the 1953 Philip K. Dick story "The Eyes Have It," who recoils in horror as he reads (perfectly commonplace) sentences describing people whose eyes can "slowly wander across the room" or "[fasten] onto" a young lady (27–28), and takes them literally. From this perspective, then, unnatural features might lurk within the pages of *any* narrative text whatsoever. This emphasis on reading methods would redirect the discussion toward what Brian McHale more aptly terms the "artificial" in all art (200).

---

1. I say "unlikely" rather than "impossible" to avoid foreclosing the interesting case where cultural differences might cause some readers to see certain parts of "nonfiction" narratives as "impossible." Some would argue that the novels of Ishmael Reed or Toni Morrison might prove quite interesting, seen through the "unnatural" lens in this way (see Kilgore, "From Unnatural").

Finally, for a few theorists, the storyworld's contents are less important than the story's telling, the structuralist *discourse* or *sjuzhet* (see, for instance, Nielsen's emphasis on enunciation ["Natural Authors" 276]). Here we may find more fertile ground for discussions of "unnatural" nonfiction, cases where the material being read makes it difficult for a reader to derive a noncontradictory storyworld, where multiple storyworld configurations remain possible even after the reader has finished reading,[2] or where the author makes use of what Walsh or Nielsen might call "fictionalizing" techniques in a manner that seems likely to distort the material. Richardson's most recent formulation sometimes seems closely aligned with this approach, emphasizing the unnatural as any textual strategies that "violate mimetic expectations and the practices of realism" or "contravene the presuppositions of nonfictional narrative" (*Unnatural Narrative* 3). This conceptualization does not, however, strictly preclude unnatural nonfictional narrative, or unnatural techniques used within nonfictional narrative, as Iversen has demonstrated in his analysis of transcribed Holocaust testimony videos. He finds, here, cases where the telling creates difficulties in comprehension and interpretation that make reconstructing coherent experientiality (following Fludernik's definition, the sense of *what it is like*) difficult, in two primary ways. In some cases, which Iversen calls "unmediated experientiality," breakdowns in narration (contradictions, corrections, or divagations) make traumatic experiences difficult for the reader to reconstruct (Iversen 102). In other cases of "demediated experientiality," similar breakdowns make the speaker's consciousness difficult to reconstruct (102). Iversen's approach suggests how and why it might make sense to understand some nonfiction narratives as "unnatural": They use textual elements and readers' expectations for narrative discourse to create an "unsettled, unsettling" (97) effect, suspending readers' sense-making interpretive activity, and this effect might be diminished or effaced entirely by trying to shoehorn their properties into naturalizing frames—including those for simple "undecidability" or "ambiguity." That is, these techniques create ontological problems with story events, not epistemological problems with the characters' knowledge about those events.

The present study adopts Richardson's approach rather than Alber's conception based on the relationship between the storyworld and the reader's world, or the even broader approach favored by Mäkelä, based on unnatural reading methods. Here, I will examine details in the texts that seem likely to create problems for story production, at a level and by a method less easy

---

2. By this I mean nontrivial differences in "what happened" at a fairly basic level; examples might include Fowles's *The French Lieutenant's Woman* (1969) or Nabokov's *Pale Fire* (1962).

to naturalize by recourse to mere uncertainty. To tackle the issue of unnatural discourse in *graphic* narrative, however, it will be necessary to consider the medium-specific affordances of the form often called "comics." Studies on comics have repeatedly called it a hybrid medium but have emphasized different properties: Will Eisner calls the medium's textual qualities paramount (8–9), while Jared Gardner (see, e.g., 57) and Pascal Lefèvre (15) hold that the indexicality or trace of the artist's drawing hand in the visual material plays the most important role (see also Fischer and Hatfield, and the work of Baetens).

For the purpose of understanding graphic *narrative* discourse, however, Scott McCloud and Thierry Groensteen each independently identify the core hybrid quality of comics: Insofar as they can be distinguished from other visual and textual arts, graphic narratives' most unique contribution is the *panel*, the segmentation of visual field that integrates the image or icon (McCloud 66, 92; Groensteen 18) with the syntagmatic structuring that the medium shares with language. So comics are *both* image *and* word, at their most basic level: the stroke of line or empty space—what Derrida calls, in different contexts, the *trait* or *passepartout* (7)—that distinguishes one image from another. As Groensteen puts it, comics create "iconic solidarity," juxtaposing "interdependent images that, participating in a series, present the double characteristic of being separated . . . and [being] plastically and semantically over-determined by the fact of their coexistence *in praesentia*" (18).

Rather than simply creating unnatural characters or events, in Alber's sense (as so many comics have done), a graphic narrative using unnatural techniques, in Richardson's sense of antimimetic or anti-conventional, would interfere with the cognitive and conventional mechanisms by which readers convert ink on the page into story elements (see, e.g., Kilgore, "Unnatural"), producing storyworlds difficult to resolve into coherent and noncontradictory events and characters. Among all the comics that engage in this kind of visual play, the most famous and obvious example also lends itself most readily to discussions of unnatural narration, not least because of its connection to the kind of traumatic events that Iversen has also studied: Art Spiegelman's *Maus* is, after all, not only a nonfiction account of some of the most infamous events of the twentieth century. It is also a memoir, or what has come to be known as autography, a literal "drawing of the self."[3]

---

3. Bradley also notes the terms "autobio comics" and "graphic memoir" (161–62).

RECONSTRUCTING THE AUTOGRAPHIC NARRATOR: ART SPIEGELMAN'S *MAUS*

Spiegelman's famous work has been so often studied that its formal properties and the major critical approaches should be familiar: It tells a nested story, relating Spiegelman's father Vladek's travails as a young Jewish man in Hitler's Germany, interpenetrated by a framing narrative relating Spiegelman's own conversations with his father, the source material for the embedded narrative. Its troubling graphic form has given rise to a variety of interpretive stances, which see its rhetorical thrust as a father-and-son psychodrama (Eakin 203); a (successful) way of coping with traumatic history and family (Elmwood 701; Adams 37; Budick 380; Chute, "The Shadow" 213; Doherty 75; and Ewert 91); a statement that reconciliation must remain forever impossible (Rothberg 670; McGlothlin 192, 194); a way of giving voice to the voiceless dead (Laga 72); and a postmodern demonstration that accuracy is both necessary and impossible (Berlatsky 155). It carries out a critique of racializing discourse (Loman 560; Ewert 100–101; Ma 117), of Holocaust testimonial discourse (Eakin), and of course also a critique of such critiques (Rothberg 670; Cioffi 121).

Thanks primarily to its graphic form—using mouse-headed cartoon characters to narrate a story of the Holocaust (see figure 4.1)—*Maus* is so distinctly *odd* that Cioffi declares that its world "by no means coincides with our own" (119), and Budick describes it as "a fiction" *tout court* (388). In fact, the *New York Times* itself initially called it fiction (Adams 46) but changed the designation after Spiegelman's scathing letter to the editors (see Doherty 69). The distinction is difficult. For one thing, the iconic mouse representation generates a variety of graphical and interpretive inconsistencies that trouble its interpretation.[4] For another, as Cioffi and Ewert and many others observe, it creates a complex temporal situation where past and present "bleed into" one another (see also McGlothlin; Klepper; Berlatsky). Although many critics identify these traits as "postmodernism" (Chute; Doherty) or "self-reflexivity" (Horstkotte and Pedri; Klepper; Laga; Berlatsky), it seems likely that beneath its real-world story, beneath the reader's common assumption that the events really happened, something "unnatural" occurs in *Maus*'s narration.

If Spiegelman told the story simply and unproblematically with animal figures, Horstkotte and Pedri, Ewert, Ma, and others would be able to close the debate, calling the mouse-people simply a matter of metaphor, and the

---

4. See also Horstkotte and Pedri; Ewert; and Ma. I would argue that it operates as what Fauconnier and Turner would call a "single-scope blend," which works like Ewert describes this metaphor: "in only one direction," applying human traits to the mice and not vice versa (95).

FIGURE 4.1. Mouse-people (Spiegelman 1: 5)

unnatural theorist would be left with little to say. But Spiegelman peppers the *Maus* texts with features that trouble the reading process, prompting readers to rebuild the storyworld in new ways. Scholarship on *Maus* that attends to such effects (see Cioffi; Klepper; McCloud; Budick; McGlothlin; and others) has mostly adopted the structuralist tradition and assumed that the story-discourse relationship achieves a static state once the reading is complete. They therefore observe that the book creates three different narrative levels, corresponding to three figures of the narrating agent: the mouse-headed Vladek, who tells his own story; the mouse-headed "Artie," who co-narrates Vladek's and his own story; and a second instance of the autographic narrator, a mouse-*masked* figure I will call "Art," who narrates in lowercase text.[5] Rather than stop here, however, I want to consider how these moments develop across the text and across the temporality of the reading process, showing how the

---

5. Interestingly, Berlatsky's otherwise more nuanced analysis of the notion of "accuracy" in the books consistently ignores the graphical distinctions between the various iterations of the Spiegelman figure, and collapses all into either the real author, Spiegelman, or his pen-and-paper avatar, Artie (162).

books' discourse—or rather the aggregate of textual features that enables story production—operates unnaturally. The reading process is dynamic and moves in several directions at once, and the reader's sense of the story-discourse relationship, I argue, changes with it.

Throughout the first 98 of *Maus I*'s 159 pages, the mouse-people conceit remains relatively stable, in spite of occasional hints that not all is well. The first major blow comes when a chagrinned Artie learns that Vladek has read "Prisoner on the Hell Planet," Artie's youthful, angry take on his mother's suicide (see figure 4.2). *Maus* faithfully embeds the whole comic, whose drawings are no less stylized, but mimic a woodcut (which, Chute notes, mimics a German expressionist style, no less! ["The Shadow" 207]), and depict *human* faces, and a photograph. Since no characters remark on the human faces, the interpolated text destabilizes the story's comfortable ontology—Berlatsky describes the effect as "vertiginous" (160)—asking the reader to tear down and reassemble at least some of it. Were the cartoon merely a matter of pen strokes, one might draw the ironic conclusion that the mouse-people autographically narrate themselves as humans (an avant-garde move indeed!), except that animals exist in our world, but in the world of *Maus,* humans do not—and of course, then there is also the photograph. Rather, "Hell Planet" most likely joins the world of the real author, making its appearance here a complex kind of metalepsis. In perceiving this metalepsis, readers will have to recognize a narrating instance not yet clearly figured in the text: an instance responsible for drawing Artie *and* for inserting the human-headed "Prisoner" text.

Before reading *Maus II,* most readers will probably assume that this narrating instance corresponds to the real author, Spiegelman, and indeed, *Maus I* lets readers "naturalize" the associated textual features by maintaining clear distinctions between the narrative layers: In the absence of discrepancies between Spiegelman's real-world biography and the one depicted here, we can integrate all of Spiegelman's in-text avatars to create a composite conception of Spiegelman-the-real-author. But this is the textual maneuver that becomes so important in *Maus II*: moments of breakdown, followed by recuperation.

In the second volume, Spiegelman applies a series of twists that repeat this iterative rebuilding process several times.[6] On the very first page, the autographic narrator "Artie" tries to decide how to draw his wife, Françoise. When she learns of his dilemma, she declares, "A *mouse,* of course!" (2: 11). And of course, on the page, she is already drawn as a mouse. In addition to providing comic relief, this playful exchange reinforces the narrative layering

---

6. Several critics identify many of the examples that follow, but they attribute them to an increase in self-reflexiveness (Klepper 98), a universalizing aesthetic turn (Ewert 101), or a feeling of "despair" over historical accuracy (Berlatsky 146).

FIGURE 4.2. A panel from "Prisoner on the Hell Planet!" (Spiegelman 1: 102)

established in *Maus I*, and yet it also begins to suggest the inadequacy of that simple construction: Using cartoon animals to represent distinctions that are ultimately ethnic (and not racial) creates serious difficulties that repeat those Vladek faces in Hitler's Germany. As Berlatsky also points out (156), this is one of many moments where the racializing metaphor of animal representations seems designed to defamiliarize classifying instincts; another appears later, within Vladek's story, when a concentration camp internee claims to be "a German," and not to belong among "these Yids and Polacks" (2: 50)—and gets drawn alternately as a mouse and a cat. Such moments can be "naturalized" by reference to the book's narrative levels, but the process of deconstruction and reintegration must always bear with it the traces of unnatural discomfort: The character on the page is *both* mouse *and* cat, and yet *neither* mouse *nor* cat—because the context of the camps flattens difference to a matter of clothing and abjection (see also Ewert [98–100] and Berlatsky, who points out that in death the character reverts to mouse form only [158]). Here, however, the unnatural ontological oscillation remains confined among the text's "mouse-people" narrative levels, and readers may feel free to naturalize the oscillation to a matter of indeterminacy.

The book's heavily studied second chapter completes the iterative process begun in *Maus I* by introducing yet another narrative level. Here, Spiegelman introduces a new self-avatar, a drawing of a human man in a mouse mask (see figure 4.3).[7] Now, the reader will need to credit the stories of Vladek and Artie to *this* figure, "Art." But Spiegelman grants "Art" further "unnatural" features: Faced with aggressive interviewers, he shrinks to child size and has to visit his "shrink," Pavel, to get "unshrunk." And during the interview, Art and the animal-masked media reps trample all over a pile of dead mouse-people (not mouse-*masked* people) that litter the cartoonist's study. In addition to these by turns comical and horrific effects, which welcome the reader into the pain and absurdity of Artie's project, these features (plus the highly stylized aspects of the sequence) demand yet another shadowy narrating level. Some narrating agent *presents* (draws as well as writes) the mouse-masked figure (see figure 4.4).[8] I therefore differ with extant criticism: I would add another narrative layer. Chute calls the mouse-mask environment the text's "own enunciative context" ("The Shadow" 208), while Ewert ascribes all narrative enunciation to "the grownup Art" (93). Like Berlatsky, Klepper elides the differences between "Artie" the mouse-person and "Art" the mouse-masked human (85) and later calls the mouse-masked figure the "hierarchically highest narrative agent" (100). McGlothlin recognizes three narrative layers, but—surprisingly—identifies the mouse-masked Art *as the narrator* for his sections (181–84), even though he is not presented, à la Escher, drawing himself.

This sequence, then, requires readers to maintain at least four diegetic levels, but also to interpret ceaseless metalepses from one level to another. It is not, however, a process of seamless or even terminable (see Klepper 100) naturalization; rather, such coherence as the autographic narrator attains arrives in interpretive fits and starts. Faced with each new detail, readers have to rebuild the storyworld (ontologically, rhetorically), and the resulting storyworld will bear traces of its unnatural roots—just as in the case of the mouse/cat character—leaving an affective aftertaste of discomfort. A skeptic might, here, merely follow the common path of retreat (often used in criticism on Nabokov's similarly bewildering narrative levels) and assert that Spiegelman wrote and drew the whole thing, but this maneuver cedes the whole field: It steps outside narration altogether.

---

7. The image appeared in the back flap of *Maus I*, but as a paratext it is much less intrusive.

8. I see the question of whether we want to identify this narrative level as a "narrator," an "implied author," or "the real author" as a matter of theoretical proclivities and exigency, and will not pursue the distinctions between these terms further here.

FIGURE 4.3. "Art" as a mouse-masked human (Spiegelman 2: 41)

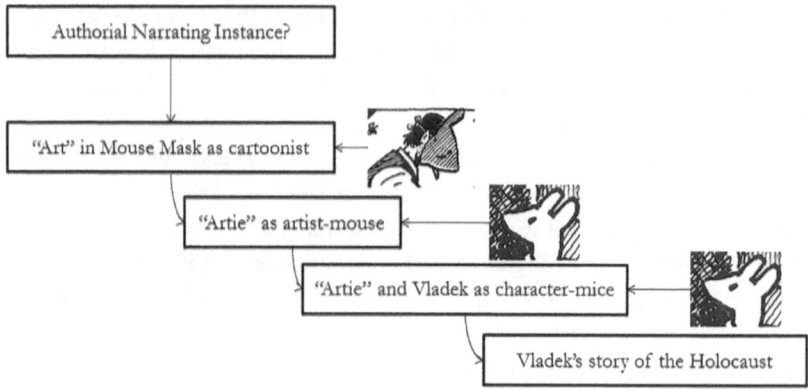

FIGURE 4.4. Narrative levels in *Maus*

But in *Maus II*, the process of iterative construction rebuilds not only story *events* but also the *act of narration* itself, the process by which Spiegelman's avatars render events in legible form. For me, rereading *Maus II* in particular, I begin to feel (as Budick [392] and Cioffi [119] also appear to feel, whereas Berlatsky does not) that none of my reconstructions of this *narrating act* are adequate. The autographic narrator—Artie/Art/Spiegelman—coheres and disintegrates continuously, and the various versions of him disassemble and reassemble themselves in my head, even after I have finished reading. In that sense, then, the act of narration, qua a reconstructed act, is "unnatural." It presents itself as according *and failing to accord* with its real-world referents—again, an ontological rather than epistemological problem. As Laga ultimately points out, *this* combination of images and words is always already inadequate, and yet their continual deconstruction and reintegration allows them to declare their inadequacy in a manner designed to inspire confidence and trust (see Laga 66; Doherty 80; Ewert 91; Berlatsky 172).

The reading situation begins to approximate what Artie himself says about the writing process: that *this* act of speech is both necessary and impossible.[9] The reader's felt experience of adjustment and readjustment, of a need to construct simultaneous with a need to reject or critique, matches the autographic narrator's (apparent, reconstructed) experience of composition. I would venture beyond Berlatsky's suggestion that the resultant text bears the "imprint" of Spiegelman's experience (153, 155, 184), and argue that this cognitive-affective experience may usefully go by the name of *empathy*. To distinguish it from more immediate, visceral, visual experiences, I call this "empathy the long way 'round."

In her analysis of more recent graphic narratives that feature anthropomorphic animals and people represented in animal forms, Suzanne Keen has suggested that graphic novels enable an empathic experience that is properly precognitive, operating faster than consciousness or cognition. She holds that graphic novels offer authors a unique affordance for accessing this precognitive realm—and notes that authors may use this manipulatively (in appropriative gestures) or more in ways "at least implying an appeal for justice, assistance, or recognition" ("Fast Tracks to Narrative Empathy" 136). Although Keen acknowledges that the precise operation of the relationship between reader and text is complex, she asserts that we can still study the textual features that seem designed to prompt this kind of engagement with the characters and, thereby, the corresponding people or animals in the real world—but this position also does imply a certain amount of tension between the assertion of an immediate precognitive experience and the properly cognitive process that readers might use to make sense of the representational relationships that these texts create.

I argue here that *Maus* affords not merely a different route to the same kind of affective experience that Keen describes, but rather that the experi-

---

9. I lack space to give adequate treatment to the notion of adequacy in *Maus*, so I would refer the reader to Berlatsky's capacious and well-theorized discussion; for me, the key textual example is a hilarious moment when Artie and Pavel discuss a quote from Samuel Beckett on silence, and the cartoon image shows the two men smoking together—in a "silence" that, given the medium, cannot help but "speak" (2: 45).

ence that goes by the name of *empathy* is a process that includes a variety of interpretive, cognitive, and emotional experiences. The quick, visceral, visual empathy that Keen describes seems to involve interpretive and cognitive dimensions as well—but they are brief, simple, and minimalized. Empathy the long way 'round carries a much heavier interpretive and cognitive load, making it perhaps less easy to reach, but perhaps also granting it a deeper resonance.

It seems to me that *Maus* gains some of its popularity and staying power because of the largely unnatural discourse-story relationship it creates (again, I want to point out that an unnatural technique like this, closer to Richardson's version of the unnatural, is a different thing from Alber's unnatural storyworlds, or Mäkelä's unnatural reading practices). Precisely because it has to operate through an extended process of mediation, this "long way 'round" has the potential to avoid what Kaja Silverman calls "appropriative identification" (see Elmwood 694), the self-serving "false empathy" (see Keen, *Empathy* xxiv) by which a reader might appropriate others' suffering to serve the needs of the self. It seems graphic narration, by redoubling the "self-doubling" process that Charles Olney describes in his studies of autobiography (see Van Dyne 106 and Watson 28), affords a uniquely effective method for evoking "empathy the long way 'round," and indeed, not every book need recruit mouse-people to invite its readers to begin an iterative reconstruction process. Unnaturalness itself need not appear as visibly as in the mouse-cat, or the mouse-masked autographic character-narrator.

RECONSTRUCTING THE ACT OF NARRATION: ALISON BECHDEL'S MEMOIRS

If not for their spatiotemporal complexity and capacious allusiveness, Alison Bechdel's autographic books *Fun Home: A Family Tragicomic* and *Are You My Mother? A Comic Drama* might be regarded as straightforward graphic memoirs, with little about them to excite a theorist of unnatural narrative. Published in 2006 to almost immediate acclaim, *Fun Home* has since become a staple of college reading, and tells a story similar in some respects to *Maus*: It relates the experiences of a child growing up in a household fractured by the twentieth century's schizoid politics of gender and sexuality. Bechdel uses a clear-line style, augmented with blue-gray watercolors and detailed cross-hatching to narrate according to a careful, nonlinear plan. Readers learn of her father Bruce's dual life, as schoolteacher and funeral home director, as heteronormative father figure and closeted homosexual, as upright educated citizen and a man who apparently engages in sexual activities with high school boys—and of course, readers also learn of Bechdel's own artistic and personal *Bildung* (see also Van Dyne 108).

Like *Maus*, *Fun Home* challenges scholars and critics, who find in its pages the same "generic elusiveness" (Freedman 126), the same problematic temporality (Warhol; Lyndenberg; Chute, "Comics Form")—in short, the same quality of *oddness*. These factors have led critics to read the text as a queer critique of heteronormative discourse (Lyndenberg; Rohy; Warhol 6–7; Chute, "Comics Form" 113; Watson), a critique of autobiographical form (Watson; Van Dyne 107), and, again like *Maus*, an attempt to cope with traumatic history. These factors, plus the book's predilection for allusion, have earned it a place in both the postmodernist (Warhol; Rohy; Freedman 133) and modernist (Freedman 138; Watson) canons, and lead Rohy to call it a "critique of realism" (349)—a near match to Richardson's recent definition of the "unnatural" as those techniques that "contravene the presuppositions of nonfictional narrative" (*Unnatural Narrative* 3). *Fun Home* sets up a reading experience that should feel familiar after *Maus*, circling around key incidents and renarrating important events over and over again, creating a recursive pattern whereby readers have to create and then modify not only the storyworld's characters and events but also the act of narration. Just as in *Maus*, *Fun Home* cues these experiences of "reconstruction" with anomalous textual elements (see also Watson 28).

To take a signal example, on several occasions Bechdel carries out a classic act of unnatural narration: She portrays in detail an event that no one living could have witnessed, her father's death in a road accident. Readers learn about Bruce's death first through direct verbal narration, juxtaposed with oblique images. At the end of the first chapter, Bechdel notes, "It's true that he didn't kill himself until I was nearly twenty," as the graphic images illustrate Bruce carefully instructing young Alison on operating a riding lawn mower (23). In the following chapter the text admits, in carefully chosen negatives and double negatives, "There's no proof, actually, that my father killed himself. / No one knew it wasn't an accident" (27; see figure 4.5). The first and last panels on the page show "rhyming" (Groensteen 7) images, first of the newspaper declaring, "Local Man Dies After Being Hit By Truck" and then of the newspaper and copy of Camus's *A Happy Death*, as found "around the house" in the days before Bruce's death (27).[10] These images ask the reader

---

10. See also Watson on Fun Home as "archive" (32) and Rohy's study on the text's Derridean "archive fever" (344).

FIGURE 4.5. First mention of Bruce's death (Bechdel, *Fun Home* 23)

to conduct several constructive moves, creating a complex set of events and existents. To imagine Bruce's death, the reader would "read into" the newspapers and the text, creating a missing event, but also a process of discovery and reconstruction carried out by the autographic narrator, *who had not seen either newspaper herself.*

On the following page, however, Bechdel forces a reconstruction by offering—in a very small lower-left quadrant panel—a graphic depiction of a moment just before Bruce's death (see figure 4.6). Here, again, the text narrates in conditionals: "maybe he didn't notice the truck coming because he was preoccupied with the [upcoming] divorce" (28). The image portrays Bruce, shirtless, in cutoff jean-shorts, carrying weeds across the road—details not yet mentioned in the text. Again, this image requires the reader to revise and rework not just the details of this event, but the *kind of narrating act* taking place. That is, from the initial textual negations and oblique images, the reader might reconstruct a reticent act of narration, and thence perhaps, a reticent narrator, but the unwitnessed event, rendered in clear and exacting detail, invites a quite different reconstruction: an *imaginative* act of narration (a positive act, rather than an act of disnarration).

Fun Home returns to this moment again and again, each time asking the reader to tear down and rebuild the sense of story and events, and of the narrating act and narrating agent behind them. Depending on the reader's predilections, the events themselves likely do not become unnatural—most readers will likely assume that some real event happened, rather than that two contradictory events happened—but *on the way there,* the events will likely flicker and rearrange, and the effect on the putative narrating agent thereby becomes unnatural. One occasion (see figure 4.7) presents an express counterfactual,

FIGURE 4.6. The first scene illustrating Bruce's death (Bechdel, *Fun Home* 28)

imagining what might have happened if the truck had missed—but also disclosing that the truck was a "Sunbeam Bread truck" (59), creating a deft tangle of fact and fiction. In the following chapter, the narration reestablishes the context, filling in details that might at first have seemed like confabulation. As Rohy has also pointed out (348), the text quietly undoes its earlier (negatively worded) certainties, offering (in positives this time), "I have suggested that my father killed himself, but it's just as accurate to say that he died gardening" and then explains his restoration of "an old farmhouse" (89)—as the images portray him weeding as cars pass on the road. Then—and in the same position on the page as the first iteration—the discourse offers a different version of the initial imagined image (figure 4.8), and then leaps to portray the swerving truck driver, as the text backs up the portrayal with reference to the truck driver's testimony: He "described my father as jumping backward into the road 'as if he saw a snake'" (89). The quotation from the driver, in particular, invites the reader to reconstruct a different narrating act and narrator, one who, like Spiegelman, documents her data.

By now a secondary pattern should be clear: The images draw nearer and nearer to their subjects, as the panel size swells to fill the page's lateral dimensions. The final two examples continue this trend, and begin to take on an increasingly symbolic relationship with the text—the detailed image of Bruce with the weeds has become, like snakes, verbal signs, cockatoos, and other textual elements, an emblem for something unsayable, something that arrives for the reader in a successive series of overlapping, renegotiating shocks (see figure 4.9). The final iteration closes in further, eliminating Bruce, the weeds, and everything else, and filling the frame with the truck's grille—an odd image-rhyme to the comic panel's grid.

FIGURE 4.7. Scene depicting a counterfactual event (Bechdel, *Fun Home* 59)

FIGURE 4.8. Third scene depicting Bruce's death (Bechdel, *Fun Home* 89)

This sequence of iterative approaches to the event of Bruce's death—and the act of narrating that event, as well as the effect of positioning the reader in the impossible locus of Bruce's last moments (think of that grille)—is merely the most obviously "unnatural" of a number of such details. Bechdel uses a similar series of shifting repetitions to portray the moment she learned of Bruce's death, the moment in which she learned of Bruce's affair with the

FIGURE 4.9. Fourth scene depicting Bruce's death (Bechdel, *Fun Home* 116)

children's babysitter Roy, her moments of sexual discovery (see also Van Dyne 113), and the moment in which she came out as a lesbian to her parents (see also Rohy 356). As the textual elements return recursively to these moments, they also ask the reader to reimagine the autographic narrator along lines similar to Spiegelman, albeit less dramatically: The narrative reading process may be able to send the reader through a circular trajectory that duplicates the work carried out in the (reconstructed) process of narration (see also Watson, in a different interpretive direction), and thence, as in the *Maus* books, creating an odd combination of what Keen calls "situational" (*Empathy* xii, 80) and "authorial" (xiii, 124–125) empathy. That is, by subjecting the reader to the autographic narrator's experience of cognitive reassembly work, the text invites the reader to share "aspects of plot and circumstance" (Keen 80) but also involves the reader intimately in the author's "empathetic imagination" (Keen xiii)—that is, again, "empathy the long way 'round."

In *Fun Home*, the sense of "unnatural" narration remains more or less confined to these recursive elements; many of the book's pages allow the reader to proceed in peace, integrating textual elements as discourse, and using them to produce storyworld conclusions, and *Fun Home* is, ultimately, not unnatural en toto—it is not an "unnatural text." But Bechdel's second memoir, *Are You My Mother?* (*AYMM*), presents more of a challenge, using a welter of "rhyming" images to keep the reader off-balance, making even more room for comprehensive revisions to the storyworld. Almost as well received as *Fun Home* and certainly just as worthy of attention, *AYMM* turns the same critical eye on Bechdel's relationship with her mother, and spins an altogether more complicated narrative. Where *Fun Home* follows the pattern established in *Maus*, revisiting events or images and layering them with details that prompt readers to rebuild the act of narration, *AYMM* turns this iterative technique nearly into a poetics: Visually "rhyming" panels abound on every page, as the narration obsessively works through three romantic relationships; two psychoanalytical therapeutic relationships; the psychoanalytic philosophies of Freud, Alice Miller, and Donald Winnicott; the life of Virginia Woolf; and of course, a lifetime relationship between Bechdel and her mother. Where *Fun Home*'s unnatural techniques revolve around the act of narration to be reconstructed from the textual material, *AYMM* creates an unsettlingly ambiguous temporality, where the time of narration advances in fits and starts, as Bechdel's narrating avatar seems to be changing and learning as she writes, redoubling readers' cognitive work, and also explaining why, as yet, this second book has received less critical attention.

As of this writing, no scholarly analyses seem available, but the book's longer reviews divide predictably between those who process and appreciate the book's ferocious cultural criticism (Roiphe; Bilger; Barber; Warren) and those who do not (Garner; Jacobs). Like the other books considered here, *AYMM* elicits observations on its complexity and difficulty (see Barber; Bilger; Bradley; Warren) and confusion over its genre. Everyone identifies it as "a memoir," and most observe that it really considers the artistic process—following Alison and Helen's lead in calling it a "metabook" (*AYMM* 285)—but some then reclassify it as an "essay full stop" (Bradley 163), a "graduate thesis about object relations" (Jacobs 75), and more like "poetry" than "the dense, wordy introspection of most prose memoirs" (Roiphe par. 7).

In *Fun Home,* the multiple frames of reference could usually be matched up, integrated with the storyworld, and interpreted by reference to "Alison's" apparent age, but in *AYMM,* the cues are subtler, and the drawings create images more similar to one another. Bechdel's in-text "Alison" avatar appears in similar positions regularly throughout the book: working at a computer, talking on the telephone with her mother Helen, and working with a therapist. Readers could be forgiven for occasionally confusing the first therapist, Joyce, with the later Carol, or the period during which Alison writes *Fun Home* (cued by a stylish Apple MacBook on her desk, among other details) with the one in which she writes the present volume itself (cued by a mammoth Apple monitor, Alison's glasses, and a hands-free headset).

This environment sets up a complex, ambiguous temporality, where anecdotes or narrative episodes are not so much *framed* or *embedded* as *interleaved* (as Warren and Bilger also note), asking the reader to keep a sharp eye out for contextualizing details and elements that invite revisions to the story and its telling—and also building up an affective charge of disorientation. These turning points are many, so I will only explore two in detail: a childhood memory when Helen stopped kissing seven-year-old Alison good-night, and a more recent memory in which Helen expresses disapproval of twenty-four-year-old Alison's book contract for "lesbian cartoons"—doubtless the first compendium of Bechdel's popular series, *Dykes to Watch Out For*. Both, I will argue, form part of the recursive pattern that may occasion the "empathy the long way 'round" observed in *Maus* and *Fun Home*.

The first case, a childhood memory, appears initially as a sudden, traumatic event in the life of a young girl. A series of panels and narrative text boxes explains the nightly ritual of "coofying," where Helen would tuck in and deliver good-night kisses to Alison and her brothers (*AYMM* 134–36). But—as the text-box narration explains the travails that Virginia Woolf and her mother faced within a patriarchal society—the graphic images show Helen declaring to Alison, "You're too old to be kissed good night anymore" (136; see figure 4.10). Whereas prior images show Helen bending over the boys, her pacific expression sketched in sleek lines of eye and brow, this final panel shows her standing upright, face now etched in exhaustion and distaste as she reaches to turn off the light. As the narration explains, the young Alison "felt almost as if she'd slapped me" but remained "stoic" and "betrayed no emotion" (137). The interaction is emblematic of the child-developmental and cultural themes elaborated like meticulous lacework by the narrative's complex temporality. Alison and Helen rehash the same interactions throughout their lives together: Helen not quite satisfying Alison's needs; Alison withholding those needs to preempt disapproval or withdrawal of affection; both women's needs struggling for expression in a heteronormative, patriarchal culture (see also Bilger 14).

This sequence presents the event as an abrupt and unforeseen calamity, and may prompt some readers to regard Helen as cold, distant, or perhaps—as the narration itself suggests through the account of Woolf—simply reacting as best she can to the gendered expectations of her time and culture. It also suggests an "Alison" character damaged in childhood by a lack of affection or contact—a rather simplistic Freudian narrative. *AYMM* does not leave the event there, however. A longer narrative segment reveals an achingly intimate account of a seven-year-old Alison drawing a nascently sexualized image of a doctor and a female child. Helen finds the drawing, but Alison, seized by fear and shame, dodges a confrontation. In a curious sequence of panels,[11] the narration reworks the withdrawn-coofying incident: "Did Mom rifle through my [drawings] while I was getting ready for bed?" the narration muses, as

---

11. For the sake of expediency, I have distorted the sequence of events slightly: The musing over when Helen discovered the drawing comes first, followed by the sequence showing the avoided conversation.

FIGURE 4.10. Helen Bechdel declining to kiss Alison good-night (Bechdel, *AYMM* 136)

the images work back through young Alison's bed-readying, and then, as the moment of withdrawal arrives, the narrating text box says, "It occurs to me now that perhaps this is why she stopped kissing me good night. / Until now, the memories have been separate: the time Mom stopped kissing me, the time Mom found the dirty picture" (144; figure 4.11). This is the moment that asks the reader to reconsider not just the event but also the act of narration.

Although the sequence is redolent with many possible interpretive maneuvers, it becomes "unnatural" in the fashion of *Maus* and *Fun Home* in its use of the word *now*, a term whose temporal locus becomes thoroughly ambivalent. The configuration of images (showing childhood) and text boxes (narrating an adult's perspective) suggests that the *now* corresponds to the time of narration, discourse time, rather than the time being chronicled, the story time. And yet, earlier parts of the book have portrayed an aging Alison engaged in the preparatory work for the book, *and actually writing it*. The *now* could refer, therefore, to any number of potential deictic centers, any number of versions

FIGURE 4.11. Realization of parallel events (Bechdel, *AYMM* 144)

of "Alison-the-narrator." In fact, because the narration comes coupled with (past) images carefully selected to correspond to the (recent) epiphany, the one time that *now cannot* refer to is the final enunciative (or rather, presentational) time, usually regarded as the time of the telling, the discourse time. The radically ambiguous *now* appears again and again throughout the text (see *AYMM* 14, 49, 87, 253, 271), and always draws readers' attention to the disjunctions that separate the narrating agent into instances as varied as the acts of narration she carries out, imposing on narrator and reader alike the pressure to build and to reject what is built. That is, unlike the narrator of *Fun Home*, who accrues self-reflexivity and meticulousness with each reconstruction, the narrator in *AYMM* begins to seem someone who (as Alison explains several times) does not merely *work* at narration, but obsessively *reworks*. The signature maneuver is one of reconsideration and restatement—embodied just after this sequence in Alison's statement to her then-therapist Jocelyn, "God, I can't believe I told you that" (145).

The second example involves a similar event, which becomes occasion for a similarly problematic reconstruction of the narrating act: This time, Helen withholds approval for a twenty-four-year-old Alison's book contract because it consists of cartoons telling expressly lesbian stories. Oblivious to Alison's mounting exasperation during one of their numerous telephone calls, Helen remarks, "I would love to see your name on a book, but not on a book of Lesbian cartoons" (182). The narrating boxes explain that even then, Alison "understood that she was upset more about [Bruce's] homosexuality than mine. / But I also understood that my mother's disavowal was about something else altogether" (182). Given the preceding pattern, astute readers may expect, first, that this crucial scene will appear again, in new contexts, and second, that this confident narratorial explanation will *also* be upended, as indeed it is.

This *scene* itself does not repeat verbatim, as others do, but the event it indexes—Helen's disapproval of the book—does. The first iteration shows Alison explaining to Helen that, as the narration puts it, she has "met an agent . . . who encouraged me to put together a book" (181). The second iteration shows Alison telling her mother that she "met with that publisher" and "signed a contract to do a book of cartoons" (227). The first iteration presents Alison and Helen interacting as though for the first time, and the details of mise-en-scène are, as usual, carefully chosen: Alison talks on a telephone in a basement apartment, dressed in shorts and a T-shirt. The second iteration also portrays the interaction as though it is their first, as Helen asks, "You mean your lesbian cartoons?" and then, "But . . . what if someone sees your name?" (228). But this time, Alison sits in an upper-story apartment, in a different shirt. The narration then presents this exchange as an epiphany, a moment in which she recognized that "whatever it was I wanted from my mother was simply not there to be had," a fact devoid of blame (229). In the panels that follow, Alison hangs up on Helen, and then an iconic panel, spanning two-thirds of the page, shows twenty-four-year-old Alison bent over the silent telephone, face contorted in—ultimately cathartic—sobs (229; figure 4.12). These two iterations resist any easy reconciliation: They seem to be two different versions of the same event, *but also* two different but similar events. The first iteration appears at the end of a mini-story about Alison's developing literary talent, while the second appears at the climax of a sequence concerning Alison's romantic difficulties. The narration does not remark on the repetition of the telephone conversations, so the reader is left with an undecidable feature (if not an aporia)—but the recursions do not end there.

A few pages later, a sequence of panels repeats the scene with the hung-up telephone, showing Alison's bent body and agonized expression. The narrating

FIGURE 4.12. Alison and the (real) telephone (Bechdel, *AYMM* 229)

boxes explain, "The day I hung up the phone on Mom was the last time she made me cry. / Things got easier after that" (233; figure 4.13). But telltale differences force a new reconstruction: The "telephone" is an amputated receiver "hung up" on a stack of books. *This* Alison is dressed in (again) a different shirt and pants, and wears glasses. The final panel clarifies the reconstruction, portraying Alison posing for a camera on a timer. Here, the panels show the artistic method by which Bechdel created both *Fun Home* and *AYMM*, by posing herself in the varied roles. As in the other two texts, the method itself becomes ambivalent, an effort toward greater verisimilitude, greater optical accuracy, but in that very effort, it becomes also a creative effort, a *making* rather than a *telling* or a *recounting*. Like *Maus* and *Fun Home*, *AYMM* is *both* nonfiction *and* fiction (and not merely either one or the other, ambiguous), in a properly unnatural sense of mutually exclusive acts of narration, rather than overlapping or patchwork effects.

FIGURE 4.13. Alison and the (reconstruction) telephone (Bechdel, *AYMM* 233)

This final iteration redoubles the temporal confusion over the act of narration, suggesting that this act, like the story material it recounts, stretches through an indefinite but lengthy period of time. The apparently straightforward archivist and memoirist of *Fun Home* has been replaced by a ruminative, obsessive reworker, a narrative agent who, very much like the Art of *Maus*, recognizes the unsayability, the impossibility of *this* act of narration, and yet at the same time feels compelled to keep saying "now." As in the other books, too, the present formulation—the notion of an obsessive reworker—is itself inadequate. Because I must present it in compact analytical prose, I must also deform what is ultimately a complex and dynamic network of images, words, and careful recursive sequences. I would argue that no one "reconstruction" of the narrator or the act of narration can become fully adequate to the ceaseless repetitions and revisions that *AYMM* demands. Like the other books, too, *AYMM* asks the reader to perform the same patient, iterative, and ultimately frustrating act of (re)construction that the narrating agent herself performs. *AYMM* inveigles the (patient) reader into repeating the autographic narrator's reconstructive act, and into *feeling* the parallels between the two processes, generating the potential for "empathy the long way 'round"—an experience that Roiphe (par. 4) and Barber (125) seem to share.

Bechdel identifies Donald Winnicott, and by extension Virginia Woolf, Alice Miller, and others, as the theoretical correlates of the story she tells in

AYMM, but the complexity and ambivalence of the narrating act it carries out incline me to identify an additional critical referent, mentioned only in the text's acknowledgments: Judith Butler. The poetics of unnatural narrative technique, in this text, helps the narrative articulate what Butler articulates in much denser philosophical prose in *Giving an Account of Oneself* (2005): that this act is both necessary and impossible, because self-narration is also self-division, and therefore change, making memoir an exercise in belated re-recognition. Nonetheless, Butler argues (40, 51), the process itself, in its necessity and impossibility, reveals the grounds by which it singles out one unique interaction between subjects—one unique intersubjectivity. That is, in a manner suggested also in Jean-François Lyotard's late work on the *différend* (see Silverman 13), the reconstructions are inadequate, but through their recognition as inadequate, they asymptotically approach adequacy. It seems to me that the graphic form is uniquely suited to this kind of presentation through impossible narration.

CONCLUSIONS

Thus far I have treated the establishment of an empathic connection as an end in itself, but of course it would also play a role in readers' ongoing relationship with these narratives, feeding back into the interpretive process. In allowing the reader to identify with the author's narrating agency in this recursive fashion, such empathy permits the reader a carefully couched way to identify with marginalized subject-positions. The experience also grants access to the problematics of relation, in both the sense of "relating to" a difficult relative (Vladek, Bruce, Helen), and in the sense of "relating" that other's experiences to an unrelated audience. This, then, is the reason these texts work so hard to generate "empathy the long way 'round": The sense of a felt connection, a shared travail, affords readers a chance of partaking of the kind of protracted self-division practiced by the narrators, rather than simply observing in bewilderment as the narrator completes a totalized design, as in *Ulysses* (in *Fun Home,* Alison reads it with a bemused "What the fuck . . . ?" [207]), or enduring a Brechtian assault, as in Acker's *Empire of the Senseless*. At their best, all three of these graphic narratives attempt to engage the full range of readerly participation that narrative makes possible, asking for more than mere consumption.

Some may object that the term *sympathy* might seem more appropriate here, particularly if the recognition of a similar experience occurs intellectually, rather than emotionally or "viscerally." It is a valid point, but the sympathy/empathy distinction itself risks reinscribing the binary discourse that separates affect from cognition (among many other binaries). The empathy/sympathy disjuncture should refer, rather, to the difference between a sense of alignment or fellow feeling, and a sense of positive regard toward one with whom readers may *not* feel aligned or "fellow," and is therefore related more to readers' self-positioning than to the reading process or the textual form.

By this point, too, it should be obvious that "empathy the long way 'round" is likely to be a precarious achievement. Its situational qualities suggest that both reader and autographic narrator are the same kind of peripatetic, struggling, thinking beings, but the cognitive-affective network outlined here may fall apart for some readers, if other textual features destabilize the sense of shared outlook or activity. This certainly seems to be the case in the critical reception of *AYMM* to date, as Garner and Jacobs express discomfort at the complicated narrative technique, and the more determinedly feminist, introspective, and metanarrative focus. In my view, these responses underestimate *AYMM* for exactly the same reasons that scholarly approaches may underestimate all three of these texts if they affix them with the label "metanarrative," "ambiguous," or "self-reflexive": Such responses collapse not just textual complexity but also the dynamic, interactive reading process made possible by these graphic and narrative techniques.

When successful, however, these books' unique form of empathy uses unnatural storytelling techniques to recuperate the traditional pejorative definition of *unnatural* once (and in some ways still) associated with the works' subject matter. In this sense, they serve one of the postmodernist projects outlined by Jean-François Lyotard, namely bringing into focus those unsayable or unperceivable differences that make mutual understanding impossible: as Flynn puts it, to "bear witness to différends by finding idioms for them" (153).

Finally, in the context of narrative theory proper, Keen's conception of "fast tracks" to empathy has joined a variety of other arguments in suggesting that graphic narratives have a uniquely "immediate" effect on readers, but in this study I suggest that farther-reaching networks of textual material also create effects as sustained and worthy of attention as conventional novels—and that these networks can be understood as extensions of traditional narratological concerns, and do not need further new terminology such as Groensteen's "*tressage*" or "braiding" (82). Furthermore, the effect of "empathy the long way 'round" suggests a modification to common theories of nonfictional narrative: If nonfiction texts can use unnatural narrative techniques—even if they do not become wholly unnatural texts—then the difference between nonfiction and fiction must arise somewhere above and beyond the activity of storyworld *comprehension*, perhaps in an activity closer to Ricoeur's "mimesis$_3$," the interpretive adoption of narrative material into the reader's lived experience (and these categories of activity cut across the structural story/discourse/referent distinctions laid out by Cohn).

As demonstrated within these narrative worlds, boundaries between critical categories become as impossible as they are necessary: We need to be able to use the terms *fiction* and *nonfiction* in some sense, but also to emphasize the continuities between the textual materials they may label. Whereas a "natural" narratology, as construed by Fludernik, among many other studies on mimesis, emphasizes the continuities between face-to-face conversational narrative and narrative in other media, the form of "unnatural" narratology I examine here emphasizes the *discontinuities* between face-to-face conversational narrative and mediated narratives (by construing the narrator and narration as collaborative constructs), and the *continuities* between fictional and nonfictional narrative (by identifying these constructs in both). That is not to say that fictional and nonfictional narrative *are* the same, but rather that they use the same cues, promptings, and encouragements, in more ways than are commonly acknowledged, including some unnatural cues that militate against the usual assumptions for nonfiction discourse. I would therefore once again side with Berlatsky, in suggesting that an absolute fiction/nonfiction binary has outlived its critical usefulness (184), and yet take a step further, suggesting that identifying unnatural narrative techniques in "less-fictional" works helps fill the space between the binary poles and clarify degrees along the continuum of fictionality—among which we might find works that fit Hutcheon's historiographic metafiction and Berlatsky's postmodernist historical fiction, among many others.

This is not to say that readers do not "read differently" when they read nonfiction; rather, readers *create story (including the narrator and the act of narration) out of textual material* in a highly similar way whether they read fiction or nonfiction, but then *use* the story differently—matching and measuring it against their experience in different ways—when primed to understand the resultant storyworld as "reality."[12] That is, in my view, *pace* some theorists in the structuralist communication-model tradition, the act of narration (or presentation) does not precede any given reading, although the act of writing (or drawing) does. Spiegelman and Bechdel obscure this situation—and prompt new levels of readerly participation—by drawing themselves drawing.

---

12. Here, I intend reality in the broadest constructivist sense, including both the reader's sense of the material's accord with his or her own sense of reality and the rhetorical sense that some person intends the material to accord with that person's or that person's culture's (rather than the reader's) sense of what is real.

WORKS CITED

Adams, Jeff. "The Pedagogy of the Image Text: Nakazawa, Sebald, and Spiegelman Recount Social Traumas." *Discourse: Studies in the Cultural Politics of Education*, vol. 29, no. 1, 2008, pp. 35–49.

Alber, Jan. "Unnatural Spaces and Narrative Worlds." *A Poetics of Unnatural Narrative*, edited by Jan Alber et al., The Ohio State UP, 2013, pp. 45–66.

Baetens, Jan. "Abstraction in Comics." *SubStance*, vol. 40, no. 1, 2011, pp. 94–113.

Barber, Mary E. "Review of *Are You My Mother* by Alison Bechdel." *Journal of Gay & Lesbian Mental Health*, vol. 17, no. 1, 2013, pp. 124–26.

Bechdel, Alison. *Are You My Mother?: A Comic Drama*. Houghton Mifflin Harcourt, 2012.

———. *Fun Home: A Family Tragicomic*. Mariner Houghton Mifflin, 2006.

Berlatsky, Eric L. *The Real, the True, and the Told: Postmodern Historical Narrative and the Ethics of Representation*. The Ohio State UP, 2011.

Bilger, Audrey. "The Other Shoe Drops: Review of *Are You My Mother* by Alison Bechdel." *Women's Review of Books*, vol. 29, no. 5, 2012, pp. 13–14.

Bradley, William. "Graphic Memoirs Come of Age." *Fourth Genre: Explorations in Nonfiction*, vol. 15, no. 1, 2013, pp. 161–65.

Budick, Emily Miller. "Forced Confessions: The Case of Art Spiegelman's *Maus*." *Prooftexts: A Journal of Jewish Literary History*, vol. 21, no. 3, 2001, pp. 379–98.

Butler, Judith. *Giving an Account of Oneself*. Fordham UP, 2005.

Chatman, Seymour. *Story and Discourse: Narrative Structure in Fiction and Film*. Cornell UP, 1978.

Chute, Hillary. "Comics Form and Narrating Lives." *Profession*, 2011, pp. 107–17.

———. "'The Shadow of a Past Time': History and Graphic Representation in Maus." *Twentieth Century Literature: A Scholarly and Critical Journal*, vol. 52, no. 2, 2006, pp. 199–230.

Cioffi, Frank L. "Disturbing Comics." *The Language of Comics: Word and Image*, edited by Robin Varnum and Christina T. Gibbons, UP of Mississippi, 2001, pp. 97–122.

Derrida, Jacques. *The Truth in Painting*. 1978. Translated by Geoff Bennington and Ian McLeod, U of Chicago P, 1987.

Dick, Philip K. "The Eyes Have It." 1953. *The Philip K. Dick Reader*. Citadel Twilight Carol, 1997, pp. 27–29.

Doherty, Thomas. "Art Spiegelman's *Maus*: Graphic Art and the Holocaust." *American Literature: A Journal of Literary History, Criticism, and Bibliography*, vol. 68, no. 1, 1996, pp. 69–84.

Eakin, Paul John. "Eye and I: Negotiating Distance in Eyewitness Narrative." *Partial Answers: Journal of Literature and the History of Ideas*, vol. 7, no. 2, 2009, pp. 201–12.

Eisner, Will. *Comics and Sequential Art*. 1985. Expanded ed., Poorhouse P, 1990.

Elmwood, Victoria A. "'Happy, Happy Ever After': The Transformation of Trauma between the Generations in Art Spiegelman's *Maus: A Survivor's Tale*." *Biography: An Interdisciplinary Quarterly*, vol. 27, no. 4, 2004, pp. 691–720.

Ewert, Jeanne C. "Reading Visual Narrative: Art Spiegelman's *Maus*." *Narrative*, vol. 8, no. 1, 2000, pp. 87–103.

Fauconnier, Gilles, and Mark Turner. *The Way We Think: Conceptual Blending and the Mind's Hidden Complexities*. Perseus-Basic, 2002.

Fischer, Craig, and Charles Hatfield. "Teeth, Sticks, and Bricks: Calligraphy, Graphic Focalization, and Narrative Braiding in Eddie Campbell's *Alec*." *SubStance*, vol. 40, no. 1, 2011, pp. 70–93.

Flynn, Thomas R. "Lyotard and History without Witnesses." *Lyotard: Philosophy, Politics, and the Sublime*, edited by Hugh J. Silverman, Routledge, 2002, pp. 151–63.

Fludernik, Monika. *Towards a "Natural" Narratology*. Routledge, 1996.

Freedman, Ariela. "Drawing on Modernism in Alison Bechdel's *Fun Home*." *Journal of Modern Literature*, vol. 32, no. 4, 2009, pp. 125–40.

Gardner, Jared. "Storylines." *SubStance*, vol. 40, no. 1, 2011, pp. 53–69.

Garner, Dwight. "Artist, Draw Thyself (and Your Mother and Therapist): Review of *Are You My Mother* by Alison Bechdel." *New York Times*, 3 May 2012, C1(L), https://www.nytimes.com/2012/05/03/books/are-you-my-mother-by-alison-bechdel.html.

Groensteen, Thierry. *The System of Comics*. 1999. Translated by Bart Beaty and Nick Nguyen, UP of Mississippi, 2007.

Heinze, Rüdiger. "The Whirligig of Time: Toward a Poetics of Unnatural Temporality." *A Poetics of Unnatural Narrative*, edited by Jan Alber et al., The Ohio State UP, 2013, pp. 31–44.

Horstkotte, Silke, and Nancy Pedri. "Focalization in Graphic Narrative." *Narrative*, vol. 19, no. 3, 2011, pp. 330–57.

Iversen, Stefan. "'In Flaming Flames': Crises of Experientiality in Non-Fictional Narratives." *Unnatural Narratives—Unnatural Narratology*, edited by Jan Alber and Rüdiger Heinze, De Gruyter, 2011.

Jacobs, Rita D. "Review of *Are You My Mother* by Alison Bechdel." *World Literature Today*, vol. 87, no. 1, 2013, pp. 74–75.

Keen, Suzanne. *Empathy and the Novel*. Oxford UP, 2007.

———. "Fast Tracks to Narrative Empathy: Anthropomorphism and Dehumanization in Graphic Narratives." *SubStance: A Review of Theory and Literary Criticism*, vol. 40, no. 1, 2011, pp. 135–55.

Kilgore, Christopher D. "From Unnatural Narrative to Unnatural Reading: Review of *A Poetics of Unnatural Narrative*." *Style*, vol. 48, no. 4, 2014, pp. 629–36.

———. "Unnatural Graphic Narration: The Panel and the Sublime." *Journal of Narrative Technique*, vol. 45, no. 1, 2015, pp. 18–45.

Klepper, Martin. "Emergent Art: Textual Identity in Art Spiegelman's *Maus*." *Anglistik: International Journal of English Studies*, vol. 18, no. 2, 2007, pp. 83–101.

Laga, Barry. "*Maus*, Holocaust, and History: Redrawing the Frame." *Arizona Quarterly*, vol. 57, no. 1, 2001, pp. 61–90.

Lefèvre, Pascal. "Some Medium-Specific Qualities of Graphic Sequences." *SubStance*, vol. 40, no. 1, 2011, pp. 14–33.

Loman, Andrew. "'Well Intended Liberal Slop': Allegories of Race in Spiegelman's *Maus*." *Journal of American Studies*, vol. 40, no. 3, 2006, pp. 551–71.

Lyndenberg, Robin. "Under Construction: Alison Bechdel's *Fun Home: A Family Tragicomic*." *European Journal of English Studies*, vol. 16, no. 1, 2012, pp. 57–68.

Ma, Sheng-Mei. "Mourning with the (as a) Jew: Metaphor, Ethnicity, and the Holocaust in Art Spiegelman's *Maus*." *Studies in American Jewish Literature*, vol. 16, 1997, pp. 115–29.

Mäkelä, Maria. "Realism and the Unnatural." *A Poetics of Unnatural Narrative*, edited by Jan Alber et al., The Ohio State UP, 2013, pp. 142–66.

McCloud, Scott. *Understanding Comics: The Invisible Art*. Lettering by Bob Lappan, Kitchen Sink and HarperPerennial, 1993.

McGlothlin, Erin. "No Time Like the Present: Narrative and Time in Art Spiegelman's *Maus*." *Narrative*, vol. 11, no. 2, 2003, pp. 177–98.

McHale, Brian. "The Unnaturalness of Narrative Poetry." *A Poetics of Unnatural Narrative*, edited by Jan Alber et al., The Ohio State UP, 2013, pp. 199–222.

Nielsen, Henrik Skov. "Natural Authors, Unnatural Narration." *Postclassical Narratology: Approaches and Analyses*, edited by Jan Alber and Monica Fludernik, The Ohio State UP, 2010, pp. 275–301.

———. "Naturalizing and Unnaturalizing Reading Strategies: Focalization Revisited." *A Poetics of Unnatural Narrative*, edited by Jan Alber et al., The Ohio State UP, 2013, pp. 67–93.

Richardson, Brian. *Unnatural Narrative: Theory, History, and Practice*. The Ohio State UP, 2015.

———. *Unnatural Voices: Extreme Narration in Modern and Contemporary Fiction*. The Ohio State UP, 2006.

Rohy, Valerie. "In the Queer Archive: *Fun Home*." *GLQ: A Journal of Lesbian and Gay Studies*, vol. 16, no. 3, 2010, pp. 340–61.

Roiphe, Katie. "Drawn Together: Review of *Are You My Mother* by Alison Bechdel." *The New York Times Book Review*, 29 Apr. 2012, 11L, https://www.nytimes.com/2012/04/29/books/review/are-you-my-mother-by-alison-bechdel.html.

Rothberg, Michael. "'We Were Talking Jewish': Art Spiegelman's *Maus* as 'Holocaust' Production." *Contemporary Literature*, vol. 35, no. 4, 1994, pp. 661–87.

Silverman, Hugh J., editor. *Lyotard: Philosophy, Politics, and the Sublime*. Continental Philosophy VIII, Routledge, 2002.

Spiegelman, Art. *Maus: A Survivor's Tale*. 2 volumes, Pantheon, 1986–1991.

Van Dyne, Susan R. "'The Slippage Between Seeing and Saying': Getting a Life in Alison Bechdel's *Fun Home*." *Teaching Comics and Graphic Narratives: Essays on Theory, Strategy, and Practice*, edited by Lan Dong, McFarland, 2012, pp. 105–18.

Walsh, Richard. *The Rhetoric of Fictionality: Narrative Theory and the Idea of Fiction*. The Ohio State UP, 2007.

Warhol, Robyn. "The Space Between: A Narrative Approach to Alison Bechdel's *Fun Home*." *College Literature*, vol. 38, no. 3, 2011, pp. 1–20.

Warren, Roz. "Watching out for Mom: Review of *Are You My Mother* by Alison Bechdel." *Gay & Lesbian Review Worldwide*, vol. 19, no. 4, 2012, p. 39.

Watson, Julia. "Autographic Disclosures and Genealogies of Desire in Alison Bechdel's *Fun Home*." *Biography*, vol. 31, no. 1, 2008, pp. 27–58.

CHAPTER 5

Metalepsis and Emotion in Unnatural Stories

DANIEL PUNDAY

SINCE ITS INTRODUCTION more than a decade ago, the scope of "unnatural narrative" has been a subject of vigorous debate. Brian Richardson has recently summarized the question of how wide a range of stories should be considered unnatural in this way: Is something that is merely physically impossible enough to make a narrative unnatural, or do such works need specifically to invoke and reject mimesis (13)? Metalepsis, however, poses no such problems for categorization. In a 2012 article in the *Journal of Narrative Theory*, Alice Bell and Jan Alber characterize "metaleptic jumps" between narrative levels as "physically or logically impossible." Metalepsis, thus, is "one manifestation of the unnatural" (166). As with so many features of unnatural narrative, metalepsis has usually been interpreted with an emphasis on the rules that have been violated, and there is broad agreement that these metaleptic violations make the work that contains them unnatural.

Although some scholars have asserted that metalepsis can help to assert the authenticity of the narrative (Alber 211), scholars have generally opposed metalepsis to what Werner Wolf has called aesthetic illusionism.[1] In this chap-

---

1. In his entry on the topic for the *Living Handbook of Narratology*, Wolf notes the common association of illusionism with seriousness: "The shunning of aesthetic distance can also be witnessed in a no less typical tendency of illusionist works toward seriousness . . . , although this does not exclude the comic from illusionism entirely. Comedy and laughter imply emotional distance, which runs counter to the strong affinity between emotional involvement and

ter, I challenge unnatural narratology's account of metalepsis's estranging effect on our emotional engagement with the story. Instead I will demonstrate the unlikely ways that metalepsis can work to deepen our emotional attachment to the story, despite its seemingly estranging effects.

METALEPSIS, IMMERSION, AND ESTRANGEMENT

Gérard Genette offered the modern definition of metalepsis in *Narrative Discourse*. Genette describes metalepsis as a violation of the normal rules governing "introducing into one situation, by means of a discourse, the knowledge of another situation" (234)—such as when the author claims to be manipulating the fates of characters, or when characters confront their authors. Genette explains the effect as follows:

> Any intrusion by the extradiegetic narrator or narratee into the diegetic universe (or by diegetic characters into a metadiegetic universe, etc.), or the inverse (as in Cortazar), produces an effect of strangeness that is either comical (when, as in Sterne or Diderot, it is presented in a joking tone) or fantastic. (234–35)

A few years later, he clarifies and adds additional possibilities in *Narrative Discourse Revisited*. These disturbances can be "set down only to humor (Sterne, Diderot) or to the fantastic (Cortazar, Bioy Casares) or to some mixture of the two (Borges, of course), unless it functions as a figure of the creative imagination" (88).

Genette himself recognizes that there are many different varieties of metalepsis. Marie-Laure Ryan's distinction between "rhetorical" and "ontological" metalepsis (205–7) is helpful in contrasting violations of levels that occur in the telling of the story, from those that actually affect the story world itself. Dorrit Cohn has more recently expressed this distinction as one between metalepsis at the level of "discourse" and "story" (105). Examples of rhetorical/discursive metalepsis include an author's mention of leaving a character waiting while turning to another, while examples of ontological/story metalepsis include those particularly postmodern devices of authors interacting physically with their characters. Clearly, rhetorical metalepsis is less disruptive to our sense of the story; as Ryan says, "rhetorical metalepsis opens a

---

aesthetic illusion. The interrelation between illusion, emotions and seriousness can be seen not only in realist fiction, but also in drama: tragedy tends toward aesthetic illusion (Aristotle's catharsis presupposes empathetic immersion), while comedy frequently suspends illusion."

small window that allows a quick glance across levels, but the window closes after a few sentences, and the operation ends up reasserting the existence of boundaries" (207). There are some forms of discourse-level metalepsis that are more disruptive than others. Monika Fludernik unpacks Genette's example of metalepsis at the level of the author's own commentary about the writing of the story: "It refers to the baring of the mimetic illusion by undermining the realistic expectation that the narrator merely tells a story over which he has no power" (384). Such a reference to the author's control does not ultimately alter the storyworld in the way that we would expect from ontological metalepsis, but it is considerably more metafictional than we see in more conventional forms of rhetorical metalepsis.

Scholarship on metalepsis over the last decade has often framed the varieties of metalepsis, especially of ontological metalepsis, using a spatial model. Fludernik distinguishes between narrational and lectorial metalepsis based on whether the narrator moves "down" into the world of the story, or whether a character moves "up" a level to that of the narrator (389). Alice Bell and Jan Alber reframe this distinction as two varieties of what they call vertical transmigrations in the storyworld. In contrast, they offer horizontal metalepsis, which might involve the movement of a character from one story to another:

> The transmigration of a character or narrator into a different fictional text is metaleptic because, as in the other two cases, it involves the transgressive violation of story world boundaries through jumps between ontologically distinct zones or spheres. (168)

Bell and Alber's spatial model for thinking about metalepsis draws on conventional ways of talking about narrative "levels" and helps to organize many of the common types of ontological metalepsis.

Because it introduces the awareness of one level of a narrative into another, we usually think of metalepsis as a device that undercuts reader or viewer immersion in the story. We have already seen this in Genette's observation that the intrusion of the narrator into the storyworld (or its inverse) "produces an effect of strangeness that is either comical . . . or fantastic" (*Narrative Discourse* 235). This vision of metalepsis is probably best exemplified by the often-cited example of Woody Allen's short story "The Kugelmass Episode," in which a man travels into the novel *Madame Bovary* to pursue a clandestine affair:

> I need to meet a new woman. . . . I need to have an affair. I may not look the part, but I'm a man who needs romance. I need softness, I need flirtation. I'm not getting younger, so before it's too late I want to make love in Venice,

trade quips at "21," and exchange coy glances over red wine and candlelight. (61–62)

The metalepsis is played for laughs, and Kugelmass's desire to introduce romance into his life in this unlikely way sends up the self-deception of a middle-aged man and the clichés that we have about our love of literary characters.

Of course, critics have long recognized that rhetorical or discourse-level metalepsis can work to support (rather than undercut) the reality of the characters and storyworld. Fludernik makes this observation:

> The term "transgression," actually, is quite inadequate to the effect of these passages since they tend to enhance the realistic illusion of storyworld representation, aiding the narratee's (as well as the reader's) imaginative immersion into the story rather than foregrounding the metafictional and transgressive (nonrealistic) properties of such an imaginative stepping into the story world. (382–83)

Although a reference to following a character across a lawn or leaving one to turn to another has a mildly metafictional effect, such passages actually work to emphasize the reality of this storyworld, in that the characters are treated as if they persist even as the story is being told.[2] It is clear that Genette's characterization of metalepsis as producing "an effect of strangeness" (*Narrative Discourse* 235) applies most unproblematically to ontological metalepsis, whose violation of levels is much harder to recuperate within a realistic and stable understanding of characters and their world.

In 1987, Brian McHale offered a provocative suggestion about metalepsis at the end of *Postmodernist Fiction*, with which critics have been struggling ever since. Metalepsis models our experience of stories as a whole, which work to pull us into their worlds. McHale writes, "If authors love their characters, and if texts seduce their readers, then these relations involve violations of ontological boundaries" (222). McHale suggests that Kugelmass's metafictional story is in some ways typical of how narratives construct and then move across narrative levels. Many critics working on metalepsis have tackled the challenge that McHale offers, perhaps Fludernik most effectively. Describing McHale's description as an example of "metaphorical exuberance": Authors "do not really step down into the fiction and make love to [their

---

2. See Fludernik 387 on how the metalepsis in this case is based on the dual temporalities being implied.

characters]. . . . Likewise, readers do not actually get 'seduced' by story or plot—not only do readers rarely engage in sexual actions as part of their reading experience, as a nonhuman entity, the text (plot, configuration, closure) cannot literally provoke stimulation" (393). She suggests, however, that such metaphorical uses can be valuable as a way to explore the nature of narrative textuality:

> What I am therefore saying is that the device of metalepsis in many instances need not actually be literally treated as an ontological contradiction (and therefore transgression), but could be regarded as an imaginative transfer into the impossible in parallel with authorial omniscience or autodiegetic narrators' precise memory of dialogues and thoughts in the past. (393)

McHale's suggestive challenge aside, the consensus is that ontological metalepsis usually estranges the reader from the text. It is no surprise, then, that Allen's "Kugelmass Episode" has come to represent this technique, since it captures the comic and deflating effects of such metafiction.

EMOTION IN METALEPTIC NARRATIVES

If ontological metalepsis is generally understood to be estranging for the reader—an effect that, of course, can be used for many different narrative, aesthetic, and rhetorical purposes—then the postmodernist fiction that makes heavy use of it should be characterized by emotional disengagement. Although many stories like "The Kugelmass Episode" do this, there is an explicit emotional appeal in a great deal of postmodernist writing that is directly in conflict with this generalization about ontological metalepsis. That is, many such stories evoke emotional situations directly, and often explicitly invite readers to respond to narrative events of loss and despair in the same way that traditional narratives would—by being "moved" by the situation of the characters represented. Popular self-reflexive narratives like Dave Eggers's *A Heartbreaking Work of Staggering Genius* or Jonathan Safran Foer's *Extremely Loud and Incredibly Close* come to mind as obvious examples of this somewhat surprising relationship between metalepsis and emotional appeal. We might likewise think of a film like *Stranger Than Fiction,* in which Harold Crick (Will Ferrell) discovers that he is a character in a novel doomed to be killed off shortly—a fate that we are invited to mourn. This unlikely relationship between metalepsis and emotional appeals is perhaps best embodied in the voice-over narration in Christoffer Boe's 2003 film *Reconstruction,* in which a novelist appears to create and then rewrite the romantic affair between his wife and a younger photographer: "It is all film. It is all a construction. But even so, it hurts."

It is this tension between ontological metalepsis and appeals to explicit emotions that I want to unpack in the remainder of this chapter. I would like to base this discussion on three well-known US fictions that represent different ways of weaving ontological metalepsis and these sorts of explicit emotional appeals: Mark Danielewski's collage novel *House of Leaves*, John Barth's short story "Lost in the Funhouse," and Walter Abish's short novel *Alphabetical Africa*.[3]

The central story in *House of Leaves* focuses on a family that moves into what turns out to be an ever-expanding house, which is larger on the inside than on the outside. The novel explicitly evokes the horror genre of the haunted house, the effect of which is described in the text itself as "uncanny" (359). The father in this family, Will Navidson, is a filmmaker and records his explorations of the space; in this regard, the novel is really about a horror film of a sort. More broadly, the narration of the innermost story about the house anticipates conventional responses to suspense stories; at one point, for example, Danielewski ends a chapter with the line, "Which is exactly when Karen screams" (40). More tellingly, the narrator offers interpretations of the events in the house that steer the reader toward an embrace of this feeling of uncanniness:

> The terrifying implication of their children's shouts is now impossible to miss. No room in the house exceeds a length of twenty-five feet, let alone fifty feet, let alone fifty-six and a half feet, and yet Chad and Daisy's voices are echoing, each call responding with an entirely separate answer. (57)

Surrounding this conventional horror story is the metaleptic play for which the novel is best known. This includes the novel's nested forms of scholarly and editorial commentary: Not only is the film located within a narrative about its reception, but that narrative has footnotes from both of its editors—Zampanò and Johnny Truant. In making uncertain both the existence of the events that are the basis for the story and the mental stability of its editors,

---

3. I am adopting a broad definition of metalepsis with these three examples, since Barth's story, in particular, might be categorized simply as metafiction. Only Abish's novel is a clear instance of characters crossing narrative levels (see also the article by Roy Sommer in this collection). However, all three involve what I am calling a "metaleptic play" that should undermine emotional involvement—inserting into the narrative an awareness of the story as an artifact (a physical book in Danielewski, a story in Barth) being constructed by an author. This range of works allows me to sketch a wider variety of strategies for negotiating emotion at the end of this chapter.

Danielewski raises questions about who is really reading and writing the inner narrative. Equally metaleptic is the novel's play with page space later in the narrative, the manipulation of which appears to be the work of Danielewski rather than that of the professed writer of the inner narrative, Zampanò. And, of course, we are invited to see the titular "house of leaves" as a metafictional reference to the book, which we inhabit as readers. Here an explicitly, conventionally emotional horror story coexists with a metaleptic textual design.

As a second example, let us turn now to the last few pages of John Barth's "Lost in the Funhouse." Nominally the story is about a car trip to Ocean City in the 1940s, which the protagonist Ambrose invests with adolescent expectations of adventure and romance. The ironic, mature voice of the narrator summarizes the perspective of an older Ambrose looking back on these expectations: "The time they went with his family to Ocean City; the *erotic fantasies* he used to have about her. How long ago it seemed, and childish! Yet tender, too, *n'est-ce pas?*" (84). Barth's way of telling this story is straightforwardly metafictional, with the author intervening into the telling of the story explicitly to discuss his storytelling choices and challenges. He discusses Gustav Freytag's model of rising and falling action (95), proposes possible conclusions, and despairs at finishing the story: "I'll never be an author. It's been forever already, everybody's gone home, Ocean City's deserted" (86). As this passage implies, this story is increasingly dependent on the author's own narrative of despair about the telling of the story. Although early in the story we are encouraged to see Ambrose's elaborate dreams about the funhouse that he will encounter as comedic and juvenile, as the story moves toward its conclusion, the sense of loss and despair becomes considerably less ironic. Barth ends with a gesture of resignation and acceptance:

> He wishes he had never entered the funhouse. But he has. Then he wishes he were dead. But he's not. Therefore he will construct funhouses for others and be their secret operator—though he would rather be among the lovers for whom funhouses are designed. (97)

Although different in style from Danielewski and somewhat more ambiguous in tone, the emotional effect of this story is far from the comic self-reflection that "The Kugelmass Episode" models. It is clear that a relatively traditional emotional investment in the events of these stories is implied despite their metalepsis.

As a final example, consider Walter Abish's *Alphabetical Africa*. Abish's book is a particularly well-known example of writing based on the adoption of artificial constraints and procedures. In this case, the constraint on Abish defines the words available to him for writing each chapter: The first chapter uses only words beginning with the letter *a*, the second with words beginning with *a* and *b*, and so on until the twenty-sixth chapter, when the letters begin to be removed, until the fifty-second chapter returns to using only *a* words. Abish tends to make his metaleptic references somewhat obliquely and metaphorically, although in places the design of the book becomes a plot element. For example, the narrator is invited to a "letter auction" at one point:

> Daily I had been complaining how I had been losing a few letters each day. I couldn't explain it. At first I didn't inform anyone about it, but after I contacted a few friends in early June I discovered how everyone else also interested in language and letters had been burglarized, chiefly and almost exclusively losing letters concerning Africa. (121)

At times Abish's novel appears to be a humorous send-up of our ways of talking about and cataloging the exotic. There are many explicit comic or absurdist elements to the narrative, such as when one character is hired "to take an inventory of the entire island" (78) or when it appears that the country of Tanzania has literally been painted to match its color on the map (43, 53). But, as we saw in Barth, there is an element of loss that runs throughout the later portions of the story. In the first chapter of the second half of the book, one character remarks, "One never knows when one does anything for the last time" (69), but it is clear that the design of the book makes this gradual loss of names and places obvious and inevitable. Throughout are warnings about loss and abandoning language (78), and by the time we get to the second G chapter, characters are described as "Growing forgetful": "Contagious forgetfulness erased all former charts" (139). Although certainly less explicitly than does *House of Leaves* or even "Lost in the Funhouse," the second half of *Alphabetical Africa* evokes an emotional context for its textual play.

"ILLOGICAL" EMOTIONAL RESPONSES

What, then, do we make of the relationship between metalepsis and emotional appeals? We know that these narrative worlds are uncertain and contradictory, and that more often than not the grounds for the reality of the events described are undermined by the conditions of their telling. That doesn't seem, however, to keep the authors from anticipating an emotional response. In this regard, I am reminded of Robyn Warhol's discussion of her own illogical response to a scene in the film *Wag the Dog*, where Woody Harrelson plays a captured US soldier in a faked war. Warhol narrates:

The photo shows Harrelson wearing a sweater with rips in the front which the commentators, in voice-over, reveal to be a message in Morse code. The commentators interpret the message: it reads, "Courage, Mom."

"Courage, Mom." The phrase floats from the Dolby speakers into the theater, and I feel a familiar burning in the back of my throat, a momentary clutch of the muscles behind my palate, a tingling in the sinuses all along my cheekbones; suddenly my eyes begin to sting as they fill with tears. "Courage, Mom." There is nothing authentic, nothing genuine, nothing "real" about the moment, nothing in the diegetic context that could explain my reaction: the film's multiple ironies add layers to the defenses my academic study of sentimentalism should have established for me years ago. (xvii)

Warhol points out a disconnect between her emotional response to a particular moment in this film and everything else she knows about the context for that moment. Despite the fact that the film explicitly undermines the reality of that moment, it has its effect nonetheless. Much the same thing seems to be happening in the metaleptic texts that I have been discussing: Despite all of the textual context that works against the reality of the story (after all, Abish is talking about the loss of letters in a book whose rules he himself created), nonetheless these stories have the power to affect us emotionally.

One reason why these stories have these emotional effects is the gap between our affective and cognitive responses to a work.[4] In *Experiencing Narrative Worlds,* Richard Gerrig reviews conventional debates about how obviously unreal or fictional events can move readers emotionally: "If, in fact, unreality should militate against emotional response, how is it that readers regularly experience strong emotions toward characters and situations that are purely authors' inventions" (180). Gerrig goes on to reject the premise of this question, however, and to argue that "the experience of emotions in response to fictions follows more-general patterns of circumstances in which affect is dissociated from cognition" (180). In a discussion of "being moved" by literary works, Patrick Colm Hogan has criticized "appraisal theories" that link emotional responses to our ability to "mentally simulate the experiences of a character from his or her point of view" (245) and calculate likely outcomes for the characters represented. More recently David Miall has offered the view of "emotion as a process":

---

4. In this essay I am not distinguishing between emotion and affect. Antonio Damasio defines the latter as containing a wider range of phenomena, and can include things like mood (342 n. 10). Because my focus is primarily on explicit appeals to commonly shared emotional states (fear, sadness from loss, and so on), these are probably best characterized as emotions.

This view, resting on recent research that has reversed the previous half-century's priorities in the emotion-cognition relationship, argues on neuropsychological evidence in particular that emotion is at the basis of, and shapes the purposes of, all cognitive activity. (324)

Miall shows that rather than our cognitive assessment of a situation being the basis for our emotional response, in fact the relationship can be reversed: "Damasio and others demonstrate the power of feeling to prompt judgments before conscious awareness has had time to assess the situation" (344).

Recent cognitive theory has pointed out, then, that we tend to overemphasize reasoning when we talk about cognitive response. Instead of starting from our appraisal of the situation, Hogan advocates a focus on "experiential triggers for emotion" ("On Being Moved" 243) that have less to do with global reasoning about the situations and futures of the characters:

> In the case of a live performance or film, we directly experience the actor's and actress's facial expressions, their gestures, tone of voice, gait, posture, and so forth—all important emotion triggers. More significantly for present purposes our emotional response is bound up with our simulation of a characters's experiences. . . . However, our emotional response is not a matter of the probability calculations that go along with that simulation. Rather, it is a matter of the concrete images we experience when engaging in that simulation. It is also a matter of the emotional memories that are activated during simulation—in the case of *Romeo and Juliet,* memories of romantic love, separation, and the death of loved ones. (246)

In his more recent book *Affective Narratology,* Hogan discusses the potential gap between our cognitive and emotional experiences in memory:

> Emotional memories, like skills memories—such as how to ride a bicycle—are "implicit" memories. Thus, when activated they do not lead us to think about some representational content. . . . [W]hen an emotional memory is activated, we may or may not think of the event with which it is associated. Rather, we feel the emotion. (5)

Hogan's observation here about our emotional response to literary works is especially important for our thinking about metaleptic texts. According to this account, there really is no contradiction between emotional involvement and metalepsis because our emotional response to characters and situations is often very local. When Robyn Warhol tears up at *Wag the Dog,* she is responding to the local situation of a son's brave concern for his mother despite his own danger, and allowing all of the irony and deception that surround this scene to remain an intellectual context in the background. Likewise, when Abish tells a story of forgetting and loss, that story is emotionally engaging even though the way in which he has constructed this loss is extremely self-referential and playful. The same is true for Barth's story of an author's struggles, or Danielewski's horror story about a haunted (paper) house. In all of these cases, even though the aesthetic illusion that immerses us in the story is broken, our emotional response to individual narrative elements remains.

TWO TYPES OF EMOTIONAL METALEPSIS

It is worth noting that some of the features of the self-reflexive fiction that I have been discussing may well be unique to the particular US postmodernism that has been the basis of my sample texts. Although my discussion has made clear that ontological metalepsis can coexist with emotional appeals to the reader, their commonness in these writings requires further explanation.

Writing in 1997, Hans Bertens argued that postmodernist fiction held emotion at arm's length. While the postmodern culture exemplified for him by Oprah Winfrey "demands emotion, raw and public emotion" (26), he claims that postmodern fiction is "astonishingly reticent in its display of emotions" (29). I think that I have shown that this is not the case—even though the emotions shown are often complicated by the ontological inconsistencies that define these worlds. Instead, I am inclined to see the exploration of emotional response as perhaps one of the goals of later twentieth-century writers. Seen from this point of view, these metaleptic texts join the scatological novels of Burroughs and an ironically pornographic book like *Willie Masters' Lonesome Wife* (Gass) as narratives that explore how readers respond to literary works. In many ways, these emotionally metaleptic texts are of a piece with Susan Sontag's call for "an erotics of art" to replace "hermeneutics":

> Interpretation takes the sensory experience of the work of art for granted, and proceeds from there. This cannot be taken for granted, now. Think of the sheer multiplication of works of art available to every one of us, superadded to the conflicting tastes and odors and sights of the urban environment that bombard our senses. Ours is a culture based on excess, on overproduction; the result is a steady loss of sharpness in our sensory experience.... What

is important now is that we recover our senses. We must learn to see more, to hear more, to feel more. (13–14)

We could say that such texts would provide especially important cases for an "affective narratology" since they make the tension between our emotional and intellectual responses to stories so knotted and complex.

I want to conclude, however, by emphasizing not the particular cultural moment that produced these texts, but the rhetorical and formal possibilities that this tension between emotion and metalepsis affords. Allow me to propose, schematically, two obvious variations on the relationship between emotion and metalepsis:

1. There are novels in which the emotional involvement occurs despite the metaleptic context. This is the case with Danielewski, I think. The self-reflexiveness of the text and the ontological games he plays with his "house of leaves" neither detract nor add to the uncanny quality of the house; instead, those other elements remain an intellectual context that supports other uses of the text. In the case of Danielewski, this appears to be an interest in the theme of "inhabiting" a book. In the case of a novel like Eggers's *Heartbreaking Work of Staggering Genius*, the metalepsis seems designed as a complement to the author's sense of placelessness and uncertainty, and to contribute to the storytelling persona. What I am suggesting in this case, then, is attention to the rhetorical uses of metalepsis alongside the emotional structure of the work.
2. There are other novels, however, where metalepsis makes possible the emotional context of the story. This is true of both Barth and Abish, who use the movement of the text toward the end of the book to create a sense of urgency and loss that is the basis for our emotional engagement in the text. Metalepsis and emotional engagement are far more deeply entwined in this case.

The first variation is not particularly challenging to the scholarship on metalepsis and unnatural narratology. Some critics have recognized that emotional involvement can be sustained despite metalepsis;[5] I noted at the outset that both Fludernik and Alber discuss how metalepsis can be used to assert the overall authenticity of the story. Variation two strikes me as more interesting and largely overlooked in scholarship; it suggests that metalepsis is a condition of our emotional investment rather than something to be overcome. Both

---

5. Werner Wolf makes this point as well in a discussion of *The Purple Rose of Cairo*, where the metalepsis of the film does not disrupt "a strong empathy for poor Cecilia" ("'Unnatural' Metalepsis" 125).

examples that I have given of this second variation focus on the coming end of the narrative, which provides a framework of loss that gives the story much of its emotional impact. Thirty years ago, Peter Brooks made this link between our awareness of the coming end of the narrative and a kind of feeling of loss. Drawing on Freud, he suggested that narrative middles could be seen as a kind of delay:

> We emerge from reading *Beyond the Pleasure Principle* with a dynamic model that structures ends (death, quiescence, nonnarratability) against beginnings (Eros, stimulation into tension, the desire of narrative) in a manner that necessitates the middle as detour, as a struggle toward the end under the compulsion of imposed delay, as arabesque in the dilatory space of the text. (107–8)

Brooks describes a metaleptic awareness on the part of the reader that maintains a dual awareness of both the events of the story and the way that they are moving toward a hoped-for but also dreaded end.

Are there ways of combining emotion and metalepsis other than a focus on time and the ending of the story? To the extent that the time-bound nature of the narrative provides a framework that these authors use, we can certainly look for other sorts of constraints. We might note, for example, that Danielewski focuses less on the passage of time and more on the space of the narrative (the house that gets bigger), which is linked to the physical space of the book. It seems that spatial constraints could be used to create a similar sense of emotional response in readers of ontologically metaleptic narratives, since like the time of reading the space of the book is a metaleptic element of the reading experience. Consider, for example, the way that Raymond Federman exploits spatial constraints in *The Voice in the Closet*. Rather than being temporally oriented toward the end of the narrative, Federman's story is spatially concerned with the page itself, since he has limited the number of letters that he can use in each line. In this broadly autobiographical story, a young Federman escapes from the Nazis who capture and kill his parents by being hidden in a closet; the "voice" in the closet of the title is thus that of Federman himself (in his role as both the young protagonist and the older author telling the story). The space of the closet is, ironically, a means of escape. In the writing of the story, Federman treats the constraints that he has adopted with a similarly mixed emotional investment; they limit him, but also promise a freedom from the temptation to fictionalize his past:

> He waits for me to unfold upstairs perhaps the signal of a departure in my own voice at last a beginning after so many detours relentless false justifica-

tions in the margins more to come in my own words now that I may speak sway I the real story from the other side.

Here the ontological metalepsis that makes the text so unusual in its design nonetheless coexists with a story of hope and escape made possible by the constraints provided by the page space.

If the time of narrative and the space of the book provide natural anchors that authors can exploit for emotional appeals in these narratives, we would expect that other external constraints would likewise be available to authors for the same purpose. Early in this chapter, I mentioned the case of the film *Stranger Than Fiction*, whose protagonist discovers that he is a character in a novel, and that he must die for the story to achieve its full aesthetic potential. In this case, director Marc Forster is drawing on the external expectations of the narrative film form: The death of significant characters is usually one of the means by which the story achieves its conclusion and meaning, just as marriage is the natural conclusion of the romance, or resolution is the natural end of a comedy. Here, again, the external constraints imposed on the story—which are independent of the particular way that the story itself treats this character—become a means by which emotion is defined that can be quite in contrast to the playfulness of the narration.

Genre, too, offers similar constraints that might be exploited. Much of Robert Coover's early short fiction explores with the way that genres shape stories—probably most famously in the genre-laden story "The Babysitter," whose multiple narrative possibilities depend in large part on the genre of the television programs (detective, western, romance) that play throughout the story. Here genre functions as an external force that imposes constraints independent of the characters themselves. Coover's theater-based stories, like "Charlie in the House of Rue," rework a Charlie Chaplin silent character whose seemingly playful slapstick has a violent and ominous undertone. The story begins with a gesture toward such familiar Chaplin gestures ("He flexes his bamboo cane, his elbows, his knees, glances around, his patch of scruffy black mustache twitching with anticipation" [87]), only to have the underlying assumption of his comic silent world violated. A few pages into the story, he encounters a "lady's boudoir" where a young woman removes her negligee; turning to go, he "smacks up against the wall: the door is gone" (90). Here the story depends on the tension between the expectations created by this genre, and the way in which it has been subtly, and not so subtly, violated. In other stories, Coover makes a similar use of the constraints and expectations provided by medium. Coover's reworking of *Casablanca*, "You Must Remember This," similarly plays on the coming end of the film ("Time goes by" [186]) in a way that invokes the medium of the film as a whole. Much as with the way that time functions in Abish's novel, the constraints of medium and genre appear to provide an occasion for loss that is independent of the (sometimes comic, often scatalogical) plot.

In all of these cases, emotion is being invoked through features that are, at least in part, independent of the story and contained, instead, in the framework through which the reader is interacting with that story—the time of the narrative, the space of the book, the medium and genre of its telling. This framework provides a second channel through which emotional appeals can be made. This two-channel form of communication helps to explain how such metaleptic narratives can nonetheless be emotionally engaging. More importantly, this bifurcation between emotional and more rational responses to the work suggests the complexity of our cognitive experience of narrative.

WORKS CITED

Abish, Walter. *Alphabetical Africa.* New Directions, 1974.

Alber, Jan. *Unnatural Narrative: Impossible Worlds in Fiction and Drama.* U of Nebraska P, 2016.

Allen, Woody. "The Kugelmass Episode." *Side Effects,* Ballantine, 1981, pp. 59–78.

Barth, John. "Lost in the Funhouse." *Lost in the Funhouse: Fiction for Print, Tape, Live Voice,* Doubleday, 1969, pp. 72–97.

Bell, Alice, and Jan Alber. "Ontological Metalepsis and Unnatural Narratology." *Journal of Narrative Theory,* vol. 42, no. 2, 2012, pp. 166–92.

Bertens, Hans. "Why Molly Doesn't: Humanism's Long, Long Shadow." *Emotion in Postmodernism,* edited by Gerhard Hoffman and Alfred Hornung, Winter 1997, pp. 25–37.

Brooks, Peter. *Reading for the Plot: Design and Intention in Narrative.* Harvard UP, 1992.

Cohn, Dorrit. "Metalepsis and Mise en Abyme." Translated by Lewis S. Gleich, *Narrative,* vol. 20, no. 1, 2012, pp. 105–114.

Coover, Robert. "The Babysitter." *Pricksongs & Descants,* Plume, 1989, pp. 206–39.

———. "Charlie in the House of Rue." *A Night at the Movies: Or, You Must Remember This,* Collier, 1987, pp. 87–111.

———. "You Must Remember This." *A Night at the Movies: Or, You Must Remember This,* Collier, 1987, pp. 156–87.

Damasio, Antonio R. *The Feeling of What Happens: Body and Emotion in the Making of Consciousness.* Harcourt Brace, 1999.

Danielewski, Mark Z. *House of Leaves.* Pantheon, 2000.

Eggers, Dave. *A Heartbreaking Work of Staggering Genius.* Vintage, 2001.

Federman, Raymond. *The Voice in the Closet.* Station Hill P, 1979.

Fludernik, Monika. "Scene Shift, Metalepsis, and the Metaleptic Mode." *Style,* vol. 37, no. 4, 2003, pp. 382–400.

Foer, Jonathan Safran. *Extremely Loud and Incredibly Close.* Houghton Mifflin, 2005.

Gass, William. *Willie Masters' Lonesome Wife.* Dalkey Archive, 1989.

Genette, Gérard. *Narrative Discourse: An Essay in Method.* Translated by Jane E. Lewin, Cornell UP, 1980.

———. *Narrative Discourse Revisited.* Translated by Jane E. Lewin, Cornell UP, 1988.

Gerrig, Richard J. *Experiencing Narrative Worlds: On the Psychological Activities of Reading.* Yale UP, 1993.

Hogan, Patrick Colm. *Affective Narratology: The Emotional Structure of Stories.* U of Nebraska P, 2011.

———. "On Being Moved: Cognition and Emotion in Literature and Film." *Introduction to Cognitive Cultural Studies,* edited by Lisa Zunshine, Johns Hopkins UP, 2010, pp. 237–56.

McHale, Brian. *Postmodernist Fiction.* Methuen, 1987.

Miall, David S. "Emotions and the Structuring of Narrative Responses." *Poetics Today,* vol. 32, no. 2, 2011, pp. 323–48.

Reconstruction. Directed by Christoffer Boe, Nordisk Film, 2003.

Richardson, Brian. *Unnatural Narrative: Theory, History, and Practice.* Ohio State University Press, 2015.

Ryan, Marie-Laure. *Avatars of Story.* University of Minnesota Press, 2006.

Sontag, Susan. "Against Interpretation." *Against Interpretation and Other Essays,* Doubleday, 1986, pp. 3–14.

Stranger Than Fiction. Directed by Marc Forster, Columbia Pictures, 2006.

Warhol, Robyn R. *Having a Good Cry: Effeminate Feelings and Pop-Culture Forms.* The Ohio State UP, 2003.

Wolf, Werner. "Illusion (Aesthetic)." *The Living Handbook of Narratology,* http://wikis.sub.uni-hamburg.de/lhn/index.php/Illusion (Aesthetic).

———. "'Unnatural' Metalepsis and Immersion: Necessarily Incompatible?" *A Poetics of Unnatural Narrative,* edited by Jan Alber et al., The Ohio State UP, 2013, pp. 113–41.

CHAPTER 6

The (Un)Natural Response

Reading Walter Abish's Alphabetical Africa

ROY SOMMER

INTRODUCTION

Unnatural narrative theory is a recent addition to the broad range of approaches that are now generally subsumed under the umbrella term of postclassical narratology (see Sommer, "Merger").[1] Three areas seem to be fundamental to an unnatural approach (see Alber et al., "Unnatural Narratives"): definitions of the object domain (antimimetic and experimental fiction), a fundamental critique of natural narratology (which is said to lend too much weight to a mimetic model of narrative), and, finally, hypotheses regarding the cognitive functions and effects of the unnatural (frame enrichment). Engaging with unnatural narrative theory in a systematic manner is a difficult task, however, as its conceptual framework is still evolving and there are "rather substantial differences" (Iversen 95) between the individual positions. Is the unnatural best thought of as a genre, or a corpus of texts, or a way of world making? How does unnatural theory reconcile the emphasis on an inductive approach (see Richardson, *Unnatural Voices*) with its theoretical claims concerning reading strategies and naturalization processes, claims that point to the ongoing debate on narrative,

---

1. I wish to thank Carolin Gebauer for her insightful comments on an earlier draft of this essay, and the two anonymous readers who encouraged me, among other things, to discuss more explicitly the limits of narrativity and the notion of the non-narrative novel.

cognition, and the mind? And, finally, can a "dual and oscillating conception of narrative" (Richardson, *Unnatural Narrative* xvi) obey the narratological principle of backward compatibility (see Sommer, "Future" 599) with classical definitions, or is it a conceptual alternative to existing frameworks?

In my contribution to the recent special issue of *Style* on unnatural narrative theory (Sommer, "Unnatural Fallacy"), I focused on the premises and claims of unnatural narratology. As I see it, unnatural narratology is a project that systematically explores a certain kind of experimental fiction that programmatically transcends the paradigm of narrative. Simply put, unnatural narrative theory is less a theory of *narrative* than a theory of non-narrative and antinarrative elements in the novel, a theory that is dedicated exclusively to a subgenre of literary fiction characterized, among other things, by thought experiments, metareferentiality, and aesthetic uses of language. Unnatural narratology, then, challenges us to reconsider the limits of narrativity and the uses of narrative in fiction, as well as the ways readers make sense of the unexpected.

My reading of Walter Abish's postmodern novel *Alphabetical Africa* (1974) focuses on the relationship between textual features that are said to render a narrative unnatural, and readers' ways of coming to terms with the unusual or unconventional: Do experimental texts prompt readers to adopt specific, unnatural reading strategies that are different from the ones required for reading, and understanding, natural narrative? There can be no doubt that Abish's novel is unnatural in Brian Richardson's sense (*Unnatural Narrative* 3–5): It is a literary text that strategically undermines mimetic reading strategies. What difference does this make?

Drawing on the categories of classical narratology, I will analyze the narrative discourse in Abish's novel to explore the potential and limitations of concepts such as homodiegetic narration and unreliability. Postmodernist interpretations of *Alphabetical Africa* will be taken into account in order to discuss alternative reading strategies that complement a narratological analysis. I will argue that the way readers naturalize openly antimimetic, or rather meta-mimetic, novels (i.e., novels that invite readers to reflect on the mimetic nature of their own reading strategies) is not fundamentally different from the way they approach mimetic fiction. From the schemata and parameters available to them, readers will have to select and apply those that seem most suited for the task at hand. What is different, however, is the outcome of the process of frame selection. Not all schemata will be equally relevant, as the text preconfigures its reception: Perhaps the most natural response to extremely unnatural narratives is not to think of them as narratives at all.

ALPHABETICAL AFRICA AS AN "UNNATURAL" EXPERIMENT WITH LANGUAGE AND NARRATIVE

The influence of French deconstructivist thinking on postmodern writers in the US manifests itself in a playful attitude toward established modes of thinking and writing, and writing about thinking. In his introduction to postmodernism, Christopher Butler points out that the "language and conventions of texts (and pictures and music) became something to *play* with—they were not committed to delimited arguments or narratives" (23). *Alphabetical Africa*, Walter Abish's first novel, published in 1974, is a prime example of a language game that challenges the conventional limits of narrative. The text is composed of fifty-two chapters, each headed with a letter from the alphabet. The first chapter ("A") only uses words beginning with this letter. The second chapter ("B") includes words beginning with either *a* or *b*. Chapter 3 ("C") adds words beginning with *c*, and so on and so forth. Chapter "Z," where all letters are available, according to the aesthetic principle, is followed by another chapter, also headed "Z," which introduces the second, longer half of the book. From this point forward, in every chapter a letter is not added but lost. The final chapter, again headed "A," is subject to the same constraints as the first.[2]

The first chapter begins with a puzzle: How is Antibes, the French city, linked to Africa? Why is the assembly of an African army described not as an event in the fictional world but as the outcome of an argument, and in which part of the African continent can antelopes and alligators coexist? Alligators do not normally live in Africa, and yet they are mentioned, like the argument, because the word begins with the letter *a*. Antibes, in the first sentence, however, corresponds to Abidjan in Ivory Coast, mentioned in the last sentence of the chapter: "Alex and Allen alone, arrive in Abidjan and await African amusements" (2). The change from past tense—"Ages ago, Alex, Allen and Alva arrived at Antibes" (1)—to present tense indicates a temporal distance between the first and last event in chapter 1. What is more, the fact that Allen and Alex arrive alone indicates that they have fallen out with Alva, who appears to have alienated them.

The aesthetic experience is determined by the linguistic principle: An excess of alliteration, which effects instant defamiliarization, turns the search for meaning into a challenge, even on the level of individual phrases and sentences. Ralf Schneider's model of structural components of character allows

---

2. To avoid confusion, the "ascending" chapters (from "A" to "Z") will be referred to as "A1," "B1," and so on, while the "descending" chapters (from "Z" to "A") will be numbered "A2," "B2," and so on.

us to distinguish between levels and activities of meaning making: Text-processing activities, including word-semantic analysis, syntactic analysis, and hypotheses concerning the semantics of larger sections, are rendered difficult; nor does bottom-up processing of textual information at this point allow us to construct a coherent mental model of Alex, Allen, and Alva. Neither personality theories nor empathic emotions, key components of top-down processing, offer a suitable alternative. The reader can resort to literary knowledge structures that inform his stance toward postmodernist fiction as a literary discourse that strives to displace and rupture automatic associations (see McHale 48), or—if he or she is not (yet) familiar with postmodernism—develop such knowledge structures in a bottom-up process. Another option, of course, is to stop reading if the text fails to meet one's expectations or preferences.

The highly metareferential and self-reflexive nature of Abish's text makes perspective taking, a conventional effect of perceived realism in literary fiction (see V. Nünning 220–21), difficult, if not impossible. Instead, immersion and empathy are called for, together with a sense of detached curiosity: Will Abish manage to construct a meaningful story with such limited linguistic means? The alphabetical pattern encourages readers to spend some time looking for errors (use of words in chapters where they do not belong). They will find that the self-imposed rules are observed strictly, with very few exceptions that are probably not intentional.[3] Is the text designed to create meaning at all, or is it a purely aesthetic exercise? Would the latter not be less of an artistic challenge, and thus rather pointless? How do Abish's self-imposed linguistic constraints influence the possibility of narrative world making?

Another set of questions raised by the unusual design of the novel concerns its truth claim: Can we trust the narrative? Should we regard Allen, Alex, and Alva as the characters' "true" names, or is their naming also subject to the self-imposed linguistic constraints? How can we be sure that the alphabet does not interfere with the setting—is it "really" Antibes and Abidjan, or are these cities randomly chosen because of their initial letter? Should we even try to read the novel referentially, or should we appreciate it as a linguistic and narrative experiment that transcends the conventions of narrative fiction—a "heterotopian zone" (McHale 45) that deconstructs space? The truth claim depends on our conception of the narrative discourse: Who narrates, and who serves as

---

3. The following is quoted from the Wikipedia entry on *Alphabetical Africa*: "Readers have noted that there are several places in the narrative where the constraint is violated. Most counts of these violations number them between four and six; however, up to 43 have been noted by astute readers. One point of dispute is whether the failures to meet the constraint are intentional, and therefore potentially meaningful, or are simply editing mistakes. It is said that when Abish was notified of the errors, he reacted with total surprise" (see https://en.wikipedia.org/wiki/Alphabetical_Africa). A list of "alphabetical errata" is available online. See http://www.complete-review.com/reviews/abishw/aafrica.htm#err.

a focalizer? Who is responsible for generalizing comments such as "Congolese cannot create a culture, can barely cook cucumbers, curds and cauliflowers" (6) or the numerous allusions to Alva's attractiveness and sexual exploitation?[4]

The first chapter introduces an author character—"author again attempts an agonizing alphabetical appraisal" (1–2)—who reappears frequently throughout the narrative. Who is this author? In the absence of a clearly identifiable narratorial voice, one might assume that this utterance is an ironical reference to the actual author, Abish himself, as he struggles with the alphabet, syntax, and semantics. A more abstract reading might regard this as an ironical reference to the author function in narrative fiction, thus complicating things further. When the first-person narrator is introduced in "I1," another interpretive hypothesis becomes plausible, as we will see below: The "author" of the early and the concluding chapters is identical with the "I" of the middle part, and thus an autodiegetic narrator, albeit a rather strange one, who appears to be heterodiegetic rather than homodiegetic, as he constantly reflects on his role as the inventor of the fictive characters.

Ironical self-reflexivity is ubiquitous in the novel: "Disgusted author eliminates Ferdinand" (13), we learn toward the end of chapter "F1." At a point where the experimental nature of this text begins to recede into the background, as the reader gets used to the textual design and the increasing number of initial letters allows for a more complex linguistic structure, we are again reminded of the artificiality of the narrative. The explicit reference to the creative process and emotional involvement of the fictive author emphasizes that the characters are the product of a linguistic effort—and thus of Abish's project, a project concerned with questions of tellability, narrativity, and fictionality. For instance, here is the "author," or heterodiegetic first-person narrator, reflecting on desire and emotions:

> Afternoon, author drops by at a favorite bar. His hands hold his destiny. He grips an African counter, and conceives another fictional character. Do both Allen and Alex desire Alva? Can desire be an essential entity for a book? He has already eliminated a few emotions. (19)

The question regarding the relationship between Allen, Alex, and Alva is rhetorical: Of course it is the author who decides what his characters feel, but he is clearly skeptical of mimesis. Using James Phelan's terminology (20), one might conclude that Abish, or rather his text-internal author character, denies his synthetic characters a mimetic dimension.

---

4. See, for instance, 4, 8, 9, 18, 20, 21, 23, 49, 50, 66, and 69.

But can we hold the actual author responsible for the patronizing remarks, sweeping statements and cultural stereotypes that also characterize the narrative discourse? Such an ethos attribution, to use the concept recently proposed by Liesbeth Korthals Altes, is equally unlikely and implausible. First, these utterances frequently contain nonsensical information, as in the example above: Why should the ability to create a culture depend on the cooking of vegetables? This is also true for the author's comparative evaluation of Ghana and Germany: "Ghanaians are erroneously convinced German gestures can cut floods, can cook beetles, can deafen Africans, but German gestures are all futile, besides being enormously funny" (14), or, in an even more generalizing gesture: "As a group Germans eat differently from Africans" (24). Silly comments like these are reminiscent of the absurdist tradition in comedy—Monty Python comes to mind. Such a reading is in line with a general appraisal of postmodern experiments that often challenge "serious" concepts of art, originality, and authorship.

As mentioned above, chapter "I1" offers some clarity with respect to the narrative voice, as for the first time the first-person pronoun becomes available, and a homodiegetic narrator introduces himself: "I haven't been here before. I had hoped that I could hire a car, but I can't drive. I have been awfully busy finishing a book about Alva" (21). The first-person narrator appears to be identical with the author of the first eight chapters, an assumption that is confirmed in the "Y1" chapter: "The book you are holding in your hand happens to be one I wrote. Yes, I happen to be the author" (62). A complex narrative situation is thus explicitly established. The narrator is the heterodiegetic source of the narrative, commenting on various aspects of the storyworld, but also on the act of writing and the associated dimensions of aesthetics and poetics: "I have an interest in books and in paper," he says. "An overwhelming interest, an interest exceeding my interest in Alva and Alex and Allen" (39). However, he also functions as an autodiegetic narrator who has to learn the truth about Alex and Allen from a diary: "I can infer from Alex's journal both his and Allen's intentions. Both are killers" (27). Later the narrator adds: "I don't believe I ever actually met Alex or Allen" (33). He cannot have met them, actually, as the narrator never ceases to remind us. The characters are linguistic constructs he is busy creating, although he later reveals that "Alex and Allen arranged everything, almost making me an accomplice" (36). Such comments, then, play with narrative conventions—the limited perspective and restricted knowledge typical of autodiegetic eye-witness observers.

The novel can thus be characterized as a hybrid blend, an "impossible" mixture of first-person narration and authorial narration. This becomes obvious in the concluding sentences of chapter "I1": "I don't care if Allen and Alex are in Africa, I don't care if both are hunting for Alva, because I am. I am. And I have an accurate chart, and a dictionary and her description" (26). Why does the narrator need a dictionary? Possibly because he does not speak French or the languages spoken in the African countries mentioned in the novel (this would emphasize his limitations as an autodiegetic narrator and character in the story). The dictionary with its alphabetical list of words is, however, also required to complete the task of writing this specific book about Alva, a linguistic experiment designed to create Alva in such a way that the traces of the creative process are not hidden, as in realist fiction, but foregrounded.[5] The narratorial voice that cunningly oscillates between autodiegetic ignorance on the one hand, and heterodiegetic omniscience on the other, supplements the alphabetical principle: Narrative structure and linguistic strategy go hand in hand.

One particularly successful reading strategy to resolve such inconsistencies—a strategy extensively discussed by narrative theorists—is the ascription of unreliability. There is no need here to review the many contributions that discuss the merits and disadvantages of the implied author, a key concept of rhetorical narratology. As in other fields of narrative theory, the conceptual alternatives appear complementary rather than mutually exclusive. As Ansgar Nünning has shown, it is possible to reconcile rhetorical and cognitive positions on the matter. All concepts seem to agree on the two points, however, that are relevant for the present purpose: Certain textual cues provoke a reading strategy that questions the narrator's reliability, and this complex phenomenon cannot be explained on the basis of textual evidence alone. It is the result of a clash between two incompatible value systems or world views: that of the narrator, and that of the reader.

There are many indications that the narrator in *Alphabetical Africa* might also be unreliable. Chapter "M1" begins with an admission: "My memory isn't accurate anymore" (32). Toward the end of "U1," the narrator even calls himself unreliable: "But I am an unreliable reporter. I can't be depended upon for exact descriptions and details" (56). The narrator also explicitly addresses, and thus tries to manipulate, his narratee, a well-established strategy that helps reinforce the effect of unreliability in classics of the genre, such as Vladimir Nabokov's novel *Lolita*, first published in 1956. However, when the second-person pronoun is introduced in the penultimate chapter of the first part (before the alphabetical principle is reversed), it quickly becomes obvious that the narrative addresses both extradiegetic and intradiegetic instances in a stra-

---

5. Dictionaries serve as a leitmotif for the desire to come to terms with the other, quite literally, but possibly also for Africa's appropriation and exploitation by European colonial powers (see, for instance, 77, 80, 81, 115, 136).

tegic move to increase ambiguity. This becomes most obvious in chapter "Y1." The opening sentences seem to refer simultaneously to the narratee—that is, the text-internal representation of the reader, commenting on his or her initial confusion when trying to naturalize the novel's unusual beginning—and to an unnamed intradiegetic character, who has been browsing a book written by the narrator in a bookshop:

> You were unaware of me at first. You look up, surprised, not having heard what I said. You remind me of someone I knew in Antibes years ago. The book you are holding in your hand happens to be one I wrote. Yes, I happen to be the author. (62)

Perhaps the strangest effect of Abish's experimental design is how the gradual lifting of linguistic constraints in the ascending chapters ("A1" to "Z1") corresponds with an increasingly coherent storyworld. In narratological terminology, one could argue that the degree of narrativity increases in the first half and decreases in the second half of the book. Conversely, the unfamiliar or unnatural qualities of the text recede, and increase, depending on how many letters of the alphabet are currently in use. Beginning with "Z2," the narrator unfolds the story of Alfred and Alva's arrival in Zanzibar, where Alfred takes over the property of Europeans who have left the country because of the political situation, while Alva begins an intimate relationship with the French consul's beautiful wife. The novel almost assumes a critical postcolonial stance, for instance when child soldiers and preparations for war are mentioned in passing:

> On the southern tip of the island a small army of men is furtively training with automatic rifles, bazookas, two-inch mortars and hand grenades. But they are not very experienced, some of the soldiers being only nine years old. (77)

This army intends to attack "the great warrior ants" as well as the "driver ants" and to "rid the island of its ants" (77). Cognitively speaking, the target domain of this recurring metaphor remains unclear (although the plight of "ten thousand Muslims" from Zanzibar is mentioned in "X2," possibly a reference to the Zanzibar revolution of 1964), so that the narrative leaves it to the reader to decide what conflict Abish is referring to—or to figure out that Abish's fictional events do not correspond to specific historical realities at all. However, the ant metaphor encourages us to reread "A1," where it was first introduced. With the benefit of hindsight, the "awesome" African army advancing against an "African anthill, assiduously annihilating ant after ant" (1) no longer appears to be a nonsensical image, but an anticipation of the representation of political events whose nature is revealed, at least partly, as the semantic veil, caused by linguistic constraints, is slowly lifted. Later we learn how Queen Quat's army invades an island, presumably Zanzibar (although the island cannot be named, because the letter is no longer available), and Alfred is captured and tortured by enemy troops who attack the outnumbered driver ants using "automatic antiant devices" (109), while the queen marks "freshly captured anthills on her map" (109). The "driver ants," mentioned at least five times (77, 81, 91, 108), may echo the Ugandan invasion of Zanzibar in 1964.

The first sentence in "X2," "X stands for experimental, and for excretion, that is for plain shit on the trail" (81), anticipates the return of linguistic restrictions, (seemingly) nonsensical humor, and metareferential irony. In Queen Quat's speech ("S2"), syntax (or rather the lack of syntactic structure) is foregrounded: "She keeps saying: Same shit same scenery same suffering saints same soup same spiel same safaris" (100). The speech continues, without syntax, punctuation, or any discernible semantic pattern, for another page. "R2" begins with a metaleptic introduction of a reader named Jaqueline who appears to be reading *Alphabetical Africa*:

> Jaqueline is an impatient reader, always hastily running her eyes down a page, always looking for a particularly eventful passage, and consequently Jaqueline misses a description of Alva on page forty-nine and on page ninety-nine. (102)

On these pages, there are indeed descriptions of Alva—but one could argue that Jaqueline has missed nothing of vital importance.[6]

The narrator's criticism can, however, also be read as a comment addressed to the actual readers, reminding them not to read for content and skip less eventful passages, and preparing them for the return of linguistic constraints. Nonreferential and antimimetic reading strategies become more relevant again, as decreasing alphabetical options reduce narrativity, paradoxically creating a more complex text in the process. Complexity increases, because having been able to naturalize the novel mimetically by ascribing the metafictional game to a narrator who is explicitly referring to himself as the author of this book, the reader will try to reconcile subsequent textual data with

---

6. "Alva's body is functional. . . . She parts her legs and becomes fully functional" (49); "Alva considers her options. She can remain or she can leave. Finally she opts for staying because she likes breakfast in bed" (99).

this interpretive hypothesis: It is the unnamed first-person narrator, however unreliable he may be, who produces the novel's narrative discourse.

"I2" is crucial in this respect, for this is supposed to contain the last occurrence of the first-person pronoun, and thus the last opportunity for the narrator to openly comment on the storyworld. First, the narrator insists on his trustworthiness and reliability, a rather conventional strategy more suited to reinforce than to dispel the reader's suspicion and mistrust.[7] Then, for the first and last time in the novel, the narrator provides the reader with information on his own upbringing. The focus is on his father, an inventor, whose "extraordinary inventions fail in improving existence" (128). We do not learn what he has invented, how he is involved in African history, economics, and politics, or why his work has been ignored in Africa ("I'm deeply dismayed by Africa's apathy and indifference as far as his incredible inventions are concerned" [128]), but the son's description focuses on the fact that his father does not care about recognition. As we have come to expect from this novel, the description oscillates between conventional mimetic characterization—"father didn't care about his ideas being accepted" (128)—and information that can hardly be integrated in a mimetic model of character, due to a lack of context:

> He's busy, and he can't bother about confusing claims concerning Africa's continental drift. He doesn't even acknowledge basic differences between countries, especially black countries, considering all inhabitants equally beyond his comprehension. (128–29)

Is the narrator's father a geologist or a racist, or both, or neither? We do not know.

The most plausible reading, however, seems to be one that foregrounds the synthetic qualities of the father, whose description quickly turns into a metafictional and metalinguistic diatribe against narrative description in general:

> He hardly ever glances at a book, because implicit in almost all descriptions in a book are differences, frequently erroneous differences, because descriptions in books are building characters by adding and adding information, erroneous and frequently divisive information, he claimed. (129)

---

7. The contradictions in the narratorial discourse become most obvious at the beginning of "I2": "I haven't ever considered distorting, dissembling and falsifying anything except for a few intimate details, colorful details in a double bed, but deletions, I assert, can't be considered falsifications despite Alva's accusations" (128).

It seems that one major function of this synthetic character, who will not reappear in the remaining chapters, is to foreground the process of character construction in fiction. Another function is, paradoxically, to emphasize the anthropomorphic qualities of the narrator—the reader experiences a transition from a disembodied narratorial voice to what Phelan has termed *character narration*.

The mimetic effect allows the reader to attribute the remaining chapters to the narrator of the novel's middle section. This interpretive hypothesis comes naturally now that a first-person narrator has been firmly established, albeit an unreliable and elusive one, who frequently turns into an extradiegetic voice and comments on the experimental nature of this metaleptic novel. The hypothesis is confirmed when, in "D2," the narrator-character unexpectedly reappears: "Am deeply disturbed by Alva's disappearance. Dangerous days. Discover city's central avenue blocked by cops and army behind barricades. Abandoning car, ably avoid all cops, as darkness covers another day's advance" (144).

The use of the copula ("am") without its complement ("I") is a recurrent feature of the remaining chapters and turns out to be fully sufficient to conjure up the narrator's presence. It is most surprising, therefore, that the personal pronoun reappears in "C2": "After considering all alternatives, I capture a couple crocodiles." (146) There has been speculation as to whether this unnecessary violation of the self-imposed rules is intentional (see footnote 3). It seems plausible to assume that it is an oversight (after all, the "of" is omitted in "a couple of crocodiles," to comply with the constraints). For the present argument it is more relevant, however, that the interpretive hypothesis (the chapters following "I2" should be read as utterances by the—now invisible—autodiegetic narrator) is confirmed, voluntarily or not. This way of naturalizing the discourse supports a reading that equates the "author" of the early chapters with the narrator. The covert narratorial voice in chapters "A1" to "H1" turns into an overt character narrator from "I1" to "I2," who then becomes less overt (but not fully covert) in the remaining chapters.

The narrative discourse in *Alphabetical Africa*, then, is unusually dynamic. Initially the text makes use of a disembodied voice. It is not yet clear whether the "author" refers to an intradiegetic author character, an extradiegetic narrator, or the flesh-and-blood author, Abish himself. We cannot even argue with certainty that this linguistic experiment is intended to tell a story, or whether it is rather designed, for instance, to foreground, explore, and subvert the process of narration. As soon as (and only when) the first-person pronoun becomes available, the novel introduces a first-person narrator who appears to be autodiegetic (although one could argue that some of the information on other characters can only be conveyed through a heterodiegetic narrative instance, if the conventional limitations of first-person narration are to be observed). Thus a disembodied voice turns into a narrator who possesses anthropomorphic traits. Once the "I" disappears, the initial uncertainty is not restored. Instead, the use of the copula encourages readers to ascribe all utterances to the first-person narrator.

Summing up, Abish's novel exhibits many of the characteristics that have recently been defined as unnatural by Jan Alber et al. ("What Really" 102–4). *Alphabetical Africa* oscillates between mimetic and meta-mimetic modes of representation; it has the disorienting and defamiliarizing effects typical of postmodernist fiction; it defies conventional story logic by superimposing a linguistic principle on the narrative discourse, causing clashes between the act of representation and represented events and existents; and it foregrounds the constructedness of narrative discourse in fiction, thus prompting interpretive reorientation. According to these definitions, then, *Alphabetical Africa* may be described as an unnatural narrative. But how does the "unnatural" narrative design affect the readers' response? In what ways do unnatural narratives urge us to create new cognitive frames and create impossible blends, as Alber et al. ("What Really" 107) argue?

My reading of *Alphabetical Africa* has demonstrated that the novel offers a highly unusual combination of linguistic and narrative strategies that challenge conventional reading strategies or, cognitively speaking, processes of naturalization. But to what extent can textual qualities really influence readers' mental models? Do unnatural forms elicit unnatural responses? Such questions transcend the possibilities afforded by experimental research in cognitive psychology. The answer can only be a plausible model. What interpretive strategies are needed, what hermeneutic maneuvers are necessary in order to naturalize the unnatural? In the following section, I will attempt a more abstract reflection on how readers may come to terms with experimental, and thus unusual, narrative designs.

NATURALIZING THE UNNATURAL: HOW DOES IT WORK?

In his seminal study *Before Reading: Narrative Conventions and the Politics of Interpretation,* Peter J. Rabinowitz claims that the act of reading is influenced by readers' expectations: "Readers need to stand somewhere before they pick up a book, and the nature of that 'somewhere,' I argue, significantly influences the ways in which they interpret (and consequently evaluate) texts" (2). Where will readers of *Alphabetical Africa* stand before picking up the book? More likely than not, they will be students of literature working on postmodernist fiction. The back cover reveals that this is Abish's "delightful first novel." Calling this book a novel, however, says more about generic conventions and, possibly, the publishers' marketing strategy than about the text itself, which could more adequately be described as a linguistic and narrative experiment. As we have seen, its diegetic universe at first appears fragmented and incoherent. A series of strange events is recounted, yet one can hardly speak of a plot. There is a narratorial voice that cannot be trusted, yet it is not unreliable in the classical narratological sense, as will be argued below. And the linguistic pattern leaves one wondering whether this novel is really interested in telling a story at all.

The first obstacle readers will have to overcome, then, is to reconcile the generic framing of the book as a novel with the linguistic principle indicated by the title. We will not find it particularly challenging to accept that poetry plays with linguistic conventions, foregrounding processes of signification and world making in radical ways. Such experiments in a novel, however, raise the reader's curiosity: Will the text really stick to the self-imposed linguistic constraints, or will the principle be sacrificed for the sake of syntax and intelligibility? How will the text be able to create meaning under such strict constraints? How will the gradual completion of the alphabet affect the reading experience? What is the aesthetic effect when the experimental principle is resumed slowly but surely, starting with "Z2"?

Apart from the formal, stylistic dimension, Abish's experiment highlights a problem that is hidden rather than revealed in the realist tradition of literary storytelling: Accepting the premise of fictionality, are we supposed to suspend disbelief and trust that the narrative discourse will facilitate storyworld projection in a reliable and coherent manner? Can, and will, the novel make a truth claim, even though it appears to deny referentiality? "Very few imaginative works," Wayne C. Booth argues in *The Rhetoric of Fiction*, "rely entirely on a desire for intellectual completion" (126). An intellectual interest in understanding the nature of a novel's truth claims is an important dimension of naturalization, according to Booth, and this appears to hold equally for experimental fiction: "Even in so-called plotless works we are pulled forward by the desire to discover the truth about the world of the book" (125).

If the reader is a narratologist, his or her aesthetic experience will be preconfigured or framed by specific expectations: Is it possible to consider the text a narrative at all, according to commonly accepted definitions of narrative? Will it possess a high or low degree of narrativity, and will that change as the linguistic constraints are suspended? More specifically, the reading will focus on how the distinction between story and discourse, a concept that is constitutive of how narratology comes to terms with narrative, is achieved: When, and how, will we be able to identify a narratorial voice that produces the diegesis? My reading implies that primacy and recency effects play an important role in establishing and sustaining a narrative discourse in *Alphabetical Africa*: Initial skepticism with respect to the origin and reliability of the narratorial voice gives way to a conventionalized reading following the structuralist and rhetorical models established by Genette (autodiegetic narration) and Phelan (character narration). This interpretive hypothesis is maintained even when the personal pronoun disappears after "I2." As noted above, this reading strategy is confirmed by the use of the copula "am" (which is absent from the first chapters of the novel).

One question, however, remains: Can a narrator be considered unreliable if the artificial nature of the narrative, and, by implication, all fictional narratives, is foregrounded so strongly? After all, unreliability and untrustworthiness are essentially mimetic notions. Whether this question is considered at all relevant depends on whether we choose to anthropomorphize the narrator within a mimetic model of narrative, that is, think of him or her as of a human being telling a story. Alternatively, we are free to treat him or her—or it—as an illusion, a linguistic construct designed to help us reflect on the limits and potentials of language, on the aesthetic and dramaturgical qualities of linguistic constraints, and on the process of naturalization itself.[8]

In the first scenario—anthropomorphization aided or cued by storytelling frames—we focus on what David Herman has called the "ecology of narrative interpretation" (13), relying on the "world-creating power of narrative" (14). The self-referential structure of the novel will, however, prevent us from simply ascribing (un)reliability to the narrator; we are faced with a question that is not meant to be answered. To use an analogy from the visual arts: The reader may approach Abish's novel like a pointillist painting, assuming that behind an unusual, "artificial" surface, a "real" world is waiting to be discovered. In the second scenario, we appreciate the novel, not unlike a cubist painting that denies its referentiality, as an antimimetic experiment that creates—and ironically undermines—the illusion of a personalized voice, and lets the reader observe the act of creation itself. The linguistic constraints act like a filter in subtractive sound synthesis, that is, a device that opens and closes to allow certain frequencies to pass through, or not. In such a reading,

---

8. Referring to Jonathan Culler's concept, Fludernik defines naturalization as "the process of recuperating local textual inconsistencies by integrating them within a more general overarching sense-pattern" ("Naturalisation" 395). I am using the term in this sense.

the question of the narrator's (un)reliability is irrelevant: the narrative frame itself becomes irrelevant.

This issue has not yet received sufficient consideration in cognitive narrative theory: While literary texts differ in their narrative design, either facilitating or thwarting mimetic readings, empirical readers differ both in their preferences for specific interpretive strategies and the conclusions they draw when certain strategies do not work. Most readers will agree that Abish offers us neither a realistic portrait of literary characters *as people* (see Forster), nor a naturalist image of Zanzibar *as an island*. His "piecemeal representation of Africa" is, as McHale observes, "full of anomalies such as the non-existent beaches of land-locked Chad" (53). It is up to the readers, however, to decide whether they become part of the pointillist camp, the cubist camp—or prefer to regard the text even more radically as the literary equivalent of abstract art. It is also up to the reader to decide whether he or she will continue looking for more suitable interpretive hypotheses, reading the novel, for instance, as a meta-mimetic and metafictional reflection on narrative world making, or simply stop reading.

A suitable hypothesis in this context is one that allows the reader to impose on the text what Monika Fludernik ("How Natural" 360) has called a "homogenous semantic framework."[9] Drawing on Tamar Yacobi's work, she distinguishes genetic, perspectival, mimetic, generic, functional, and existential principles that may inform a reader's attempt to make sense of a text. More specifically, these strategies help readers come to terms with perceived oddities by reducing complexity in various ways. The strength of this argument is that it does not prescribe or even predict the outcome of the process of naturalization. It acknowledges that there is a wide range of interpretive strategies readers may employ, and thus a variety of readerly responses. The desire to homogenize informs most scholarly approaches to fiction, probably even the most radical deconstructive readings that seek to homogenize difference, and certainly narratological readings whether they focus on natural or non-natural aspects of narrative. We may choose and change our system of description, but we cannot, as Nelson Goodman once observed, escape the system (any system) altogether: "If I ask about the world, you can offer to tell me how it is under one or more frames of reference; but if I insist that you tell

---

9. See Fludernik, "How Natural" 360: "What all of these strategies amount to is the attempt to impose a homogenous semantic framework on the text, to standardize the interpretative effect, in other words, to motivate deviance from the norm or from current templates by explaining the difference as signifying additional information that enhances or deepens our understanding of the text."

me how it is apart from all frames, what can you say? We are confined to ways of describing whatever is described" (2–3).

CONCLUSIONS

Like many other theories, narratology, as a frame of reference for the study of narrative, confines us to a certain way of analyzing novels and other types of fictional and factual texts that can be defined, narratologically, as narratives. There are two common ways of defining a narrative: by establishing minimal conditions met by all and only narratives, as structuralist narratology has it, or by establishing a core of necessary or compulsory conditions supplemented by optional, facultative criteria that may or may not be relevant for a given narrative. On the basis of a classification of a given oral, verbal, or audiovisual text as a narrative, narratological criticism usually directs critical attention to the narrative design of a text, focusing on structure and form rather than theme and style.

My reading of *Alphabetical Africa* reveals some standard procedures of narratological criticism, for instance a systematic description of narrative discourse and the use of narratological terminology. In classical narratological fashion, it focuses more on how the text works than on what it means. More specifically, it hypothesizes that after the initial confusion caused by alphabetical constraints, the emergence of an autodiegetic narrator facilitates an experiential reading of the novel, despite the ubiquity of absurd propositions. It also raises the question, however, whether the ascription of unreliability, a reading strategy that often works in similar circumstances when coming to terms with discursive discrepancies in realist fiction, is really an option in this particular case.

I have argued that not only the reliability of the narrator but also the viability of a referential reading as such is undermined to such a degree that the limitations of a narratological approach are revealed: The reading experience clearly transcends naturalization in terms of experientiality, even if this is theoretically possible. Readers looking for that kind of "natural" experience would probably not be satisfied. Other frames of reference, in Goodman's terms, are therefore needed to do justice to the complexity of Abish's linguistic experiment: Reading *Alphabetical Africa* as a postmodern novel (see McHale) or as, in Bakhtin's sense, a dialogic text (see Schirato) are tried and tested strategies that allow us to fully appreciate the literary qualities of the novel. Of course, postmodern or Bakhtinian readings do not contradict or replace a narratological approach, but complement it nicely (or vice versa—narratology can also be seen as a tool that serves generic, historical, or poetic approaches to literature).

What does this mean with respect to the arguments of unnatural narrative theory? With respect to terminology, unnatural narrative has been introduced to refer to antimimetic, literary experiments. While one can discuss whether *non-natural* (or even better, possibly, *antinatural*) would be a more suitable term, it certainly is good to have such a category. Where I differ on principle from what the unnatural argument seems to imply, however, is in the scope of the concept. Unnatural narratives do not elicit unnatural responses: What they do is cue readers, naturally, to choose a different frame of reference. Narrative is simply not the most relevant category when it comes to naturalizing a novel like *Alphabetical Africa*. The natural response to such a literary work, which I would define as a dominantly non-narrative or even antinarrative experiment, is to realize that narrative, and narratology, whether natural or unnatural, is not the only frame, or framework, that allows us to come to terms with literary fiction.

My analysis suggests two conclusions that are consistent with my recent theoretical critique of unnatural narratology's premises and claims (Sommer, "Unnatural Fallacy"). First, it can be assumed that readers, when dealing with an experimental, antimimetic, or unnatural narrative—that is, a narrative that in one way or another deviates from expectations raised by generic conventions—will first seek to apply tried-and-tested strategies for naturalizing and narrativizing the text. One such strategy might be doubting a narrator's reliability. If this fails, as in Abish's case, readers will try other strategies, such as approaching the text as a linguistic experiment.

Second, there are cases where a narrative act, or rather the simulation of a narrative act, does not constitute a narrative. The complex relationship between narration and narrative therefore deserves further scrutiny. As Abish's example shows, the mere use of a narrating voice may have a mainly, or even exclusively, metareferential function. The old analogy between writing and painting mentioned above helps to illustrate this point. On the representational, mimetic end of the wide range of possibilities, we find the long tradition of figural painting. By varying degrees of abstraction, art moves through impressionism, pointillism, and Cubism to abstract art.

Similarly, the novel, as a broad generic concept, accommodates quasi-autobiographical storytelling and various forms of fictional narration, as well as linguistic experiments that challenge and extend the limits of the genre in ways that to some may seem unnatural. How should narrative theory respond to the heterogeneity of the novel? Assuming as a premise that *all* novels are best described as narratives encourages a reductionist approach to the weird, the wonderful, and the wonderfully weird. The non-narrative novel is not an oxymoron, as Richardson's ("Rejoinders" 501) response to my argument seems to imply, but a rare species in a predominantly narrative environment, and like all rare species it deserves closer scrutiny. Instead of stretching its core concepts to "narrativize" even the most experimental literary text, narrative theory should, then, team up with complementary theories of the novel and of fictionality in order to do justice to the wide variety of literary devices novels may use to manipulate, augment, and enrich our experience of the world.

WORKS CITED

Abish, Walter. *Alphabetical Africa*. New Directions Publishing, 1974.

Alber, Jan, et al. "Unnatural Narratives, Unnatural Narratology: Beyond Mimetic Models." *Narrative*, vol. 18, no. 2, 2010, pp. 113–36.

———. "What Really Is Unnatural Narratology?" *Storyworlds: A Journal of Narrative Studies*, vol. 5, 2013, pp. 101–18.

Booth, Wayne C. *The Rhetoric of Fiction*. 1961. U of Chicago P, 1983.

Butler, Christopher. *Postmodernism: A Very Short Introduction*. Oxford UP, 2002.

Fludernik, Monika. "How Natural Is 'Unnatural Narratology'; or, What Is Unnatural about Unnatural Narratology?" *Narrative*, vol. 20, no. 3, 2012, pp. 357–70.

———. "Naturalisation." *Routledge Encyclopedia of Narrative Theory*, edited by David Herman et al., Routledge, 2005, pp. 395–96.

Forster, Edward Morgan. *Aspects of the Novel: The Timeless Classic on Novel Writing*. Harcourt, 1955.

Goodman, Nelson. *Ways of Worldmaking*. Hackett Publishing, 1978.

Herman, David. *Story Logic: Problems and Possibilities of Narrative*. U of Nebraska P, 2002.

Iversen, Stefan. "Unnatural Minds." *A Poetics of Unnatural Narrative*, edited by Jan Alber et al., The Ohio State UP, 2013, pp. 94–110.

Korthals Altes, Liesbeth. *Ethos and Narrative Interpretation: The Negotiation of Values in Fiction*. U of Nebraska P, 2014.

McHale, Brian. *Postmodernist Fiction*. Methuen, 1987.

Nünning, Ansgar. "Reconceptualizing the Theory, History and Generic Scope of Unreliable Narration: Towards a Synthesis of Cognitive and Rhetorical Approaches." *Narrative Unreliability in the Twentieth-Century First-Person Novel*, edited by Elke D'hoker and Gunther Martens, De Gruyter, 2008, pp. 29–76.

Nünning, Vera. *Reading Fictions, Changing Minds: The Cognitive Value of Fiction*. Winter, 2014.

Phelan, James. *Living to Tell about It: A Rhetoric and Ethics of Character Narration*. Cornell UP, 2005.

Rabinowitz, Peter J. *Before Reading: Narrative Conventions and the Politics of Interpretation*. Cornell UP, 1987.

Richardson, Brian. "Rejoinders to the Respondents." *Style*, vol. 50, no. 4, 2016, pp. 492–513.

———. *Unnatural Narrative. Theory, History, and Practice.* The Ohio State UP, 2015.

———. *Unnatural Voices: Extreme Narration in Modern and Contemporary Fiction.* The Ohio State UP, 2006.

Schirato, Anthony. "Comic Politics and Politics of the Comic: Walter Abish's *Alphabetical Africa.*" *Critique: Studies in Contemporary Fiction,* vol. 33, no. 2, 1992, pp. 133–44.

Schneider, Ralf. "Towards a Cognitive Theory of Literary Characters: The Dynamics of Mental-Model Construction." *Style,* vol. 35, no. 4, 2001, pp. 607–40.

Sommer, Roy. "The Future of Narratology's Past: A Contribution to Metanarratology." *Emerging Vectors of Narratology,* edited by John Pier et al., De Gruyter, 2017, pp. 593–608.

———. "The Merger of Classical and Postclassical Narratologies and the Consolidated Future of Narrative Theory." *DIEGESIS: Interdisciplinary E-Journal for Narrative Research,* vol. 1, no. 1., 2012, pp. 143–57, http://nbn-resolving.de/urn=urn:nbn:de:hbz:468-20121121-124341-0. Accessed 12 Feb. 2016.

———. "Unnatural Fallacy? The Logic of Unnatural Narrative Theory." *Style,* vol. 50, no. 4, 2016, pp. 405–9.

CHAPTER 7

Transcending Humanistic and Cognitive Models

Unnatural Characters in Fiction, Drama, and Popular Culture

BRIAN RICHARDSON

INTRODUCTION

Although character theory has existed since the time of Aristotle, antimimetic characters, which have been around since before Aristotle, still need to be adequately comprehended by narrative and dramatic theory.[1] For the most part, character theory has been dominated by a substantially mimetic sensibility that sees characters as largely or entirely like persons; in the words of Baruch Hochman, "both characters and people are apprehended in someone's consciousness, and they are apprehended in approximately the same terms" (7). Many characters, from those of Aristophanes to Bugs Bunny, fail to fit this description; these figures in fact violate the humanistic concept of a person. In the 1970s and 1980s there was a period during which non- and antimimetic characters were acknowledged and begun to be theorized. Roland Barthes stressed that characters were "paper beings" (*Image* 111) and argued that it is wrong to take the character "off the page in order to turn him into a psychological character (endowed with motives)" (*S/Z* 178). During the next twenty years, a number of other theorists explored the possibilities of non- or antimimetic characters; these included Joel Weinsheimer, Thomas Docherty,

---

1. I wish to thank Jan Alber, James Phelan, and Peter Rabinowitz for providing many insightful comments and important suggestions on earlier versions of this essay; they are greatly appreciated.

Brian McHale, James Phelan, Aleid Fokkema, John Frow, and, more recently, Per Krogh Hansen. This represented an important advance in the theory of character, and one that I fully support.

Now, however, these advances are often being ignored as the older mimetic bias seems to be returning to the critical scene, led by cognitivist and mind-oriented narratologists like Marisa Bortolussi and Peter Dixon, Richard J. Gerrig and David W. Allbritton, Ralf Schneider, and David Herman (125–31).[2] In a recent text, Herman returns to the humanist position articulated by Hochman, affirming that literary characters are "more or less prototypical members of the category 'persons'" (125), and again: "characters in novels can be viewed as *model persons*; these fictional individuals are at once shaped by and have the power to reshape broader conceptions of what a person is and how persons can be expected to respond in particular kinds of circumstances" (127).[3] Such a stance necessarily ignores the many characters that are significantly different from persons; worse, it may even preclude a theoretical treatment of such entities.[4]

The stakes, then, are significant; this chapter will attempt to expose the limitations of overly narrow theoretical approaches, draw some necessary attention to unnatural characters in a number of genres and media, and suggest a more adequate theoretical model to encompass them, one that attempts to restore the multifaceted approach to character even as it adds to those facets. I define unnatural characters as figures that contain antimimetic features that defy the realm of human possibilities and elude conventional types; they are, in fact, impossible persons. I will begin by identifying five types of unnatural or impossible characters: (1) incomplete or contradictory figures and impossible fusions of multiple persons, (2) multiple versions of the same individual, (3) parodic personae, (4) fabricated entities, and (5) metacharacters, or characters who know that they are fictional beings. Particular attention will be devoted to this last type, which has not yet been adequately theorized. I will provide an extended account of such figures in experimental fiction, science fiction, drama, film, and other media and analyze in some depth their elaborate development in Raymond Queneau's *Le vol d'Icare* (*The Fall of Icarus*;

---

2. Gerrig and Allbritton, analyzing James Bond, do note some distinctively fictional aspects of the novels, such as their formulaic construction, but stress the ways in which readers ignore those features and respond to the characters as if they were people.

3. For a critique of rhetorical and cognitivist positions, see Herman et al. (238–40).

4. There is nothing inherent in cognitive approaches to narrative that demands that characters be treated as persons; it is the limited application of the theory and not the theory itself that I am criticizing here. Jan Alber (104–48) and H. Porter Abbott (123–30) have shown how cognitive theory can be effectively employed in the analysis of unnatural figures and texts. One hopes that more cognitivist research will help explain how the mind processes robustly unnatural characters when it encounters them.

1968), a work that is a kind of meditation on character. Last, I will look at ways in which the physical enactment of otherwise mimetic characters in drama, film, or video can make them unnatural. A theoretical conclusion argues for an expanded notion of character, emphasizes the essential difference between fiction and nonfiction, and affirms the fundamental disparity between humanlike personages and distinctively fictional characters. Another goal of this essay is to expand the application of unnatural narrative theory and analysis to periods, figures, and genres that have not hitherto been discussed from this framework. In addition, I hope to open new avenues of exploration in this field by investigating performative aspects of unnatural productions, that is, the ways in which a representation in a performance can transform a mimetic character into an antimimetic one.

FIVE WAYS OF BEING UNNATURAL

I consider unnatural characters to be not merely impossible beings, but beings that violate or parody the conventions of realism. These are *anti*mimetic figures, to be distinguished from the merely *non*mimetic figures such as talking animals or flying horses or other conventional types found in standard works of fantasy and common fairy tales.[5] I wish to clarify at the outset that what I call an unnatural character need not (and probably cannot) be antimimetic in *all* aspects, but only in enough to make them humanly impossible. Many of the examples below will be perfectly human except for a single, major antimimetic element, such as the fact that they know themselves to be fictional characters.

Imperfectly Human Characters

Numerous postmodern characters demonstrate their unnaturalness by having too few consistent attributes to render themselves as humanlike personages, or they have too many contradictory features to plausibly form a single character, or they may be a fusion of two or more individuals. Still others may have many of the right traits but in the wrong combination.

Too few traits: The theater offers prominent examples of characters so minimally human that they do not constitute represented persons at all. One may begin with the unusual figures that populate the dramas of Gertrude Stein. As Marc Robinson says of her first mature play, "What Happened"

---

5. By "convention," I mean a widely and easily recognized pattern that has been utilized thousands of times over many years.

(1913): "The characters, if there are characters, haven't names, unless a series of numbers in parentheses is meant to signify presence. Otherwise, the voices are devoid of descriptive elements that would determine identity" (13). Character here is quite literally reduced to a cipher. Tristan Tzara's 1921 Dadaist play, "Le coeur à gaz" ("The Gas Heart") is limited to six figures: Eye, Mouth, Nose, Ear, Neck, and Eyebrow. They exchange nonsensical comments and show no discernible identities as persons or as body parts. Still more extreme is Beckett's "Quad" (1981), which deconstructs character altogether. It presents four actors or "players," as alike as possible, their gender unimportant, each of whom paces in a straight line along fixed trajectories. There is no speech, no individualization, no characterization. Manfred Pfister, in his seminal *Theory and Analysis of Drama,* writes: "In drama, the presentation of a figure [character] without even the most rudimentary plot and the presentation of a plot that does not contain even the most drastically reduced form of figure is inconceivable" (160). Yet this is exactly what Beckett seems to be doing in this work. Perhaps the most radical form of antihumanist presentation occurs in Peter Handke's 1966 *Sprechstück* "Publikumsbeschimpfung" ("Insulting the Audience"). His actors face the audience and state: "We don't tell you a story. We don't perform any actions. We don't represent anything. We don't put anything on for you. We only speak" (9). These figures, especially Handke's, exist near the very border of narrative: The events are minimal and the causal relations among them dubious. They are saying things and acting onstage, but the causal connections that produce the repeated patterns are difficult to discern and are independent of ordinary human causal matrices. Nevertheless, events take place and transformations occur.

The notion of a minimal character is developed in Felipe Alfau's story "Identity" (1936), in which the narrator encounters a figure who is hardly noticeable and can rarely be remembered. The figure complains, "I know I will never be important as a human being, and I have thought that I might gain fame and importance as a character" (5–6), specifically "as the most unimportant character in fiction" (Alfau 6). Thomas Docherty (28–42), Aleid Fokkema (*Postmodern Characters* 57–71), and others have discussed such deliberately "incomplete" personae. As Fokkema notes, "terms like 'cipher,' 'figure' or—the most striking metaphor—'cartoon,' imply that characters in postmodern works lack the manifestations of a 'self' which are crucial for representation. Such terms are based on the traditional concept of character, which ought to be 'round,' rich, and particular" (60).

Contradictory characters: Other characters have an impossible number of contradictory attributes. In Alain Robbe-Grillet's *La Maison de Rendez-*

vous (1965), Edouard Manneret is depicted in numerous impossible ways. Like the other characters in the novel, he is more a comic book–type figure than a human personality. He has no psychology to speak of, and his actions are contradictory. As Ilona Leki observes, "Manneret is alternately a drug dealer, a dealer in the slave trade, a writer, an artist, or a doctor experimenting with various drugs on Kim, who is perhaps his daughter" (83). He also dies several times in the book, always in a different way. He has no personality but is little more than a series of incompatible narrative functions, sometimes the murder victim, sometimes the killer, and so on. In the end, he is little more than a contradictory group of attributes predicated of a single name. Other characters in the novel do not even have this stability; the young European woman, for example, is alternately identified as Lauren, Loren, Loraine, or Laura.

An even more extreme example of multiple, discrete entities presented as a single character is found in Martin Crimp's audacious play *Attempts on Her Life: 17 Scenarios for the Theatre* (1997). Crimp does not merely refuse to provide a single, consistent self-identity; his play challenges the very idea of individual identity by depicting a series of discourses about a woman (or several women) named Anne, or Anya, Annie, or some other variant. They are presented as different people with different life stories in different situations: the girl next door, a performance artist, a rich woman, a terrorist, a scientist, a porno actress, a character in a script, even a new make of car (the Anny, naturally). In a revealing comment on one of her performance art pieces, a voice notes: "She says she's not a real character like you get in a book or on TV, but a *lack* of character, an *absence* she calls it, doesn't she, of character" (25).

This work cannot, however, be dismissed as a mere collection of unconnected vignettes. There are several strategies, beginning with the drama's title, that invite the audience to bring many of these disparate stories into a plot and thereby partially unify its fragmented subject. These include the many, seemingly contradictory messages that are received by Anne's answering machine in the play's first scene, which prefigure the story fragments presented in many of the subsequent scenes. The fourteenth scene, a musical number, likewise affirms the existence of a single character ("she") even as it subverts any essence or ground for any unified personality or figure:

> She is royalty
> She practices art
> She's a refugee
> In a horse and cart.
> She's a pornographic movie star

A killer and a brand of car
A KILLER AND A BRAND OF CAR!
She's a terrorist threat
She's the mother of three
She's a cheap cigarette
She is Ecstasy. (59)

Similarly, many details recur from one scene to another that suggest a closer connection than mere random association. Warfare, international travel, ashtrays, affairs with married men, terrorism, and repeated imprecations appear to connect various scenes. When we are told that Anne, the suicidal performance artist, offers a dialogue of "blood, saliva, and chocolate" (50), we are reminded of the car, the Anny, that will never be made "slippery by blood," "slippery by saliva," or "sticky by melted chocolate" (34). None of these recurrences, however, is particularly distinctive. By the end of the play, we have no resolution, and the central question for narrative theorists (as well as spectators) remains: Is there a single story about a single figure capable of embracing the entire work, or are there simply seventeen independent stories about different women? The work itself simultaneously advances and precludes both positions. One may read it allegorically or metadramatically, as a critique of the concepts of a fixed, stable character, or as an account of the ways in which subjectivity is constructed by the self-interested discourse that surrounds it.[6]

The work itself offers yet another interpretive option. The penultimate scene, in which a pornographic film is being prepared, suggests a number of correspondences between the fictional film and the play itself: "Of course there's no story to speak of . . . Or characters. . . . Certainly not in the conventional sense" (65–66). After her period of work, the voices suggest that the porno actress could go on to be a number of things, including a model, painter, swimmer, chemical engineer, humanitarian, psychologist, writer, and so on (69–71). Building on this suggestion, one might be tempted to interpret the various Annes and Annies of the play as potential characters that one woman might assume during the course of her life; all would be aspects of a single, potential *fabula*, variants of which we are on the process of observing. Such an interpretation, however, merely assuages some audiences' desires for a mimetic, humanistic recuperation as it does violence to the irreducible het-

---

6. Jan Alber states that the play "can be read as an allegory on the objectification of women in the globalized world" and adds that "the play uses the various versions of Anne, which are projected by nameless representatives of powerful institutions, to reveal the hidden uniformity behind the promises of diversity in the age of globalization" (136).

erogeneity of the multiple Annies of the work; ultimately, it both is and is not a single identity (see also Alber 133–39).

Fused characters: Equally radical are fused characters, individuals who merge with others during the course of the narrative. Stray, private thoughts of Stephen Dedalus unnaturally "wander" into the mind of Leopold Bloom at various points in *Ulysses* (see Richardson, *Unnatural Narrative* 127–28), and the thoughts and minds of many of the characters of Beckett and the authors of the *nouveau roman* (Claude Simon, Robert Pinget) are contaminated more extensively by intrusions from or mergers with other characters. Especially unnatural fusions of identities occur in Beckett's *The Unnamable* (1953), as I discuss in *Unnatural Voices* (95–103), and in Rushdie's *The Satanic Verses* (1981), where the protagonists exchange identities (see Fokkema, "Postmodern Fragmentation"). In the "mutual dream scene" in Tony Kushner's *Angels in America, Part I: Millennium Approaches* (1991), one character, Harper, appears in the dream of another character, Prior, even as Prior appears in Harper's hallucination. They debate the ontology of this impossible interpenetration:

HARPER: Are you. . . . Who are you?
PRIOR: Who are you?
HARPER: What are you doing in my hallucination?
PRIOR: I'm not in your hallucination. You're in my dream.
[. . .]
HARPER: There must be some mistake here. I don't recognize you. (31)

Not surprisingly, the characters are unable to resolve this most unnatural situation.

Neither, of course, can the more mimetic-minded narrative theorists. Even Uri Margolin, who is entirely comfortable discussing character "as simply a verbal artistic product, a paper person fashioned forth in some artistic-historical context" (70), has difficulty discussing unnatural character constructs with contradictory features. "Endowing a character with simultaneous incompatible properties (tall and short, young and old) turns him into a bundle of mutually exclusive strands which cannot be jointly realized in any universe" (73), he observes, even though he immediately (and contradictorily?) adds, "Such are the impossible characters of postmodern narrative" (73).[7]

Inhuman combinations of traits: Just such an impossible entity appears in Maya Sonenberg's "Nature Morte" (1986), the story of the first cubist child,

---

7. James Phelan makes a similar point in *Reading People, Reading Plots* (1–3); I believe my analysis is equally applicable to this position.

a baby born to an unwed mother from Avignon in 1911. Visually, he is odd: "He was flat, or no, just when you saw him from the side or back. He looked real skinny then, but from the front, well, it was almost as if you could see all of him" (36). The other boys do not want him to play baseball with them since if he manages to hit the ball, "it seems like before he's even started to run, he's back at home plate" (40). His relationships to space and time are skewed. The boy's "world is solid. He breathes in space that solidifies as it approaches. His body forms planes of space and flesh that adhere to the walls, to the window panes, and to the floorboards" (40–41). Though his body seems to lack a third dimension, his mind transcends all three: He is even able to watch his own birth (41). Surely, figures like these need to be conceptualized in any theory of fictional characters.

Multiple Individuals

We may also note cases in which the same character is multiplied. In Stanisław Ignacy Witkiewicz's *The Madman and the Nun* (1923), Walpurg, the protagonist, hangs himself at the end of the first scene of the third act. As his corpse is being carried away, he reenters the stage. There are thus two Walpurgs present at the same time. His lover tries to understand the scene before her: "Darling! Is it really you? And what's that? (*She points at the corpse.*) O—what does it matter, I'm so happy I'll probably go mad" (30).

Qurratulain Hyder's epic novel of northern India, *River of Fire* (1999 [1959]), covers some 2,400 years as it stretches from the Mauryan empire to the partition of 1947. Its narrative centers on a few central characters who continue to reappear with similar names in successive historical periods. Thus, Gautam begins as a religious student in the fourth century BCE who falls in love with Champa, the daughter of the chief minister; she returns his love, but their fate is tragic. He reappears several centuries later as Syed Abdul Mansur Kamaluddin, a Persian, and falls in love with a local woman, Champavati, who also eludes him. In the nineteenth century, under the British occupation, he returns as Gautam Nilanbar Dutt, and is charmed by a young woman, Champa Jan. In the twentieth century, Gautam is a college student and meets Champa and the others at and around the university. This provides their last opportunity to finally love each other as they deserve to. Hyder thus recreates recurring characters over time. She is not merely offering an example of the doctrine of reincarnation; in the Hindu tradition, souls can be reborn into any form of life and are not paired up over the centuries (in addition, Hyder is not a Hindu). Instead, she utilizes it as a kind of trope, offering the possibility that individuals—and nations—can finally end cycles of warfare and enforced separation and instead live together harmoniously.

In "August 25, 1983" (1983), Borges has constructed a fiction in which his sixty-one-year-old self appears to slip through time and stumbles upon his much older self. Borges makes the most of these logically impossible incongruities:

> There, in my narrow iron bed—older, withered, and very pale—lay I, my eyes turned up vacantly toward the high plaster mouldings of the ceiling. Then I heard the voice. It was not exactly my own, but the one I often hear in my recordings, unpleasant and without modulation.
> "How odd," it was saying, "we are two yet we are one." (489–90)

A number of authors of time travel fiction create scenarios in which individuals are able to interact with earlier versions of their selves or their progenitors; the *reductio ad absurdum* of this stratagem appears in Robert Heinlein's 1959 story, "All You Zombies," in which, due to trips back in time, a man becomes his own father and mother.

Parodic Characters

While mildly parodic characters may merely draw attention to a quirk in a character's behavior, more extreme parodic figures are antimimetic if they expose the lack of realism of an author, school, or genre. In showing how artificial or unlifelike an earlier author's character is, the parodic figure is thus necessarily an unnatural figure. In Witkiewicz's *The Water Hen* (1921), the protagonist is shot and killed on two separate occasions, once at the beginning and once at the conclusion of the play, as the endings of Ibsen's and Chekhov's dramas about symbolic birds and suicidal youths are mercilessly satirized. The characters of parodic works do not particularly resemble human beings, and analyses of the motives and behavior of people will not help much in explaining the actions of these figures. They are instead responses to antecedent texts, texts that may well have been selected for critique because of their perceived failures of verisimilitude. Such characters and events may trace their own, antimimetic patterns as well. As Jan Kott explains his dramaturgy:

> The new type of play Witkiewicz proposes in [his] *Introduction to the Theory of Pure Form in the Theater* will not imitate real life, but the pure arts of painting and music. Unhampered by such obsolete notions as believable

characters and consistent plots, the dramatist will be free to deform reality for purely formal ends and use all the elements of the theater as the musician uses notes or the modern painter colors and shapes. (Witkiewicz 34)

For an extreme case of second- or even third-degree parody, we may turn to Tom Stoppard's *Travesties* (1975). Most of its action takes place within the wayward memory of the aged Henry Carr—which is itself an unrealistic, postmodern representation of memory. He also has other eccentricities, such as a highly stereotyped image of James Joyce, whom he knew in Zürich in 1917. Thus many of Joyce's speeches are trivial; often they are presented in the form of limericks. As "Joyce" says when he appears onstage:

> Top o' the morning!—James Joyce!
> I hope you'll allow me to voice
> My regrets in advance
> For coming on the off chance—
> B'jaysus I hadn't much choice! (33)

At one point, Carr seems to guess that which he should not be able to know—that limericks are being spoken by the characters around him in order to represent his confused understanding—when he asks the character Joyce, without any plausible realistic motivation, whether he comes from Limerick (33). Some quotations from *Ulysses* (which Joyce was writing at the time) are worked into the dialogue. Aspects of Dada are likewise spoofed in the figure and speech of Tristan Tzara. In addition, the often misremembered events of Carr's past merge with the plot of *The Importance of Being Earnest* (1895); the play and the characters increasingly turn into those of Wilde's. It is only by appreciating the major literary intertexts behind this work that we can comprehend the figures of this play. The characters are not drawn from life, but from books, and in this case it is a genealogy very little mediated by any pretensions to mimeticism.

Fabricated Entities

A final category that I will call fabricated entities includes fictional entities that are not found in the real world or in established genres and are not readily reducible to conventionalizing formulas. To some extent this is a flexible and even, at times, an imprecise category; its boundaries are fluid, and different readers will perceive and assess the constructed nature of such entities differently. A compelling example is Gregor Samsa from Kafka's "Die Verwandlung" (1915). He is, simultaneously and impossibly, both a giant insect and a conscious human being, and this particular mix cannot be reduced to or explained by the conventions of science fiction, fantasy, or the character's dreaming (see Iversen 96–98). Caryl Churchill's skriker is another central example. The figure is an extremely creative preternatural being only very loosely based on a traditional malevolent fairy; her language is extraordinarily playful and employs aural and thematic associations as it dips in and around standard English:

> When did they do what they're told tolled a bell a knell, well ding dong pussy's in. Tell them one thing not to do, thing to rue won't they do it, boo hoo's afraid of the pig bag. Open Bluebeard's one bloody chamber maid, eat the one forbidden fruit of the tree top down comes cradle and baby. (*Plays: Three* 245)

Additional such specimens include John Barth's sentient spermatozoon in "Night-Sea Journey" (1968) and Ian McEwan's sophisticated, cunning fetus in *Nutshell* (2016). Karen Russell has fabricated a number of compelling entities in her collection *Vampires in the Lemon Grove* (2014), including a scarecrow, women who are part silkworm, and a misunderstood vampire. Marie Darrieussecq presents a woman who is transformed into a pig in her widely discussed novel, *Truismes* (1996; see Iversen); Melanie Rae Thon compellingly creates an animated river in *The Voice of the River* (2011). A more sustained such example appears in *Solaris*, a novel by Slanisław Lem (1961), later made into films by Andrei Tarkovsky (1972) and Steven Soderbergh (2002). In each incarnation, the sea that surrounds the planet Solaris is a conscious, living organism—a most unnatural character—and one that is particularly prone to fabricating various mimetic entities. It also constructs three-dimensional humanlike figures out of the astronauts' memories and fantasies. Thus, the protagonist, Kris Kelvin, meets his dead wife, Rheya, on the planet. It is as if she is resurrected, though she has not aged in the ten years since her death. Kelvin realizes that, however lifelike she is in every humanly possible way, she is merely an embodiment of his memories. She also becomes more humanlike the longer she is with him. At first, she does not realize she is merely a simulacrum. When she discovers this fact, she is horrified and attempts to commit suicide by drinking liquid oxygen. Though her flesh is burned and her breathing nearly stops, she is quickly regenerated and her body is restored to its normal condition. Understandably, she is rather confused about her ontological status: "Is this me?" she asks (141). "Rheya? But . . . I am not Rheya. Who am I then?" (141). She tries to clarify her thoughts and motives by explaining, "What else could I think, except that was Rheya!" (141). Such epistemological hesitation is more than appropriate for speculating over such unnatural entities.

Metafictional Characters

Some of the most interesting and most insistently fictional characters are those who know that they are fictional beings; despite their prevalence over the past century, these entities still have not been adequately theorized. Brian McHale is one of the few scholars to have discussed this kind of character (121–24). He importantly differentiates the degree of the characters' awareness of their fictional status, a knowledge that is crucial to their identity and to our responses to their situations. The *locus classicus* of this type is Pirandello's 1921 drama, *Six Characters in Search of an Author*, in which the characters show up at a theater and ask for an author to complete their story. They state that they were born characters; as the Father says: "One is born to life in many forms, in many shapes, as tree, or a stone, as water, as butterfly, or as woman. So one may also be born a character in a play" (217). Another early example appears in "A Character," in Felipe Alfau's 1936 story collection, *Locos* (17–38). Here, a character not only escapes from his author, but vies with him to narrate his life along a different trajectory. The narrator begins, "The story I intend to write is a story which I have had in mind for some time. However, the rebellious qualities of my characters have prevented me from writing it" (19). After writing the first sentence that names the character, the narrator is distracted. At this point, the character takes over: "Now that my author has set me on paper and given me a body and a start, I shall proceed with the story and tell it in my own words" (20).

Along with Flann O'Brien's *At Swim-Two-Birds* (1939), which has received considerable critical attention, perhaps the most elaborate play with fictional characters is found in Raymond Queneau's *Le vol d'Icare* (1968). The plot begins as the novelist Hubert notices that his central character, Icarus, is missing. A few days earlier, another novelist had read the first few pages of the manuscript and praised the character; Hubert goes directly to his home to determine whether he has stolen him. But Icarus is not there, neither under a pseudonym nor under a different identity. He is in fact in a tavern, learning how to be a person in *fin de siècle* Paris. He does not know much, being only "ten or fifteen pages old" (18). He further suspects Hubert will not easily be able to substitute another personage for him, since he feels he is irreplaceable (41).

This proves to be the case. Hubert acknowledges that although he could continue with some of the other characters, he is fond of Icarus and will not proceed without him. He laments the fate of a novelist without characters, and goes on to speculate, "Perhaps that is how it will be for all of us, one day. We won't have any characters. We shall become authors in search of characters. The novel will perhaps not be dead, but it won't have characters in it any more. Difficult to imagine" (60)—though this is exactly what many authors of *nouveaux romans* were doing at the time Queneau was writing his novel. Such a stance is presented in the author Jacques, who, rather like Robbe-Grillet, is interested in "description for description's sake." He adds, "If I had to, I could do without characters" (91). By contrast, another novelist in the book does not care if he loses a character—he has an inexhaustible supply of them: "I have a file full of characters, hundreds of them, on the strength of which I can go on producing works based entirely on adultery and on ultra modern fin-de-siècle sentiments" (92). This comment points to the idea of similar actants that, though minimally individuated, can perform the same role in different narratives. This idea is alluded to in the description of the detective hired to find the missing character: "He has appeared in many novels under different names. A second Vidocq" (14). This statement may imply a characterological joke, since the historical Eugène François Vidocq was the model for Balzac's Vautrin as well as characters by Victor Hugo, Alexandre Dumas, and Eugène Sue. Other statements provide a running commentary on the nature of characterization.[8] Hubert cannot give the detective much information about Icarus because he had not developed his personality. He explains, "The modern novel, as you are aware, does not begin by exhibiting the principal character, it leads up to him gradually" (15). Elsewhere, two characters argue over whether a figure in a novel is the same as its dramatization in a play.[9]

Icarus never loses sight of his status as an entity made of words. He notes, sounding vaguely like Mallarmé,

---

8. Frank Wagner discusses the novel's intertextuality, noting also the impossible allusion that appears when the situation of the lost character is described as "pirandellian," many years before Pirandello would begin writing.

9. Hubert vigorously asserts their difference: "Is the third rate actress whining 'Adieu, Our Little Table" the same as the Abbé Prevost's Manon Lescaut? . . . No: they are two different characters" (69). Here the performed aspect of characters is introduced; I will discuss this later in the essay.

> The ink flows on the white paper in shallow, fertile rivulets from which friends, relations and enemies are born, as well as indoor plants, in the corners of apartments furnished with rep and velvet, mahogany and Cordova leather. The quill conducts a little world of objects and names towards a destiny which escapes me. (24)

When he visits a bookseller and asks to hold one of the volumes, the man tells him to make himself at home ("Faites comme chez vous"; 49). Icarus, whose former habitation was literally a book, takes this as a derisive joke. Later, Mme. De Champvaux, Hubert's dissatisfied lover, encounters him; she is delighted to learn that he is "handsome, poor, and idle! As in a fashionable novel! . . . What a marvelous day!" (94). Further into the text, another woman falls in love with him and wants them "to be the hero and heroine of a romantic novel" (177). If fictional characters wish to escape from their books, the people around them want to live as in a novel.

As the narrative progresses, more characters escape from other authors. Adelaide, the character that Icarus was intended to be united with, vanishes from Hubert's novel along with her father in order to find him. This action is not without its risks; her father warns: "You want us to abandon this abode where we're so nice and warm, this novel where we're so well nourished, and our kind M. Hubert?" (124). His daughter is not dissuaded. After she meets up with Icarus, she laments her decision, even as she tries to make it work (175). Other characters are able to find and identify each other in a way that, to use a comparison made by a character, is not unlike the way gay men identify other gay men. Eventually, however, all disperse. Many return to their former authors; Adelaide and her father wind up in the pages of a rival writer. Icarus even offers to go back to Hubert if the novelist is willing to make a number of changes in his plot concerning his future love life. Hubert refuses; he has abandoned the novel and is writing a new one with more docile characters. At the end, he changes his mind, and goes to find Icarus. The character is now piloting an early airplane; he takes it higher and higher. Finally, he loses control and the plane crashes. The character meets his end. Hubert's last words, however, enthusiastically state: "Everything happened as was anticipated: my novel is finished" (192). Icarus's life, Hubert's novel, and Queneau's book conclude simultaneously.

A poignant version of this general situation occurs in Marc Forster's film *Stranger Than Fiction* (2006). Harold Crick, the protagonist, hears a voice that narrates the events of his life as he is experiencing them. The narrator, who starts off sounding like conventional voiceover, speaks in the third person and in the continuous present and the past tense. Crick is the only one in the storyworld who can hear these words. He visits a psychiatrist and complains about the voice in his head, but she cannot help him. This may serve as an exemplum of the status of nonmimetic characters: Human psychology is not always especially relevant to their situation. Crick then visits a narratologist (who displays a copy of *Poetics Today*), who helps identify the narrative trajectory he is enmeshed within. While he is in the professor's office, Crick sees a video of novelist Karen Eiffel, and realizes that hers is the voice he keeps hearing. Later, Crick hears the voice say that he is to die; he shouts to the heavens, "This isn't a story to me; it's my life. And I want to live!" as the difference between person and character is vividly underscored. He subsequently visits the novelist to plead for his existence; instead of assenting, she gives him a copy of the novel to read. It will clearly be her masterpiece. When he has finished reading it, he becomes resigned, agreeing that as a work of literature, it is necessary for the protagonist to die. Never before in the history of literature has a character agreed to give up his life for art.

This scene points to a distinctive aspect of the most affecting situation involving metacharacters: the drama of their discovery of their fictionality and its mortal consequences. McHale has suggested that the degree of their self-knowledge is especially significant (121). He further notes that some characters, "confronted with the evidence of their own fictionality, fail to draw the obvious conclusion; they hear their master's voice—sometimes literally—but without recognizing it" (121), and provides examples of such misrecognition in works by Gabriel Josipovici, Vladimir Nabokov (*Transparent Things*, 1972), Alasdair Gray, and John Barth. I suggest that the transformation of their awareness is still more compelling, as can be seen in the example above from Forster's film.

McHale writes that "a character's knowledge of his own fictionality often functions as a kind of master-trope for determinism—cultural, historical, psychological determinism, but especially the inevitability of death" (123). One might well argue the opposite—that it suggests a possible freedom from these determinisms, as is the case of characters who escape from their creators or convince them to spare their lives. In any event, the appropriate analogues to actual human experience are partial or tenuous; we do not normally worry whether we are literally the invention of someone else or, to take an example suggested by Nabokov and offered by characters themselves from Muriel Spark's Caroline Rose in *The Comforters* (1957) to Harold Crick, the suspicion that we are mad.[10] The trope of death, explicitly invoked by metafictional char-

---

10. McHale observes that Rose "hears voices, and even a typewriter at work, but cannot convince herself that she is merely undergoing a nervous breakdown" (122). It may be noted that Crick's general situation often resembles that of Rose.

acters since Miguel de Unamuno's protagonist in *Niebla* (*Mist*; 1909), further underscores the difference between people and characters: The characters are conscious of their own fictionality and thus are able to be conscious of the dual nature of their existence, both as humanlike figure and fictional creation. They personify the twofold nature of most fictional characters, existing as both fictional construct and mimetic representation.

Perhaps the most important relations are the negotiations between the ostensibly realistic and avowedly fictional characters in these works. Paradoxically, many of the metacharacters (other than Alfau's and, to some extent, Queneau's) are presented through a fairly realistic characterization; other than their ontological status, they often substantially resemble the "real" characters around them; Pirandello's characters frequently critique the mimetically inadequate performances of the actors who impersonate them. Despite the fact that from the standpoint of the real world, both the figure of the fictional author and their characters are equally fictitious, we are intrigued by such cross-world transgressions, their status, duration, extent, and number. A character's moment of discovery of his or her fictional status is always important, and the response to this discovery is typically dramatic if not climactic. We are concerned whether the protagonists successfully escape to live undiscovered among "real" people, or are able to persuade their creators to spare their lives. Above all, audiences are concerned to learn whether the metaleptic rupture is closed, and all figures return to their "natural" plane of existence within the fictional world. This is another example of the curious situation discussed by Daniel Punday in this volume, in which metalepsis does not distance but rather helps us identify with the characters. Paradoxically, however, in order to maintain the possibility of empathy, metafictional characters need to resemble their "real" counterparts in most ways: We will not care about Crick's fate if he were to simply shrug his shoulders and say, "Well, after all, I'm only a character. Maybe my creator will reincarnate me into a better entity in her next book?" Metafictional characters, in some respects the most antirealistic of personae, nevertheless produce significant affective results through mimetic behavior. We also note that just as fictional characters can escape from their stories and enter the "real" world of their novelists, the opposite can also happen, as when the "real" character Kugelmass enters the fictional storyworld of *Madame Bovary* in Woody Allen's "The Kugelmass Episode" (1977).

Many different genres include works that present characters who are aware of their own fictionality. These include the frame-breaking techniques of Aristophanic comedy, animated cartoons (especially the Looney Tunes features), popular films such as the Bob Hope–Bing Crosby "road" movies of the 1940s and 1950s, Monty Python films, some hyperfiction, and many comics.[11] Karin Kukkonen describes one such figure, Splash Branigan, from *Tomorrow Stories* (1999–2002): He "is an anthropomorphic, sentient, and opinionated blob of ink used in the production of comics" (108), a figure that regularly moves between storyworlds and narrative levels by climbing in and out of the blob itself—a variant of which is also found in other comics.

To conclude this section, we may note the paradoxical, semi-metafictional characters in Kamel Daoud's *Meursault, contre-enquête* (*The Meursault Investigation*; 2013), a retelling of the events of Camus's *L'Etranger* (1942) from the perspective of the brother of the Arab who was shot by Meursault. The narrator-protagonist laments to his narratee:

> I'm sure you're like everyone else, you've read the tale as told by the man who wrote it. He writes so well that his words are like precious stones, jewels cut with the utmost precision. A man very strict about shades of meaning, your hero was; he practically required them to be mathematical. (2)

One the one hand, the narrator is a character in the fictional storyworld created by Camus; on the other he knows the value of Camus's prose and the effect his book has produced in the real world. The fictional Meursault does not intend his account to be published, and there is no indication that he is a great stylist—a Borgesian paradox worthy of Pierre Menard, since even though the words of Meursault and those of Camus are identical, only the latter are brilliantly composed; Meursault's, by contrast, are presented as merely the workman-like prose of an unexceptional individual. This is the same principle or convention that decrees that Shakespeare's characters cannot know that they are speaking brilliant verse, as Gregory Currie has explained in his account of limitations of representational correspondence (58–64, 78–79).[12] In Daoud's text, the character once again presents himself as living both within and outside of the text's designated storyworld.

---

11. It should not be assumed that all cartoons are antimimetic. Some may be largely mimetic (*Charlie Brown*); others conventionally antimimetic (Mother Goose cartoons).

12. Othello even apologizes for being a poor speaker: "Rude am I in my speech, and little blessed with the soft phrase of peace" (I.iii.83). This, however, may be a deliberate rhetorical stratagem.

ENACTED AND EMBODIED CHARACTERS

Characters portrayed by actors onstage can greatly affect a play's depictions and its reception; dramatic representation by its very nature can readily complicate, enhance, or dissolve the unity of a character.[13] Bertolt Brecht made use of this difference, and encouraged his actors to distance themselves while onstage from the characters they portrayed; when the scene being enacted did not include their characters, the actors who played them were encouraged to sit at the edge of the stage, watching and smoking as the play continued. Actors' presence thus adds another layer to the representation of characters, and the enactment can alter, invert, or transform the story being presented. In a performed play or a film, characters are portrayed by actors whose resemblance to the roles they portray may be imperfect. We see this frequently in plays put on by high school students where the older adult characters are played by actors who are clearly teenagers. Generally, we ignore these disparities and treat them as part of the general imperfection of enacted representation.

But some playwrights drive a wedge between actor and character and thereby produce an unnatural effect. This is especially obvious when salient physical differences, such as the gender, race, size, or age of the performers, visibly differ from those indicated by the story. As I have discussed elsewhere (*Unnatural Narrative* 93–95), Aristophanes parodies the fact that men played the roles of women in Greek drama by having one male character try onstage to disguise another man as a woman in his comedy, the *Thesmophoriazusae*. A male character played by a man is thus depilated and cross-dressed onstage in order to resemble the storyworld's women, who are also played by men (though presumably with greater verisimilitude).

Shakespeare provides much metadramatic humor when his female characters, who are played by boys, go on to disguise themselves as boys. In *As You Like It*, Rosalind, in drag, states, "I thank God I am not a woman, to be touched with so many giddy offences" (3.2. 340–42). The gender of the actor seems to substantially erase that of the character. Similarly, the original boy actor portraying Cleopatra unnaturally fulfills the fate that her character hopes to escape:

> The quick comedians
> Extemporally will stage us and present our Alexandrian revels . . .
> And I shall see

---

13. For a very useful discussion of this phenomenon, see Pentzell.

> Some squeaking Cleopatra boy my greatness
> I' th' posture of a whore. (5.2, 216–21)[14]

Numerous similar transformations can be written into a script; a number of them are suggested in Carlos Fuentes's intriguing note on the casting of the roles of Maria and Dolores in his drama "Orchids in the Moonlight." He writes, "Ideally, the roles would have been interpreted by the Mexican actresses Maria Felix and Dolores del Rio. Even more ideally, one and then the other would have alternated in the parts" (145). Then again, Fuentes continues, they could be played by actresses who resemble the originals, or by women who don't look like them at all, or by two men. Each of these possibilities can affect the resulting characterization, underscoring, distancing, or negating of the character's extraliterary identity, as the possibilities of representation range from identity to homage to parody. Here, the performative dimension of characterization is most insistently visible.

One of the most compelling superimpositions of story and performance appears in Roger Vadim's incestuous cinematic adaptation of Poe's story "Metzengerstein" (1832). As Jeff Stafford explains in his program notes:

> Vadim's take on "Metzengerstein" added a gender twist to Poe's original story, transforming the cruel protagonist, Count Frederick, into Contessa Frederica, a decadent aristocrat who lusts after her distant relative, Baron Wilhelm. . . . Vadim played up the perverse aspects of the story by casting his wife Jane [Fonda] and her brother Peter as the would-be lovers and expanding the brief narrative with visual details about the assorted orgies and sadistic games being conducted at Frederica's castle.

Such compelling or blatant interactions between fictional characters and the nonfictional persons who portray them have been around for some time. During the Restoration, plays would be written featuring a sexually innocent young woman who was intended to be played by an actress who was a notorious courtesan. Such an unnatural casting partially negated the naiveté of the character, and knowing members of the audience would chortle over many suggestive lines that took on additional, venereal meanings in such performances. Again, the point of the casting was to pit the actor against the character in an unnatural manner for a deliberately discordant effect.

---

14. These issues are discussed by numerous critics, such as Lorraine Helms and Anne Herrmann. For a bibliographical note, see Helms 197 n. 4.

In realistic or mimetic casting, the actors' body types are intended to replicate those being represented; if there is too great a discrepancy, makeup, prostheses, and various other devices are employed to make the actor resemble the character. If the actress still looks too young to plausibly be a grandmother, the audience is supposed to ignore the discrepancy. For scenes set in the character's childhood, different actors are employed to represent the same person in order to better produce a verisimilar effect. In antirealist works, however, the opposite principle prevails, as the enactment transforms or parodies the characterization established by the story. In Luis Bunuel's *Cet obscur objet du désire* (1977), two very different looking actresses, Angela Molina and Carole Bouquet, portray Conchita, the central female character, in different scenes. In this case, the difference is there to be noticed, appreciated, and reflected on.

In *Cloud Nine* (1979), Caryl Churchill foregrounds the ability of official British discourse to create the gendered personalities it requires by having the paradigmatic Victorian wife played by a male actor. As she (he) states:

> The whole aim of my life
> Is to be what he looks for in a wife.
> I am a man's creation as you see,
> And what men want is what I want to be. (*Plays: One* 251)

A fictional woman who is clearly intended to be played by a man is quite simply a different character from one represented along traditional gender lines.[15] In the second act of the play, twenty-five years pass for the characters and each is portrayed by a different actor, one whose actual gender now corresponds to that of the character portrayed. Another unnatural feature of the casting of this work is that it allows the younger Betty to literally embrace her older self onstage at the end of the play, providing a powerful, literal image of the reunion of a divided self.

This kind of antimimetic casting has been effectively employed by makers of television commercials. There is a series of related commercials for the Snickers candy bar in which the enacted version includes impossible transformations that center on the theme of losing one's individual identity. In one instance, Betty White, an octogenarian actress, is seen muddling along in a pickup football game. One of her teammates tells her that she is playing like Betty White. This figure then eats a Snickers bar and is transformed back into

---

15. Another compelling example of cross-gender casting that works against cultural stereotypes of gays occurs in Kushner's *Angels in America,* in which all the roles for straight men are played by women; the intended effect of this is both to de-effeminize gay men and to "denaturalize" heterosexuality.

his real self, an athletically fit young man. The theme of the commercial is articulated in a voice-over: "You're not you when you're hungry" (Snickers). There are several variants of this commercial, including one that features several young men riding in a car with the actual Aretha Franklin. Ms. Franklin is complaining repeatedly, and one of the men explains that he always acts like a diva when he is hungry. After the candy bar is bitten into, a young white man takes the space vacated by the actual star singer. Here, gender, age, race, and body shape are impossibly transformed as the physical enactment of the scene literalizes the metaphor of "acting like a diva" in a way that none of the characters can perceive or imagine.

Enacted presentation is able to extend or trope literary representation in still other ways. Eugene Ionesco, for example, has performed the character "Ionesco" in a production of his play *Improvisation, or The Shepherd's Chameleon* (1956), and Muhammed Ali has played himself (sometimes rather unconvincingly) in a movie of his life; this leads to the apparent paradox that in the film *Ali* (2001), actor Will Smith could portray the young Ali more convincingly than could Ali himself. The interfacing of the presentational and the representational is a common feature of performance art, where the performer may remain aloof from, comment on, or tend to merge with the figure represented. In autobiographical performances, still more ontological wrinkles complicate the permeable boundaries between actor, character, and author as well. As Henry M. Sayre observes in a discussion of these issues, "It is . . . the emergence of the personal into character and role that allows character or role to assert itself as more than mere image" (79). Typically, autobiographical performance artists must present authentic enactments of their public (and, presumably, actual) selves.

Another way of transforming or dissolving characters is through the theatrical practice of "doubling," in which different roles are played by the same actors.[16] This practice can generate powerful effects onstage if, in the case of *Macbeth,* the actor playing Macduff is noticeably the same as the one who had played King Duncan. This produces a jarring effect as the actor playing the man just killed by Macbeth returns unnaturally to portray Macbeth's next deadly nemesis. This also gives an additional, metadramatic meaning to his line:

> The time has been,
> That, when the brains were out, the man would die,
> And there an end. But now, they rise again . . .

---

16. For an excellent study of possible or likely doublings in Shakespeare, see Booth.

And push us from our stools. This is more strange
Than such a murder is. (3.4, 79–84)

The character may be dead, but the man playing him returns immediately as a new character in a similar role.[17] Modern playwrights frequently employ such casting; Caryl Churchill is particularly effective in establishing important identities and highlighting significant contrasts between different characters by having them played by the same actor.

Unnatural Graphic Fiction

A comparable situation arises in graphic narratives that employ multiple representational modes. Thus, in Art Spiegelman's *Maus* (1991, 1992), Jews are depicted as mice and Germans as cats. But, as Christopher Kilgore writes elsewhere in this volume, when "a concentration camp internee claims to be 'a German,' and not to belong among 'these Yids and Polacks' (2: 50) . . . [he is] drawn alternately as a mouse and a cat." Such depictions "can be 'naturalized' by reference to the book's narrative levels, but the process of deconstruction and reintegration must always bear with it the traces of unnatural discomfort: The character on the page is *both* mouse *and* cat, and yet *neither* mouse *nor* cat" (p. 76). Eric Berlatsky similarly discusses the self-referential conversations between the narrator and Françoise concerning her graphic representation: "If Françoise is to be drawn as a bunny, she will be read as 'sweet and gentle' (*Maus II* 11), but if she is portrayed as a frog, she will [embody] a French stereotype" (156). Berlatsky further observes that "characters are sometimes depicted as anthropomorphic animals but are also, particularly in the outermost diegetic frame, sometimes depicted as humans in animal masks" (156). Such figures deconstruct mimetic representation and shift the focus instead to the act and ideology of fabricating actants.

Unnatural Game Characters

One might argue that a player's ability to select different contradictory roles in interactive fiction and in games is itself an unnatural practice insofar as it defies the consistencies expected of normal human personalities. This unnatural effect (or "u-effect") is intensified when the game itself helps determine the

---

17. For analysis of the unnatural elements of this play, see my *Unnatural Narrative* 104–10.

avatar's identity. In the *Fighting Fantasy* gamebook series (1982–1995), "readers generate a set of basic characteristics (Skill, Stamina, and Luck) by rolling two six-sided dice, using and adjusting these values throughout their reading of the text" (Wake 194). The creation of the player's identity thus comes about in what seems something like a speeded-up version of Borges's Babylonian lottery. Importantly, these characteristics partially determine the reading paths available, most notably during the numerous encounters with the monsters populating the underground domain (Wake 194). Both character and destiny are thus transformed by a throw of the dice. Paul Wake discusses additional unnatural aspects of gamebooks in his essay in this volume. We also note that similar strategies precede many role-playing video games. The purpose of *Second Life* is to create and enjoy an avatar of yourself; there is also a game called *Create a Person* that invites the player to do just that: "Create your own customized person in this fun game. Choose from many different facial features and clothing to create yourself, your favourite celebrity, or just have fun making different people."

Animated Cartoons

Animated cartoons regularly feature unnatural characters that are unusual combinations or blends of stock figures and are frequently used for parodic effect. The "essence" of a cartoon character is usually very limited and frequently exaggerated to preposterous degrees; in other aspects, the characters move in changing arabesques around this center. We can see these features present in Chuck Jones's Looney Tunes cartoon "Duck Amuck" (1953), which thematizes the concept of character. The narrative begins with Daffy Duck in front of a castle, brandishing a rapier, dressed and speaking like a stylized seventeenth-century French musketeer. As he walks, the scenery ceases as the space around him turns blank. He breaks the frame of the storyworld and calls out to the animator to provide the scenery. As he walks, he sees around him first a barn in a rural setting, then an igloo in the arctic, and finally a palm-lined beach. He adjusts his personality to each setting, first becoming a genial farmer, then a daring cross-country skier, and last a female hula dancer. He also depicts a frustrated actor unhappy with the faulty production. Then the blank setting returns and, gradually, his body is removed by a large eraser. Enraged, he shouts out, demanding to know where he is. At this point he is drawn back into the screen, but is confronted by new problems. Unknown to Daffy, a large paintbrush then depicts him as a mechanical quadruped. He senses something is off and states, "I don't quite feel like myself" (3:30).

Soon, he physically pushes against a black curtain that also resembles a blob of ink in order to retain his existence. The screen now shows flipping images, like the separate shots of movie film. These jam, and two half-images are visible. The two Daffy Ducks begin to talk to each other, and one grows angry with his simulacrum: "If you weren't me, I'd smack you right in the puss" (5:25). Just as Daffy seems to return to a normal setting, a giant paintbrush creates a door around him, and then slams it shut, ending the cartoon and eliminating its central character. The camera seems to pull back to disclose the identity of the troublesome animator, who is revealed to be Bugs Bunny. Together, the various transformations in this cartoon exemplify a number of the types of unnatural characterizations that I have inventoried above. This should indicate once more that there is nothing inherently literary, recondite, or postmodern about unnatural characters and scenes; they are all around us.

CONCLUSION

The numerous unnatural examples discussed above exist across genres and media, stretch for two and a half millennia, and range from the most austere to the most popular forms. I hope it is obvious that any theory of character that ignores all such figures is significantly impoverished and painfully incomplete. Unnatural characters largely defy mimetic recuperation and generally elude essentially mimetic theories of character. We can only view as inaccurate statements like:

> Even though literary characters and real people are ontologically distinct, they are processed in much the same way. In other words, literary characters are processed *as if* they were real people, and real people are processed in terms analogous to the categories brought to bear on the interpretation of literary characters. (Bortolussi and Dixon 140)

This claim may be plausible for realistic characters as well as for certain characters in fantasy or science fiction, but it is simply not true of most of the characters discussed above, in particular the metacharacters who know themselves to be fictional characters. As the narrator of Alfau's story "Character" affirms, "A character is entirely the opposite of a real being, although it is sometimes our business to try to convince the reader to the contrary" (27). Humanists and cognitivists with overly simple theoretical models of character need to account for statements and characters like this. There is nothing wrong about a mimetic theory of character; we need a theory that can identify distinctively mimetic components.[18] The main problem arises when theorists falsely claim that a merely mimetic theory is in fact a theory of fictional characters, when it is, at best, only half of such a theory.

The implications of this essay are straightforward: Any plausible theory of character must include two very different components—one for characters and aspects of characters that resemble or imitate human beings, and another for aspects of characters who resist, defy, transgress, or reconstruct identities in ways that move far beyond realist or humanist models. The type of dual model offered by Joel Weinsheimer remains an excellent starting point: Characters can resemble people, but they are also verbal constructs that may have little or no grounding in actual human behavior. Discussing the limitations of either of these positions taken in isolation, John Frow asks that "we understand fictional character both as a formal construct, made out of words or images and having a fully textual existence, and as a set of effects which are modeled on the form of the human person" (vi).[19]

Antimimetic characters represent an extreme and transparent kind of exclusively fictional entity and must be included in any comprehensive theory of character—or even for a merely mimetic theory: As we saw in the case of Daoud's text, there may well be some completely antimimetic components in an otherwise realistic character. Similarly, almost no characters are entirely antimimetic: Their impossible attributes are rather grafted on to perfectly realist ones. Gregor Samsa is an entirely plausible representation of a Central European traveling salesman of the first decades of the twentieth century; he is also, impossibly, a giant bug who still hopes to catch the train to get to work. Similarly, a totally mimetic character can be transformed into an antimimetic one when a performance or other form of enactment destroys any mimetic illusion and thus transforms it into a more complex entity. Antimimetic aspects may be introduced at some point in the text and then laid aside, as happens in *Meursault, contre-enquête*; they may start at the beginning and continue throughout the text, as in Beckett's *The Unnamable*; they may appear at the end of an otherwise realistic presentation of characters, such as the personification of the author who appears late in John Fowles's *The French Lieutenant's Woman* (1969) and goes on to provide multiple incompatible endings; or the characters may be largely mimetic but situated within entirely anti-

---

18. I hasten to add that we also need to be skeptical about ideological fictions or generic clichés masking as mimetic representations.

19. This general position has been vigorously argued for from a rather different approach by Julian Murphet. Catherine Gallagher traces a form of this difference back to the Renaissance in her chapter "The Rise of Fictionality" (350–54). Her analysis suggests that there are a number of neglected though excellent members to be added to the class of unnatural characters.

mimetic sequences of events, as in Robert Coover's "The Babysitter" (1969). This is only to say that some characters are born unnatural, some achieve unnaturalness, and some have the unnatural thrust upon them. Concerning the range of antimimetic devices possible in narrative, we see that character is rather like other components such as narration, plot, space, and narrative itself: Mimetically impossible features can intrude upon the text at any point.

I believe that a thorough account of character needs to go still further than the opposition discussed up to this point: A tripartite theory, like that of James Phelan, which promotes mimetic, synthetic, and thematic aspects of character, is particularly useful (1–14). Phelan's synthetic component includes exclusively textual aspects of character, as well as functional aspects that are required by the logic of the narrative. I would like to see this aspect expanded further to include the unnatural examples I have assembled above. My preferred model would also include an intertextual component for works that rewrite earlier texts. It seems evident that a character may be derived from four possible sources: It may re-create lived experience, personify an idea, exist as an exclusively fictional creation, or revive a character from an earlier work of fiction.[20]

It goes without saying that many characters perform several of these functions at the same time. Shakespeare's major figures are particularly effective in fusing the first three of these functions, and they have been widely praised for their mimetic fidelity, structural cunning, and ideological skepticism. It is also true that these functions may fail to merge, as when a rapid and rather unbelievable reformation is thrust upon a character in order to provide a satisfactory closure, and the synthetic tramples over the mimetic.[21] These two components may also be deliberately opposed: In Pinter's *The Basement* (1967), we see the status, speech, and personalities of Law and Stott become transposed, as each one takes on the character and situation of the other during the course of the play as all pretenses of realism are abolished, the better to foreground the symmetrical reversal of the situation of the battling protagonists. A multiform theory of character is especially useful as it allows us to model otherwise seemingly opposed critical approaches: those based on verisimilitude, on aesthetic considerations, on ideological valences, and on interventions in literary history. It seems clear that an expansive theory of character that takes into account the multiple aspects of fictional characters and their functions, fusions, and oppositions is the kind that is most needed at this time in narrative theory, especially if we are to embrace the challenging, bracing, and often brilliant figures that constitute unnatural characters.

---

20. For a fuller outline of this position, see Herman et al., 132–38.
21. The sudden reformation of the rakish protagonist of Colley Cibber's *Love's Last Shift* (1696) was so unconvincing that John Vanbrugh immediately wrote a sequel, *The Relapse* (1696), that offered a more verisimilar story and consistent character.

WORKS CITED

Abbott, H. Porter. *Real Mysteries: Narrative and the Unknowable.* The Ohio State UP, 2014.

Alber, Jan. *Unnatural Narrative: Impossible Worlds in Fiction and Drama.* U of Nebraska P, 2016.

Alfau, Felipe. *Locos: A Comedy of Gestures.* Random, 1990.

Barthes, Roland. *Image, Music, Text.* Translated by Stephen Heath, Hill and Wang, 1977.

———. *S/Z: An Essay.* Translated by Richard Miller, Hill and Wang, 1974.

Beckett, Samuel. *Three Novels: Molloy, Malone Dies, The Unnamable.* Grove, 1958.

Berlatsky, Eric. *The Real, the True, and the Told: Postmodern Historical Narrative and the Ethics of Representation.* The Ohio State UP, 2011.

Booth, Stephen. "Speculations on Doubling in Shakespeare's Plays." *Shakespeare: The Theatrical Dimension,* edited by Phillip C. McGuire and David C. Samuelson, AMS Press, 1979, pp. 103–41.

Borges, Jorge Luis. *Collected Fictions.* Translated by Andrew Hurley, Penguin, 1998.

Bortolussi, Marisa, and Peter Dixon. *Psychonarratology: Foundations for the Empirical Study of Literary Response.* Cambridge UP, 2003.

Churchill, Caryl. *Plays: One.* Routledge, 1985.

———. *Plays: Three.* Nick Hern, 1998.

Create a Person [internet game], 2002. https://www.newgrounds.com/portal/view/65462.

Crimp, Martin. *Attempts on Her Life.* Faber and Faber, 1997.

Currie, Gregory. *Narratives and Narrators: A Philosophy of Stories.* Oxford UP, 2010.

Daoud, Kamel. *The Meursault Investigation.* Translated by John Cullen, Other P, 2015.

Docherty, Thomas. *Reading (Absent) Character: Towards a Theory of Characterization in Fiction.* Oxford UP, 1985.

Fokkema, Aleid, *Postmodern Characters: A Study of Characterization in British and American Postmodern Fiction.* Rodopi, 1991.

———. "Postmodern Fragmentation or Authentic Essence?: Character in *The Satanic Verses.*" *Shades of Empire in Colonial and Postcolonial Literature,* edited by C. C. Barfoot and Theo D'haen, Rodopi, 1993, pp. 51–64.

Forster, Marc. *Stranger Than Fiction.* Mandate Pictures, Three Strange Angels, 2006.

Frow, John. *Character and Person.* Oxford UP, 2014.

Fuentes, Carlos. "Orchids in the Moonlight." *Drama Contemporary: Latin America,* edited by Marion P. Holt and George W. Woodyard, PAJ Publications, 1986, pp. 143–86.

Gallagher, Catherine. "The Rise of Fictionality." *The Novel Vol 1: History, Geography, and Culture,* edited by Franco Moretti, Princeton UP, 2006, pp. 336–63.

Gerrig, Richard J., and David W. Allbritton. "The Construction of Literary Character: A View from Cognitive Psychology." *Style,* vol. 24, no. 3, 1990, pp. 380–91.

Handke, Peter. *Kaspar and Other Plays.* Translated by Michael Roloff, Noonday, 1975.

Hansen, Per Krogh. "Formalizing the Study of Character: Traits, Profiles, Possibilities." *Disputable Core Concepts of Narrative Theory,* edited by Göran Rossholm and Christer Johansson, Lang, 2012, pp. 99–118.

Helms, Lorraine. "Playing the Woman's Part: Feminist Criticism and Shakespearean Performance." *Performing Feminisms: Feminist Critical Theory and Theatre*, edited by Sue-Ellen Case, Johns Hopkins UP, 1990, pp. 196–206.

Herman, David, et al. *Narrative Theory: Core Concepts and Critical Debates*. Ohio State University Press, 2012.

Herrmann, Anne. "Travesty and Transgression: Transvesticism in Shakespeare, Brecht, and Churchill." *Performing Feminisms: Feminist Critical Theory and Theatre*, edited by Sue-Ellen Case, Johns Hopkins UP, 1990, pp. 294–315.

Hochman, Baruch. *Character in Literature*. Cornell UP, 1985.

Hyder, Qurratulain. *River of Fire*. New Directions, 1999.

Iversen, Stefan. "Unnatural Minds." *A Poetics of Unnatural Narrative*, edited by Jan Alber et al., The Ohio State UP, 2013, pp. 94–112.

Jones, Chuck. "Duck Amuck." 1953, www.dailymotion.com/video/x2j6pt1.

Kukkonen, Karin. *Contemporary Comics Storytelling*. U of Nebraska P, 2013.

Kushner, Tony. *Angels in America: A Gay Fantasia on American Themes. Revised and Complete Edition*. Theater Communication Group, 2013.

Leki, Ilona. *Alain Robbe-Grillet*. G. K. Hall, 1983.

Lem, Stanisław. *Solaris*. Translated by Joanna Kilmartin and Steve Cox, Harcourt, 1987.

Margolin, Uri. "Character." *The Cambridge Companion to Narrative*, edited by David Herman, Cambridge UP, 2007, pp. 66–79.

McHale, Brian. *Postmodernist Fiction*. Methuen, 1987.

Murphet, Julian. "Character and Event." *SubStance*, vol. 36, no. 2, 2007, pp. 106–24.

Pentzell, Raymond J. "Actor, *Maschera*, and Role: An Approach to Irony in Performance." *Comparative Drama*, vol. 16, no. 3, 1982, pp. 201–26.

Pfister, Manfred. *Theory and Analysis of Drama*. Translated by John Halliday, Cambridge UP, 1991.

Phelan, James. *Reading People, Reading Plots: Character, Progression, and the Interpretation of Narrative*. U of Chicago P, 1989.

Pirandello, Luigi. *Naked Masks: Five Plays by Luigi Pirandello*, edited by Eric Bentley, Dutton, 1952.

Queneau, Raymond. *The Flight of Icarus*. Translated by Barbara Wright, New Directions, 1973.

———. *Le vol d'Icare*. Gallimard, 1968.

Richardson, Brian. *Unnatural Narrative: Theory, History, and Practice*. The Ohio State UP, 2015.

———. *Unnatural Voices: Extreme Narration in Modern and Contemporary Fiction*. The Ohio State UP, 2006.

Robinson, Marc. *The Other American Drama*. Johns Hopkins UP, 1997.

Sayre, Henry M. *The Object of Performance: The American Avant-Garde since 1970*. U of Chicago P, 1992.

Schneider, Ralf. "Toward a Cognitive Theory of Literary Character: The Dynamics of Mental-Model Construction." *Style*, vol. 35, no. 4, 2001, pp. 607–40.

Second Life [game]. www.newgrounds.com/portal/view/65462.

Shakespeare, William. *The Complete Works of Shakespeare*. 5th ed., edited by David Bevington, Pearson Longman, 2004.

Snickers. "You're Not Yourself." *YouTube,* https://search.yahoo.com/yhs/search?p=snickers+commercial+not+yourself&ei=UTF-8&hspart=mozilla&hsimp=yhs-001.

Sonenberg, Maya. "Nature Morte." *Cartographies.* Ecco, 1989, pp. 35–42.

Stafford, Jeff. "Spirits of the Dead." *Turner Classic Movies,* www.tcm.com/this-month/article/495637|0/TCM-Imports-September-Schedule.html.

Stoppard, Tom. *Travesties.* Grove, 1975.

Wagner, Frank. "Intertextualité et théorie." *Cahiers de narratologie,* no. 13, 2006, n. pag.

Wake, Paul. "Life and Death in the Second Person: Identification, Empathy, and Antipathy in the Adventure Gamebook." *Narrative,* vol. 24, no. 2, 2016, pp. 190–210.

Weinsheimer, Joel. "Theory of Character: *Emma.*" *Poetics Today,* vol. 1, 1979, pp. 185–211.

Witkiewicz, Stanisław Ignacy. *The Madman and the Nun and Other Plays.* Translated by Daniel C. Gerould, U of Washington P, 1968.

CHAPTER 8

(Un)natural Temporalities in Graphic Narratives

RAPHAËL BARONI

INTRODUCTION

Unnatural narratology has recently focused our attention on unnatural representations of time, among other unnatural story elements such as weird narrators, impossible points of view, or talking animals.[1] Unnatural temporality can either consist in a specific organization of the *sjuzhet,* or it can relate to the characteristics of the *fabula*. In the first case, the "unnaturalness" could be defined in contrast to the norms of narrative representations, which are supposed to be organized, even when not referring to a chronological order of the *fabula,* as a linear sequence of information, where interactivity, synchronized information, or other kinds of variable *sjuzhet* seem to contradict the conventional forms of narrativity. In the second case, unnatural temporalities may involve a *fabula* where characters experience situations that contravene our basic experience of time—which is supposed to be a flow of events, with an unchangeable past, a future reduced to a pure virtuality, while only the present

---

1. This chapter is partly based on a previously published article: "(Un)natural Temporalities in Comics." Some parts of the argument developed in the second part of the chapter appeared also in another article: "L'exploration temporelle comme modalité du voyage imaginaire." I am grateful to the editors for allowing me to reuse some material of these previous versions, and for the journals where I published the original articles to have authorized me to use this material once again.

is actual—even if these apparently weird situations have been conventionalized by popular culture.[2] At this level, unnatural temporalities may involve any form of time manipulations; among those, as enumerated by Rüdiger Heinze (38), we find time travel, time loops, or diverging timelines, most often, the last two scenarios being directly related to the former.

In this chapter, these supposedly unnatural ingredients of narratives will be tested against the semiotic specifics and the cultural tradition of comics. First, I shall argue that a variable *sjuzhet* should be considered as a natural quality of the medium, because of the nonlinear organization of story elements, which are spread on a page and meant to be read in different orders. Conversely, linear *sjuzhets* will be considered as unconventional forms of comics, usually related to digital culture. Nevertheless, I shall show how a contemporary author such as Marc-Antoine Mathieu has used the characteristics of the medium in order to produce creative alterations of the conventional order of the reading experience. Then, on the level of the *fabula*, I shall show that many examples of time travel that we find in European comics until the 1980s are a mere extension of the motif of the "extraordinary journey," and therefore they do not engender time paradoxes, nor do they appear as completely unnatural to their readers. In commenting on a page of *Watchmen*, I will conclude that to some extent, time travel in comics should not be considered as an impossible experience of time, but rather as a reflection on the way temporality is experienced in graphic narratives, which presupposes a spatial representation of the flow of time.

THE VARIABLE *SJUZHET*: A CONVENTIONAL FEATURE OF COMICS?

The semiotic nature of comics should encourage us to question one of the most basic properties that is supposed to be conventional at the level of the *sjuzhet*. As stated by Richardson:

> In a typical work, the *sjuzhet* is the narrative in the sequence that it appears in the text: it is usually co-extensive with its presentation, whether page by page or, in an oral narrative, word by word. It is widely affirmed that narrative and its reception are sequential processes and that simultaneous events

---

2. Alber explains that there are "physical, logical, or epistemic impossibilities that have over time become familiar forms of narrative representation (such as speaking animals in beast fables, magic in romances or fantasy narratives, the omnimentality of the traditional omniscient narrator, or time travel in science fiction)" (sec. 2).

must therefore be presented and processed sequentially, not simultaneously. ("Unusual and Unnatural" 167)

The idea that a "typical" *sjuzhet* is sequential should be questioned for its mediacentric presupposition, because when Boris Tomashevsky (66–78) first introduced this concept, he was dealing with the sequential organization of novels, not of graphic narratives. Moreover, transmedial narratology has made us aware of the difficulty of applying concepts forged in literary studies to other media, especially to visual arts.[3] Even though, for Will Eisner or Scott McCloud, comics are described as sequential art, Pierre Fresnault-Deruelle has more accurately defined the medium as a complex combination of the linear organization of the panels in the strip and the tabular configuration of the page (7). Even the succession of the panels in a strip is not necessarily or entirely sequential. As illustrated by the strip by Pascal Jousselin seen in figure 8.1, the co-presence of the panels is one of the most salient differences between literature and comics, and it allows the production of effects that could not be achieved in another medium.[4]

On panel 2, the left character criticizes comics, which are described as a low form of literature. After saying, "What comics can achieve that literature cannot do? Nothing! Not one thing!" the character is being slapped by the other man, whose action overlaps panels 2 and 3, and thus, he seems innocent in panel 3. The chronology of the story is unnatural, because the characters can act simultaneously in two different time frames, and only this medium could achieve this very simple effect, because in a strip, there are two levels of organization for the *sjuzhet*: first, the sequential organization of the four panels, referring to the chronology of the *fabula*, and second, the whole strip apprehended as a single picture. In this higher level of organization, the panels can be seen as simultaneous images spread on a page, and therefore, we are invited to consider nonlinear connections among them. Groensteen has called this operation "braiding," a specific nonlinear articulation between visual elements in the spatio-topical system of comics that functions throughout the repetition of motifs or of page layouts, or of any kind of connection that we can draw between separated images, independently from their sequential order:

> Unlike film, where images appear on the screen one at a time, each disappearing to give way to the next, comics is made up of a plurality of images that are co-present before the reader's eyes. They share a segmented space and, being printed and therefore stable, remain visible, available for a sec-

---

3. See, for example, Thon.
4. The image was published in the journal *Fluide Glacial* in April 2014. It appears on the author's blog, http://cestdelareclame2.blogspot.fr/.

FIGURE 8.1. Pascal Jousselin (2014). © Pascal Jousselin. Reproduced with kind permission of the author.

ond reading in order, for example, to check a detail. The panels may, then, be apprehended simultaneously, and they may also enter into dialogue with each other across the page; they lend themselves to different levels of articulation over its surface, and they are at the intersection of the multiple trajectories that the eye may follow. They can also enter into dialogue with panels not currently visible, establishing relationships among non-adjacent pages. (*The Art of Braiding* 88–89)

So, braiding effects can be viewed as a way of encouraging the reader to enrich the signification of graphic narratives by weaving between different images, just like regular meters, rhymes, repetitions, or typographical effects may enrich the meaning of a poem.

While Richardson uses the notion of the "variable sjuzhet" in order to discuss the organization of some postmodern or experimental novels, he wisely mentions the case of visual media that can achieve similar effects:

Narrative paintings, in which several scenes of the life of an individual are depicted on a single canvas, can be read in several possible sequences. Graphic novels can employ several different reading progressions, including top to bottom, left to right, and right to left, as well as unmoored sequences. As Thomas A. Bredehoft explains, Chris Ware's *Jimmy Corrigan: The Smartest Kid on Earth* presents a page of images delineating crucial backstory of the *fabula* that can be read in different ways. ("Unusual and Unnatural" 169–70)

It is interesting to note that Richardson mentions Chris Ware, an author well known for being one of the most creative artists in contemporary alternative comics. Thus, *variable sjuzhets* might seem to belong to humorous comic strips (as Jousselin's), or to avant-garde graphic novels (as Ware's), as if they were a characteristic feature of transgressive or experimental works. However, we could find similar examples in popular comics from all periods and belonging to all genres. Every time that a page organization offers meaningful alternatives to the linear progression, it produces a kind of *unfixed sjuzhet*, because the reader is invited to read or view the panels several times and in different orders. While the co-presence of other panels on a page may disturb some sequential effects—for example, the building of suspense or surprise[5]—many authors have learned to deal with this constraint, which is also an opportunity to build specific effects, which may enrich the narration. For example, in the most basic formula, the last panel is often used as a cliffhanger,[6] and the first or the central panels, which occupy hierarchical positions on the page, can play specific roles. The author can play with the size or shape of the panels, or with symmetrical compositions, in order to catch the eye of the reader and build hierarchies beyond a strict linear progression. In the strip in figure 8.2, taken from Hergé's *On a marché sur la lune*, we can see that the linear progression is also altered in a productive way.

FIGURE 8.2. Hergé, *On a marché sur la lune* (1954). © Hergé/Moulinsart 2019.

While the first two panels are clearly organized as a sequence of events, the last three images offer an alternative: They form a kind of sub-strip embedded in the main strip, but at this level, the relation between the panels adopts a hierarchical organization rather than a linear one. Each panel relates to simultaneous events occurring in different places, the overlapping of the dialogue bubble on the three images signifying that they should be seen as a single narrative unit. The situations shown on the left and on the right feature an axiological opposition (good versus evil), and consequently, they should be processed simultaneously, or more precisely in any order that readers may choose.

---

5. For more extensive reflections about suspense in comics, see Baroni, *La Tension narrative* ch. 13 or Boillat and Revaz.

6. See Terlaak Poot.

These comics are "conventional," not because they lack creativity, but rather because the aesthetics of "la ligne claire" adopted by Hergé aims to avoid any anti-immersive effects. According to this principle, the nonlinear progression is not supposed to surprise readers or to shock them by breaking some narrative rules, but on the contrary, it wonderfully exploits the semiotic potentials of the medium without altering the flow of the narrative. In early comics, such as the page in figure 8.3, by Winsor McCay, we find several examples of creative exploitations of a hierarchical organization of a series of panels. In this case, we see that panels 13 and 14 form a sequence of events while being at the same time the simultaneous picture of a landscape overlapping the gutter between the panels.

On another scale, the deformation of the panels of each strip, which imitates the deformation of the bed of Nemo in his dream world, can be observed only when looking at the page as a whole, instead of considering each strip as isolated and successive portions of the narrative. Eventually, the last two panels exploit their relative position—one above the other, instead of the regular positioning of one beside the other—so when Nemo falls from his bed, he also falls from one panel to the next.

With all these examples, we have seen that many nonlinear relations between panels can relate to nontemporal configurations of the storyworld—such as axiological oppositions, the configuration of a landscape, or the imitation of the relative position, size, or shape of objects—and all these parallels can be noticed without altering the very basic properties of the medium and its immersive power on the audience. The tension between tabular and sequential dimensions is not just a defamiliarizing effect achieved on rare occasions by few comics, but is instead a very basic, and even the most specific, property of the medium. As explained by Benoît Peeters, in comics, there is an absolutely specific space, which he calls the "périchamp" (literally, the "peri-field," namely, the field surrounding the panel):

> It is formed by the other panels of the page, or of the double page; this space, being simultaneously different and adjacent, inevitably influences the perception of the panel seen by the reader. No glance can seize a panel as a solitary picture; in a more or less obvious way, the other panels are always already there. . . . As any particularity of a media, this data may reinforce or impair a project. Great authors of comics are those who have coped with this specific constraint by organizing the double page according to what we may call topological preoccupations. (21)

Consequently, the reader of a comic who skips ahead (or below) to later panels cannot be compared to the reader of a novel who flips a few pages ahead,

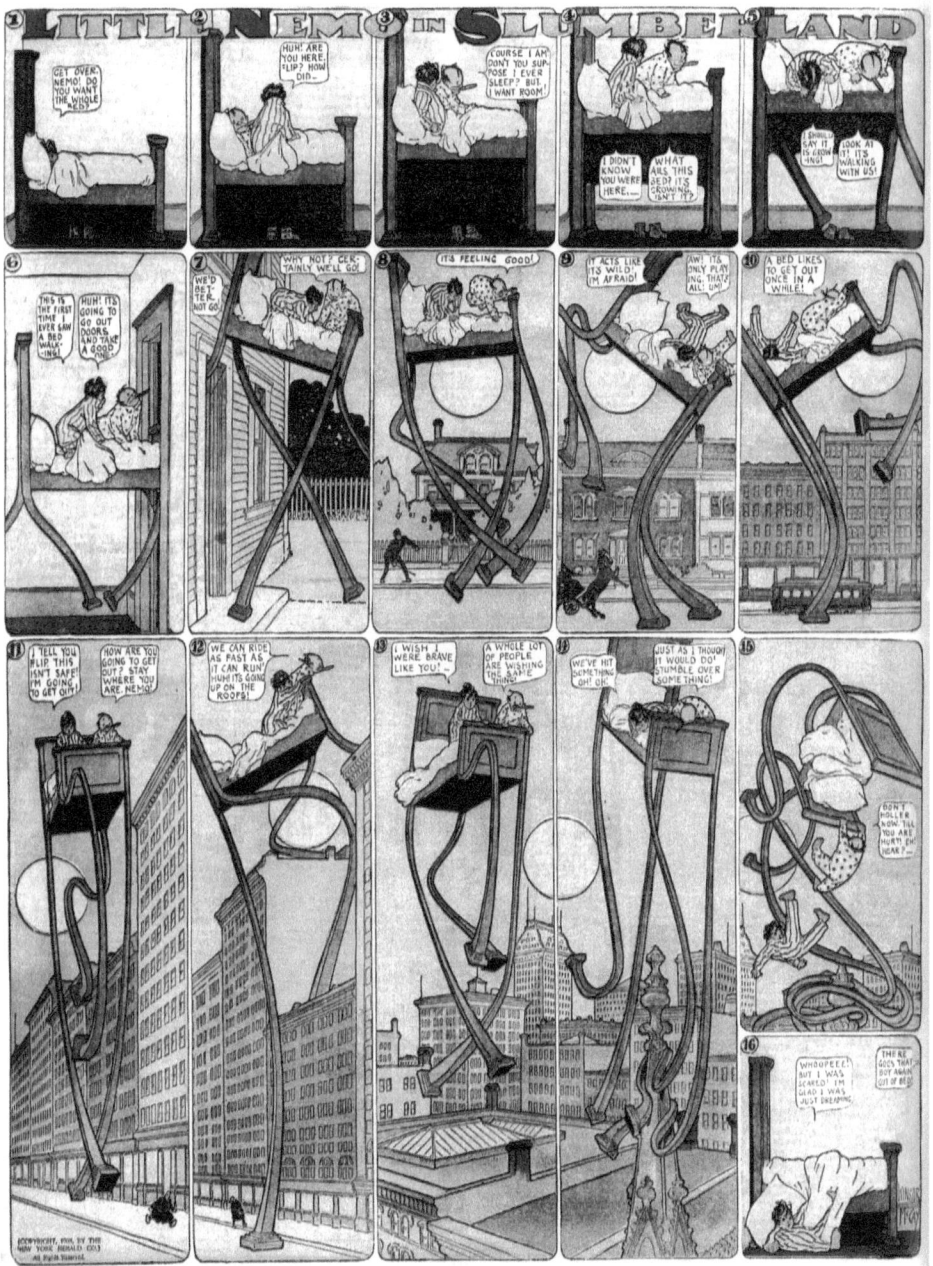

FIGURE 8.3. Winsor McCay, *Little Nemo in Slumberland* (October 29, 1905)

because to look at the whole (double) page before reading the linear sequence of the panels, or simply to navigate back and forth throughout the comic book, is not a transgression of the standard progression; it is exactly what is expected from a cooperative reader, even in popular comics. As explained by Groensteen:

> Comics are fundamentally a kind of literature that hides nothing, offered to a full possession, with nothing left aside: we discover it just by leafing through it, we navigate on its surface without obliterating what was seen before, and with keeping an eye on what is coming next. (*Bande dessinée et narration* 82)

In contrast, we should consider "fixed sjuzhets" as qualities inherent to movies or to most verbal narratives, because they are processed sequentially, while the spatial organization of the page in comics is, by definition, a more or less "unfixed" or "variable sjuzhet," with multilinear paths, more or less preconfigured by the page layout.[7] In fact, it is only in unconventional comics that the story is really processed as a pure linear progression. *Bludzee* is a typical case: Published by Lewis Trondheim in 2009, it became the first French comic strip specifically designed to fit the screen of a smartphone, thus taking the logical option of showing only one panel at a time. In digital comics of this kind, because of the size of the device used to access them, readers must scroll from one panel to another, and therefore, they are never able to grasp the entire sequence as a whole. In this case, narrative tension increases and suspense and surprises are easier to process, but this quasi-cartoon loses some of the essential qualities inherent to comics.[8] In his book *Reinventing Comics*, Scott McCloud defines the format adopted by these linear webcomics as the "infinite canvas," because there is potentially no limit to the linear succession of images; he opposes this form to the "small rectangular canvas we call the page" (221). McCloud sees this evolution as a liberation from the constraints imposed by the page layout, which, in his view, breaks the continuity of each strip and forces the author to deal with "topological preoccupations," to employ once more the term of Peeters (22). But other scholars see that enthusiasm as a symptom:

---

7. As explained by Jan Baetens (47–55), images can express time just as texts can make sense of their spatial configuration, especially in poetry.

8. We find similar examples of the formula "one panel = one page" in "Tijuana Bibles," a genre of pornographic comics produced between 1920 to 1960, whose format was designed to fit the pocket of the reader for more discretion. The arousal function of these "bibles" may also benefit from this mode of presentation. "Flip-books" are also other versions of the same formula, but this latter case underlines the proximity of this narrative form with animated cartoons.

It is striking to see that McCloud, in *Understanding Comics,* is not interested in the page as a unit, with a format adapted to what the human eye, at a distance of thirty centimeters, can conveniently apprehend all at once, with all its relations of composition and proportion; it is even the great blind spot of his theory. One understands better, therefore, why he welcomes the advent of the potentially infinite canvas as a liberation. (Groensteen, *Bande dessinée et narration* 80–81)

At this point, Groensteen argues that purely sequential graphic narratives may not be called "comics" anymore, because they would belong instead to a new kind of media, somewhere in between comics and filmic representations:

> As long as the notion of page remains, all subsequent links of juxtaposition, of organization, of enumeration, all the effects of dialogue, of braiding, and of seriality between the panels, are preserved, and comics continue to appear in their own space-topic system. Instead, the display panel by panel tears apart this construction, deterritorializes each image, masking or ruining all ties on the surface of the page. (*Bande dessinée et narration* 72)

Coming back to the discussion concerning unnatural temporalities and their relation to the configuration of the *sjuzhet* in traditional graphic narratives, we may stress that the linear organization of the infinite canvas corresponds in fact to a drastic limitation. Conversely, the page offers fantastic resources for achieving inimitable unnatural effects. Along with the example of Jousselin, some experimental authors have exploited the paginal organization of the medium in order to produce fascinating intertwining temporalities. In *L'origine,* the first opus of the adventures of Julius Corentin Acquefacques, Marc-Antoine Mathieu invents a Kafkaesque and highly metaleptic narrative where characters get progressively conscious that they live in a storyworld invented by an author. On page 40, a scientist explains to the protagonist that their two-dimensional world is embedded in a three-dimensional world; therefore, he explains, if there were a hole in their two-dimensional world, they could see through that hole a fragment of time superimposed on their present and belonging to another page of the book in the three-dimensional world (figure 8.4). He calls this hole an anti-panel ("une anti-case"), which is supposed to offer them a window where they could "read the past or the future."

Of course, on pages 41 and 42, the author has created a real hole in the center of the comics, so the reader can actually read through the page a panel situated either on page 40 or on page 43, thus creating a prolepsis and an

FIGURE 8.4. Marc-Antoine Mathieu, *L'origine* (1990). © Delcourt, 1990.

analepsis that realize the prediction of the scientist. And when it happens on page 42, the protagonist sees that the same event has been reiterated, and the scientist comes to the conclusion that this repetition proves his theory.

In this fascinating case, the hole in the page is highly unconventional, but in reality, the author has simply exploited one of the essential characteristics of the medium: the two-dimensional superimposed pages of a graphic narrative and the unlinear connections that we can braid between the separated moments of a timeline. Almost the same effect could have been achieved by simply repeating the same pictures on pages 41 and 43 and on pages 40 and 42, but then it would have been just another classical case of braiding. By using a real hole, and by making the characters aware of the repetition, the author has managed to open a real "window" in the timeline, and yet he continues to point toward the classical features of analogical comics, namely those published in real books. In some ways, the theories of the mad scientist may then become a course for teaching the original configuration of time displayed by comics.

TIME TRAVEL AS AN EXTENSION OF EXTRAORDINARY JOURNEYS AND UTOPIA

As we have seen, it is not easy to define the naturalness of any narrative element if we put aside the context and fail to consider not only the semiotic properties of the medium but also its specific cultural tradition. This is also true when we deal with thematic elements of the *fabula*, such as time travel, which is supposed to be one of the most obvious cases of physical impossibility explored by popular culture. Peter Rabinowitz has explained the difficulties it raises for narrative theory because, on one hand, we have to consider "the order of the events as experienced by the protagonist, the Time Traveller"—an order that he calls "the path of the protagonist"—and on the other hand, we must account for the chronology of the world in which the protagonist travels (183).

This problem becomes more salient with the possibility of changing a timeline while traveling back in the past, according to the well-known "paradox of the grandfather" first formulated by Barjavel (*Le voyageur imprudent*, 1944). In short: If a man kills his grandfather before his parents were born, he may not live to kill him, thus, the grandfather should be alive, and so on. The solution of the paradox usually involves a loop or a theory encompassing diverging timelines: The killer may be born in one world, but after killing his grandfather, he continues to live in another world, where he was not born, and thus, two incompatible events can coexist in parallel universes. In this case, diverging timelines and time travel are combined into a single motif. This virtuality has become very popular in novels and in movies, with pioneering works by Robert Heinlein (*By His Bootstraps*, 1941), René Barjavel (*Le voyageur imprudent*, 1944), and Chris Marker (*La jetée*, 1962), and later, it was popularized by the blockbuster *Back to the Future* (1985). Here again, Brian Richardson sees an important challenge for narrative theory, because we need "a greatly expanded concept of fabula. Most important is to go beyond the unilinear fabula and to add the concept of a multilinear fabula, a fabula with one or numerous forkings leading to different possible chains of events" ("Unnatural Stories and Sequences" 28).

Notwithstanding, we may question the so-called unnaturalness of time travel in the corpus of European comics,[9] at least before the apparition of time paradoxes in comics by the 1980s, especially in series like Pierre Christin and Jean-Claude Mézières's *Valérian, agent spatio-temporel* (*Valérian, Spatio-Temporal Agent*), or in the series by Andreas, *Rork*. First, we must consider that many modalities of what can be identified as "time travel" do not engen-

---

9. The storytelling tradition of American comics is different. In a daily strip published in April 20, 1935, the series Brick Bradford introduced a spaceship named the "time-top," which was also a time machine. This series uses the motif as a mere opportunity to diversify the environments for the adventures lived by the hero and his companions. Otherwise, the proliferation of "multiverse" in comic books, starting from the late 1950s, was mainly due to the need to expand franchise universes. It can sometimes lead to a reboot, as illustrated by the famous series of DC Comics entitled *Crisis on Infinite Earths*, published in twelve episodes between April 1985 and March 1986. The format of the comic book is also more suitable for complex scriptwriting at the scale of a single episode, which includes sometimes occasional time paradoxes.

der time paradoxes, like the exploration of a prehistoric sanctuary, as in *Voyage au centre de la terre* (*Journey to the Center of the Earth*; 1864) or in *The Lost World* (1912). There is also no longer a paradox when a mysterious sleep leads a character to awaken in a future world, as in Wells's *When the Sleeper Awakes* (1899). In this case, as the traveler has no way back, his only "unnatural" attribute is that, as in *Sleeping Beauty*, he has been aging at a different speed from his environment.

An important source for time travel has been utopian narratives, like *L'an 2440: Rêve s'il en fut jamais* (*The Year 2440: A Dream if Ever There Was One*; 1770), a novel published by Louis-Sébastien Mercier in the eighteenth century. In this novel, the author imagines a trip into the twenty-fifth century, which appears, when he is ultimately bitten by a snake and wakes up, as a mere illusion. Here again, since the trip was only a dream, no paradoxes ensue. So, not only has time travel been conventionalized by popular culture, but many instances do not disturb narrative logic. Furthermore, in the French comics tradition, the majority of time travel episodes have been interpreted as a mere extension of the classic motif of the "extraordinary journey," as exemplified by many novels and illustrated collections since the eighteenth century, until the famous Hetzel collection *Voyages extraordinaires* (*Extraordinary Journeys*). As summarized by François Rosset, these stories followed an invariable topos:

> The discovery of a imagined land is recounted most often in the context of a journey in the real world: a storm, a pirate attack, a shipwreck, a twist of fate diverts the traveller from his or her intended route, and casts him or her into a place where there are no obligations, where anything is possible. (46)

Among the numerous incarnations of these nonparadoxical modalities of time travel, grounded in the genre of *utopia* and in the *topos* of the "extraordinary journey," we can note many famous examples, like *Zig et Puce au XXIe siècle* (*Zig and Puce in the Twenty-First Century*; 1935) by Alain Saint-Ogan, which reproduces the motif of dream-travel imagined by Mercier. In 1942, with *Le rayon U* (*The U Ray*), substantially inspired by *Flash Gordon*, Jacobs illustrates the modality of a dinosaur sanctuary discovered after "a twist of fate" that diverts the travelers from their intended trip. In 1957, in *L'énigme de l'Atlantide* (*The Atlantis Mystery*), the same author mixes the utopia of a futuristic world, Atlantis, with a prehistoric sanctuary hidden in a cave, including the presence of pterodactyls (18). This story is a good example of the continuity between science fiction comics and the *topos* of the "extraordinary journey," since it is largely inspired by *Voyage au centre de la terre* and, even more, by *Vingt mille lieues sous les mers* (*Twenty Thousand Leagues under the Sea*), where we find the exact same combination: monstrous creatures guarding the ruins of Atlantis, illustrated by Alphonse de Neuville for the Hetzel edition (Verne 296–97).

Concerning the modality of a cryogenic sleep leading to a future world, we can mention, of course, the first-ever science fiction comic, *Buck Rogers in the Twenty-Fifth Century* (1928), but also, in the French tradition, the influential series *Les naufragés du temps* (*Space Force: Shipwrecked*) by Jean-Claude Forest and Paul Gillon (1964). Here again, the title of the series highlights the continuity between the *topos* of the shipwreck and that of time travel, but it adds a melancholic tone, because those "shipwrecked by time" (the literal meaning of the title) are characters living with no hope of return.

In all these cases, not only does time travel seem to belong to a tradition much older than the newer genre of science fiction, but the modality of the trip entails no special challenges to narrative logic. It is even natural in the sense that it does not transgress any essential physical rule, nor does it create a multilinear *fabula*. In the real world, we can dream of a future and then wake up, just as Zig and Puce do. And when Jules Verne invented *Voyage au centre de la terre*, the hypothesis of a dinosaur sanctuary was not considered to be completely irrational—the Galapagos Islands explored by Darwin can, indeed, be considered as a sanctuary of this kind. With the evolution of technology and science, we can even consider cryogenic sleep to be a realistic possibility, and relativist theories in physics also consider realistic the possibility that a protagonist could age at a different speed from the world out of which he or she originates, at least if he or she travels fast enough. This latter possibility was explored in the 1970s and 1980s in comics like *La guerre éternelle*[10]—an adaptation of the novel *The Forever War* by Joe Haldeman—or the adaptations of the series *Planet of the Apes*.[11] Even in adventures involving real *time machines*, time paradoxes are often reduced to the strict minimum in the comics tradition, while the representation of dinosaurs or of futuristic worlds, utopian or dystopian, continues to play the leading role, as in *Le piège diabolique* (*The Time Trap*; 1962) by Jacobs.

We can conclude that in French comics, at least until the middle of the 1980s, the graphic potential of time travel predominated over the narrative complexities involved in the recounting of unnatural temporalities, which were more often explored by literature and by movies. As explained by Groen-

---

10. The story was adapted by Joe Haldeman for the script; it was drawn by Marvano and colored by Bruno Marchand. Dupuis published the story in three volumes between November 1988 and November 1989.

11. The story by Pierre Boule, published in 1963, was first adapted for the screen by Franklin Shaffner in 1968. Marvel published a comic adaptation of the movies between February 1977 and August 1978. It was translated into French and published in Europe by LUG.

steen: "The specific imaginary in comics is a *graphic imaginary*. But we must assume that each medium has its own imaginary, and therefore, that a filmic imaginary, a literary imaginary, etc. also exist" ("Médiagénie et réflexivité"). Concerning the graphic imaginary, Groensteen insists on the specific interest in picturing exotic worlds:

> Comics spawned many imaginary worlds. For an illustrator, indeed, it is tempting to become a demiurge and to shape a coherent world, inventing geographical locations, social organizations, sets, costumes, means of locomotion, etc. with no technical or financial constraints, with no other limitations than those of his or her own talent! ("Médiagénie et réflexivité")

By sticking to the *topos* of the "extraordinary journey" instead of embracing the paradoxes of a multilinear *fabula*, French comics underline the fact that many authors saw time travel as a mere opportunity to illustrate imaginary worlds, to bring extinct species back to life, or to imagine the fabulous or dystopian cities of the future. By doing so, comics authors were the direct inheritors of a long tradition initiated by illustrators such as Alphonse de Neuville or Edouard Riou, who were giving shape and flesh to the worlds invented by Jules Verne. Here again, this cultural specificity is directly related to the semiotic potentials of the medium. The freedom offered by drawn pictures for the exploration and depiction of exotic worlds was then unrivalled, especially at a time when digital effects did not exist in movies.

We must also admit that some authors of this period cautiously avoided confronting the scriptwriting difficulties inherent to a multilinear *fabula*, either because they feared that their young audience could not follow the story, or, more probably, because they were afraid of not being able to write coherent stories involving such paradoxes, especially in the serialized forms of publications that predominated until the end of the 1960s. It is revealing that one of the first true time paradoxes in French comics appeared almost accidentally: The authors of *Valérian, agent spatio-temporel* had to change the timeline of their story because, when the series began in 1967, they imagined a cataclysm that was supposed to happen in 1986, but as the series was about to continue beyond this date, they felt the need to explain to their readers why it would not happen; otherwise, the science fictional anticipation would have turned into an uchrony. Scriptwriter Pierre Christin was very excited by this narrative challenge, while cartoonist Jean-Claude Mézières expressed great concern about this turning point in the adventures of Valérian.[12]

---

12. For a more detailed survey, see Baroni, "L'exploration temporelle."

It is also interesting to notice that with the development of digital effects, the exotic worlds first imagined in comics have spread into movies, while, in a reverse movement, contemporary comics are now favoring naturalistic stories, like reportage, autobiography, or autofiction. As explained recently by Alain Boillat, the digital revolution has greatly contributed to the transformation of cinema into a "world-building machine," thus occupying a field that used to be dominated by comics. I think that this new rivalry might be one important factor, among others, in explaining the recent reorientation of comics toward natural or even trivial worlds, while many Hollywood blockbusters seek their inspiration in older comics.

DR. MANHATTAN'S FABULOUS VISION OF TIME AND THE READER'S EXPERIENCE OF COMICS

I shall continue by briefly mentioning perhaps one of the most convincing examples of a fusion between the representation of an unnatural temporality and the conventional features of the medium. On the first page of the fourth chapter of *Watchmen*, centered on Dr. Manhattan (figure 8.5), Alan Moore and Dave Gibbons were able to illustrate, in a way that no other medium could do, the temporal experience of Dr. Manhattan, who gained, after an accident, the fabulous power of embracing the flow of time, past and future, all grasped in a single glance. As highlighted by the authors, this almost inconceivable experience of time is actually the natural experience of any reader of comics, since, by default, the future is already visible when we begin to read the page, and what has already been read is still readable.

The isomorphism of the panels and the repetition of colors and motifs encourage the reader to weave between different images, independently of the linear progression of the story. It is particularly obvious on this page, where we see repetitions between panels 2 and 9, or simply because we find the same photograph, evidently displayed at the center of the page, in each panel, like an iterative embedded panel. In the second panel, Dr. Manhattan looks at this picture and claims: "In twelve seconds time, I drop the photograph to the sand at my feet, walking away. It's already lying there, twelve seconds into the future. Ten seconds now." By saying that, Dr. Manhattan seems to express an unnatural experience of time, because he pretends that something situated in the future is "already lying there." But in fact, he only describes our own reading experience, since we can already see the photograph lying on the sand: First because, in panel 2, the image is desynchronized with the text, thus showing an anticipation (prolepsis) of what is going to happen, and

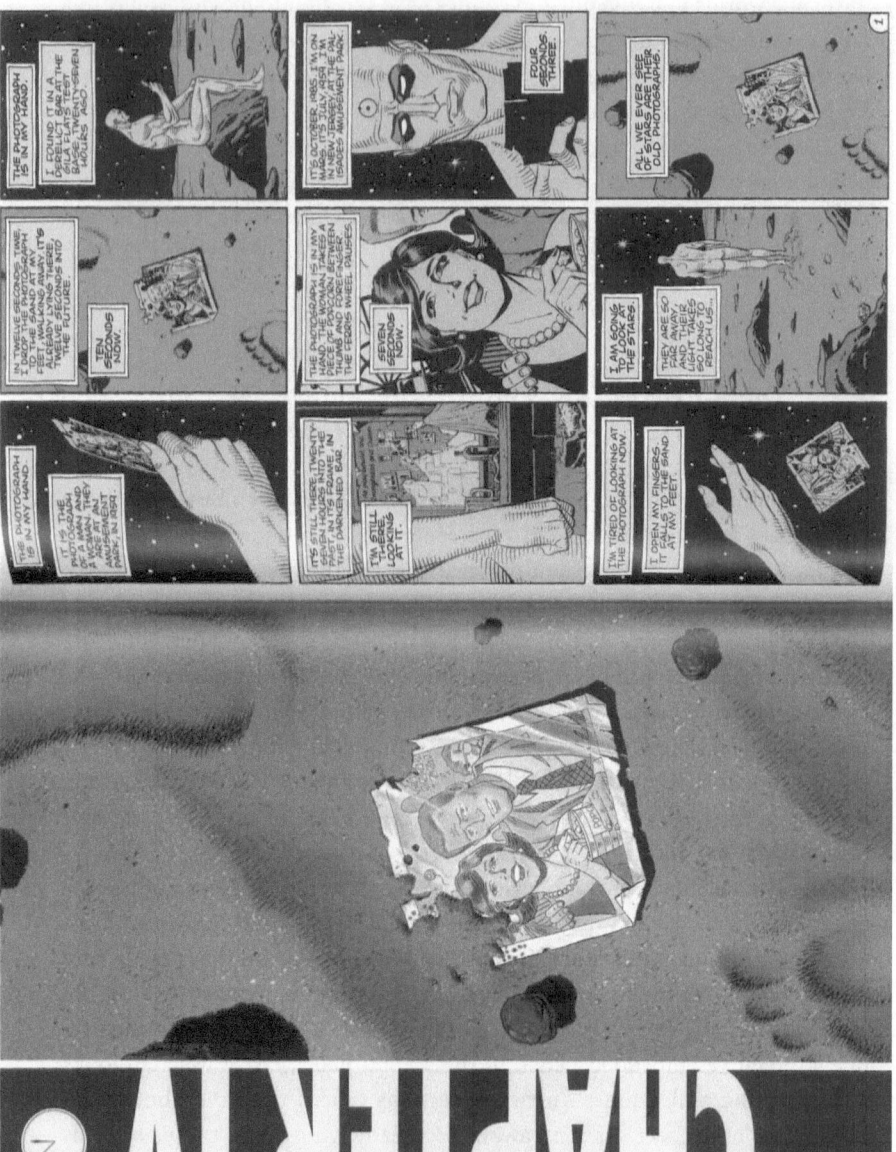

FIGURE 8.5. Alan Moore and Dave Gibbon, *Watchmen* (1986). © DC Comics, courtesy of DC Comics.

second because we can see that the exact same image is already lying ahead, in the last panel of the page, *seven panels into the future*. These two panels are also a reiteration of the cover of the chapter, and they show a footprint in the red sand of Mars and an old photograph of Dr. Manhattan and his wife, both indexical references to past events, making the character simultaneously present and absent.[13]

There is also a cinematic continuity between panels 1 and 7. These two images represent the same action, shown in the same angle, as if these representations were placed in a continuity, like adjacent photograms on a motion picture film. The reader is thus encouraged to overlap the interval of the countdown, suggesting an alternative narrative path, which would effectively reduce this waiting time to nothing. This vertical path is thus another way of justifying Dr. Manhattan when he asserts that the interval of time can be neglected and that the action described in this parenthesis is already accomplished. When he concludes by saying, "All we ever see of stars are their old photographs," he indicates that his dechronologized vision goes beyond the aesthetic of comics: It is merely the experience of anyone looking at a photograph or just staring at distant suns, whose images have traveled through space and time at the limited speed of light.

Thus, even in a graphic narrative that takes up the conventions of superhero comics, where both time travel and the unnatural powers of characters have been highly conventionalized, the authors have found a way to undermine these conventions by paradoxically showing that the vision of time of Dr. Manhattan is quite natural. This supernatural power strikes us as odd because, in this context, the capacity of the character simply reflects our experience of time when it is mediated by comics, by an old photograph, or by a considerable distance that dissociates the picture of an object from its actual presence.

GRAPHIC NARRATIVES AS UNNATURAL MEDIA?

In this chapter I have proposed to revise some principles guiding unnatural narratology by highlighting a danger of overgeneralization based on a conception of narrativity anchored in literary narratives. I suggest the acknowledgment of the importance of media specificity when we have to evaluate what is natural and what is not. We see that the frontier between mimetic and nonmimetic, conventional and unconventional, is very difficult to determine, and

---

13. On the same semiotic basis, André Bazin described the filmic image as a "présence/absence" (95–98).

at the very least, it has to be contextualized within a specific cultural tradition and by considering the semiotic constraints of the medium. Indeed, as I have shown, time travels are mostly interpreted as a mere exploration of exotic worlds in the graphic imaginary of comics, and unfixed *sjuzhets* are not necessarily unnatural in graphic narratives, at least not in the sense that they could be considered as atypical effects in the context of this medium.

Yet, as I have mentioned, some unlinear effects are more unnatural than others, either because they engender a metalepsis or an incoherence in the storyworld (Jousselin; Mathieu), or because "decorative" or "productive" page layouts[14] make braiding more obvious than usual (McCay). With its regular organization, and despite the fact that it concentrates several effects of braiding, the page of *Watchmen* relates to neither of these marked cases, because these effects are relatively discrete and can remain unnoticed for some readers. Indeed, Groensteen concedes that it is "possible to read a comic without noticing the presence of braiding" ("The Art of Braiding" 94), and he adds that some authors are less concerned by this effect than others:

> Some authors make the decision, a perfectly legitimate one, to restrict themselves to a classic unfolding of the narrative, based on linear linking devices, of a causal, deductive nature, where the meaning of each panel is beholden only to the previous ones. . . . I do not fetishise braiding, nor do I set it up as the criterion of the quality or artistic success of a comic. (89)

Of course, my aim was not to claim that comics are not a sequential art, because otherwise, this medium could not be able to tell a story. Comics have emerged as a new medium by differentiating themselves from mere illustration, precisely because authors like Rodolphe Töpffer found a way to give more autonomy to a combination of text and images for telling a linear story. Some have argued that suspense is impossible in this medium, or that it could be achieved only through the use of cliffhangers in serialized narrations (see Gauthier). Instead, I have argued elsewhere that if the short suspense of an action scene can be compromised at the scale of the page, narrative tension can easily function at the scale of the book, and effects based on curiosity are also less compromised by the visual display of events (see Baroni, *La tension narrative* 327–41). As explained by Groensteen (*Système de la bande dessi-*

---

14. For this typology of page layouts, see Peeters. Groensteen has proposed a different typology in *Système de la bande dessinée* based on the difference between regular/irregular and obvious/discrete. He has also reevaluated the aesthetic quality of regular page layouts by insisting on the fact that they accentuate braiding effects and allow more striking effects when an irregularity occurs.

née 73), in comics, the sequence is paced by the distance between panels: Adjacent panels in a strip mark a shorter period, while sequences of panels belonging to different strips or to different pages mark a longer period. In addition, the simultaneous display of separated events only concerns the unity of the double page, while other events remain hidden beyond this limit (which does not mean that braiding effects cannot be achieved at the scale of the entire book).

In any case, for a mindful reader, the page designed by Moore and Gibbons has managed to show, without altering our immersion in the flow of the narrative, how the medium has the potential to offer an unnatural (and almost supernatural) experience of time, simply because it displays simultaneously successive events in the space of the (double) page. In this sense, graphic narratives, like the supernatural powers of Dr. Manhattan, contradict an experiential form of temporality described by Saint Augustine or by the phenomenology of Husserl, Heidegger, or Merleau-Ponty. In an unmediated experience, past is what is no longer present, future is what has not happened yet, and present has no extension; the only "presence" of these time perspectives is based on mental projections: protentions and retentions.

The page of Moore and Gibbons refers to several experiences that contradict this apparently unescapable flow of time. But these experiences are not *unusual,* they are simply *mediated.* In this sense, the argument of Ricœur (31–51), who considers *emplotment* as the transformation of time by its inscription into the form of a narrative (especially when this narrative has the shape of a book), is ideally expressed by the medium of comics, because when a series of events is spread on the surface of the page, the narrative configuration can be immediately grasped as a whole. In comparison, cinematic or dramatic representations are obviously much closer to the phenomenal experience of time. Of course, in these representations, too, there is a mediation induced by the segmentation of time, by a succession of scenes or shots, and by the art of staging, of directing, or of film editing. But, when compared to comics or to novels, the duration of a scene remains undeniably closer to an unmediated experience.

CONCLUSIONS

One could come to the conclusion that some media are more natural than others, at least when we are considering their mimetic quality, for example when we evaluate the iconic resemblance between time or space representations and the referred events or objects. But here again, we should avoid naturalizing our conception of media transparency based on an ideal of "immediacy" (see, for example, Bolter and Grusin, or McLuhan). Of course, visual media may appear as more "transparent" for representing space, while the degree of temporal iconicity seems stronger in movies than in comics. Yet, our aesthetic experiences teach us that novels or comics can be as immersive as films or drama; it all depends on the quality of the work, on our personal taste, and on our familiarity with the media conventions. As explained by Cavell, a medium becomes transparent when habits or automatisms have naturalized the relation between a medium, a category of signs, and a content.[15] Besides, the concept of *naturalness* in unnatural narratology has not been developed to compare the aesthetic experience of the audience with an unmediated experience of real events. Instead, when we are concerned with the level of the *fabula*, we compare fictional entities with real entities, and when we are concerned with the level of the *sjuzhet*, we compare conventional narratives with unconventional narratives.

More explicitly, on the one hand, Jan Alber's definition of *unnaturalness* is based on the kind of stories "representing storytelling scenarios, narrators, characters, temporalities, or spaces that could not exist in the actual world." In this case, the page of Moore and Gibbons is "unnatural" only because it involves a supernatural character, who can live on Mars without a space suit, and who can see the past or the future as if they were present. So, at this level, we are not concerned by the difference between the reader's aesthetic experience and an unmediated one.

On the other hand, for Richardson, "unnaturalness" often correlates with Viktor Shklovsky's notion of defamiliarization. Thus, there is a distinction to be made between nonmimetic and antimimetic elements, the latter being based on "the degree of unexpectedness that the text produces, whether surprise, shock, or the smile that acknowledges that a different, playful kind of representation is at work" (*Unnatural Narrative* 3). In this conception, the "unnaturalness" of antimimetic elements can only be defined in comparison with more mimetic narratives. But, on this level, we can wonder if we should limit the comparison to narratives belonging to the same medium, or if it is possible to evaluate the antimimetic quality of any kind of narrative by basing the discussion on a reference to a prototypical form of narrativity belonging to a reference medium.

If there is such a thing as a reference medium, it is likely that many narratologists would define it as a verbal narrative, either because of the origin of their discipline, which has prospered in literary departments, or because of the doubtful assumption that conversational narratives are more essential to

---

15. For a synthesis, see Van Looy and Baetens 9.

humans than any other mimetic form of storytelling. But if the transparency of the mimesis becomes central to the discussion, one could also decide that the reference could be a narrative involving a less obvious form of mediation, like drama, cinema, video game, or virtual reality. Nevertheless, I still think that the decisive criterion should remain Shklovsky's defamiliarization, and therefore, it would make more sense to compare what can be truly compared, and to remain on a level where we discuss the difference or convergence between narratives belonging to the same media. Therefore, the discussion concerning the respective "naturalness" of different media should probably remain out of the scope of unnatural narratology. And on this scale, *The Origin* should probably be considered as more unnatural than *Watchmen* or *Little Nemo in Slumberland*.

WORKS CITED

Alber, Jan. "Unnatural Narrative." *The Living Handbook of Narratology*, edited by Peter Hühn et al., Hamburg University, 2014, http://www.lhn.uni-hamburg.de/article/unnatural-narrative. Accessed 28 Dec. 2018.

Andreas. *Rork: L'intégrale 1*. Editions du Lombard, 2012.

Baetens, Jan. *Formes et politique de la bande bessinée*. Peeters Vrin, 1998.

Barjavel, René. *Le voyageur imprudent*. Denoël, 1944.

Baroni, Raphaël. *La tension narrative*. Seuil, 2007.

———. "L'exploration temporelle comme modalité du voyage imaginaire dans la bande dessinée franco-belge (1930–1980)." *Image [&] Narrative*, vol. 16, no. 2, 2015, pp. 96–113.

———. "(Un)natural Temporalities in Comics." *European Comic Art*, vol. 9, no. 1, 2016, pp. 5–23.

André Bazin. *What is Cinema?*, vol. 1, 2nd edition, translated by Hugh Gray, University of California Press, 2004.

Boillat, Alain. *Cinéma, machine à mondes: Essai sur les films à univers multiples*. Georg, 2014.

Boillat, Alain, and Françoise Revaz. "Intrigue, Suspense, and Sequentiality in Comic Strips: Reading *Little Sammy Sneeze*." *Narrative Sequence in Contemporary Narratology*, edited by Raphaël Baroni and Françoise Revaz, The Ohio State UP, 2016, pp. 107–29.

Bolter, Jay David, and Richard Grusin. *Remediation*. MIT UP, 2000.

Cavell, Stanley. *The World Viewed*. Harvard UP, 1979.

Christin, Pierre, and Jean-Claude Mézières. *Valérian, agent spatio-temporel*. Series of albums published from 1967 to 2010.

Forest, Jean-Claude, and Paul Gillon. *L'étoile endormie*. Les Humanoïdes Associés, 1981.

Fresnault-Deruelle, Pierre. "Du linéaire au tabulaire." *Communications*, vol. 24, 1976, pp. 7–23.

Gauthier, Guy. "Dans la bande dessinée." *CinémAction*, vol. 71, 1994, pp. 161–64.

Groensteen, Thierry. "The Art of Braiding: A Clarification." *European Comic Art*, vol. 9, no. 1, 2016, pp. 88–98.

———. *Bande dessinée et narration*. PUF, 2011.

———. "Médiagénie et réflexivité, médiativité et imaginaire: Comment s'incarnent les fables." *Belphégor*, vol. 4, no. 2, 2005, www.dalspace.library.dal.ca/handle/10222/47702. Accessed 28 Dec. 2018.

———. *Système de la bande dessinée*. PUF, 1999.

Haldeman, Joe. *The Forever War*. St. Martin's P, 1974.

Haldeman, Joe, and Marvano. *La guerre éternelle*. Dupuis, 1988.

Heinlein, Robert. "By His Bootstraps." *Astounding Science Fiction*, October 1941.

Heinze, Rüdiger. "The Whirligig of Time: Toward a Poetics of Unnatural Temporality." *Poetics of Unnatural Narrative*, edited by Jan Alber et al., The Ohio State UP, 2013, pp. 31–44.

Hergé. *On a marché sur la lune*. Casterman, 1954.

Jacobs, Edgar P. *Le piège diabolique*. Editions du Lombard, 1962.

———. *Le rayon U*. 1943. Dargaud, 1974.

———. *L'énigme de l'Atlantide*. 1956. Editions du Lombard, 1977.

Jousselin, Pascal. Unnamed comic strip. *Fluide Glacial*, April 2014.

Marker, Chris. *La jetée*. Argos Films, 1962.

Mathieu, Marc-Antoine. *L'origine*. Delcourt, 1990.

McCay, Winsor. *Little Nemo in Slumberland*. *New York Herald*, 29 Oct. 1905.

McCloud, Scott. *Reinventing Comics: How Imagination and Technology Are Revolutionizing an Art Form*. Perennial, 2000.

McLuhan, Marshall. *Understanding Media: The Extensions of Man*. 1964. MIT Press, 1994.

Mercier, Louis-Sebastien. *L'an 2440: Rêve s'il en fut jamais*. 1771. La Découverte, 1999.

Moore, Alan, and Dave Gibbons. *Watchmen*. DC Comics, 2008.

Peeters, Benoît. *Lire la bande dessinée*. Flammarion, 2003.

Rabinowitz, Peter J. "They Shoot Tigers, Don't They?: Path and Counterpoint in *The Long Goodbye*." *A Companion to Narrative Theory*, edited by James Phelan and Peter J. Rabinowitz, Wiley-Blackwell, 2005, pp. 181–91.

Richardson, Brian. *Unnatural Narrative: Theory, History, and Practice*. The Ohio State UP, 2015.

———. "Unnatural Stories and Sequences." *Poetics of Unnatural Narrative*, edited by Jan Alber et al., The Ohio State UP, 2013, pp. 16–30.

———. "Unusual and Unnatural Narrative Sequences." *Narrative Sequence in Contemporary Narratology*, edited by Raphaël Baroni and Françoise Revaz, The Ohio State UP, 2016, pp. 163–75.

Ricœur, Paul. *Time and Narrative—Vol. 1*. 1983. Translated by Kathleen Blamey and David Pellauer, U of Chicago P, 1984.

Rosset, François. "Tempêtes opportunes et dragons véritables: Les voyages imaginaires." *Souvenirs du futur*, edited by Marc Atallah et al., Presses polytechniques et universitaires romandes, 2013, pp. 40–54.

Saint-Ogan, Alain. *Zig et Puce au XXIe siècle*. Hachette, 1935.

Shklovsky, Victor. *Theory of Prose*. Translated by Benjamin Sher, Dalkey Archive Press, 1990.

Terlaak Poot, Luke. "On Cliffhangers." *Narrative*, vol. 24, no. 1, 2016, pp. 50–67.

Thon, Jan-Noël. *Transmedial Narratology and Contemporary Media Culture.* U of Nebraska P, 2016.

Tomashevsky, Boris. "Thematics." 1925. *Russian Formalist Criticism: Four Essays,* Translated by Lee T. Lemon and Marion J. Reis, U of Nebraska P, 1965, pp. 61–98.

Trondheim, Lewis. *Bludzee.* 2009–2010, http://www.bludzee.com. Accessed 28 Dec. 2018.

Van Looy, Jan, and Jan Baetens, editors. *Close Reading New Media: Analyzing Electronic Literature.* Leuven UP, 2003.

Verne, Jules. *Vingt mille lieues sous les mers.* Hetzel, 1871.

Wells, H. G. *When the Sleeper Wakes. The Graphic,* 1898–1903.

CHAPTER 9

The Unnatural Conventions of the Interactive Gamebook

PAUL WAKE

INTRODUCTION

The gamebook, popularized by R. A. Montgomery and Edward Packard's Choose Your Own Adventure series in the US and Steve Jackson and Ian Livingstone's Fighting Fantasy series in the UK, was a significant literary genre of the 1970s and 1980s.[1] As the compound designation suggests, gamebooks combine story and game, their forking path narratives inviting the reader, usually addressed in the second person, to navigate their pages by selecting from a limited range of options in order to generate a single story from multiple possible options. In this, gamebooks join the corpus of what Christoph Bode describes as "Future Narratives," their nodal structures allowing "the reader/player to enter situations that fork into different branches and to actually *experience* that 'what happens next' may well depend upon us" (Bode and Dietrich 1). In addition to their future-oriented structures, as games they require their readers to regulate their reading (play) according to a basic set of rules that will necessarily include the selection of lexia along with one or more of the following features: a "user's guide," "victory

---

1. I would like to thank my colleagues Matthew Carter and Sam Illingworth, and the very knowledgeable and supportive members of the members of the Fighting Fantasy Facebook group, for their generous comments on the history and structures of the print gamebook.

conditions" (implicit or explicit), iterative reading, character generation, dice rolling, basic computation, code breaking, annotation, map making, and inventory management.

So defined, the gamebook immediately invites a diagnosis of "unnaturalness" (see Alber et al., "Unnatural Narratives" and "What Really"). Such a diagnosis might be made in relation to a number of definitions of unnatural narrative, including Jan Alber's emphasis on the presence of "nonactualizable elements" (*Unnatural Narrative* 3), namely "physically, logically, and inhumanly impossible scenarios and events" (*Unnatural Narrative* 14); Brian Richardson's focus on antimimetic elements that "violate the parameters of traditional realism" (Alber et al., "Unnatural Narratives" 115); and Stefan Iversen's connection of the unnatural with "clashes between the rules governing a storyworld and scenarios or events producing or taking place inside this storyworld" (Alber et al., "What Really" 103).

Through its reading of gamebooks, this chapter sets out to extend our understanding of the category of the "unnatural" in two ways. First, the addition of the gamebook genre to the "unnatural canon" (if such a term is permissible) brings attention to a significant genre that has to date been the subject of relatively little critical discussion. Second, this chapter challenges the stability of the "unnatural" as a category by defining the gamebook as a form of writing that is predicated on the dynamic relation that pertains between "natural" and "unnatural" writing—or, more specifically, as a genre that relies on the rapid habituation of readers to otherwise unnatural literary practices. In this I am responding to debates about "conventionalization" and "naturalization," locating conventionalization as function of genre (Fludernik, "How Natural" 367) and extending Alber et al.'s suggestion that while literary forms and techniques "become conventionalized over time"—in this case "you" narratives—this "does not necessarily mean that they have become *naturalized*" ("Unnatural Narratives" 131). To this end, the chapter begins with an account of the gamebook's origins, outlining the ways in which the genre might benefit from an "unnatural" analysis through a reading of Edward Packard's *The Cave of Time* (1979). With the gamebook's "unnatural" history established, the chapter turns to Steve Jackson's Fighting Fantasy gamebook *Creature of Havoc* (1986) in an exploration of the ways in which gamebooks, despite functioning through the rapid conventionalization of their apparently unnatural narrative forms, rely on the unnatural "as unnatural" in order to achieve a necessary move from empathetic to identificatory reading.

THE GAMEBOOK: A HISTORY

A history of the gamebook might well begin with Jorge Luis Borges's short story "The Garden of Forking Paths," published in 1941. Though conventional in form, Borges's story explores the foundations of the genre in its description of Ts'ui Pên's fictional novel, *The Garden of Forking Paths,* a work that is both "book" and "maze" (50) and that is made up of "diverse futures, diverse times which themselves also proliferate and fork" (51). Julio Cortázar's *Rayuela* (1963; *Hopscotch* [1966]) is another key text in the history of the genre. Described as a "proto-" or "paper" hypertext (Kacandes 200), Cortázar's novel gestures toward the gamebook's forking path form in its "Author's Note":

> This book consists of many books, but two books above all. The reader is invited to choose between these two possibilities: The first can be read in a normal fashion and it ends with chapter 56. . . . The second can be read by beginning with chapter 73 and then following the sequence indicated at the end of each chapter. (vii)

While Cortázar's novel offers only a single choice—which of the two story paths to follow—it remains significant in the history of the gamebook, unsettling the notion of a single author-determined reading path and prefiguring two of the genre's key features in its inclusion of numbered lexia and a user's guide in the form of the "Author's Note." Another early exponent of interactive fiction in print, again an author associated with literary experiment, was John Sladek, whose "Alien Territory" appeared in Michael Moorcock's *New Worlds* magazine in 1969 (the same year saw the publication of B. S. Johnson's "book-in-a-box" *The Unfortunates*).[2] Prefaced by a user's guide entitled "HOW TO READ THIS STORY" and constructed of thirty-six lexia connected by arrows across its horizontal and vertical axes, Sladek's short story provides a clear antecedent to the gamebook (lacking just the possibility of multiple endpoints). It does, however, differ radically in terms of effect. Where the gamebook's "unnatural" mechanics typically function to generate immersive identificatory reading, Sladek's story of war and the media uses a deliberately alienating layout that is, as Rob Latham puts it, "highly rationalized and oddly

---

2. John Sladek's "The Nose: A Programmed Book," composed 1968–70, but not published until 2001, is another example of the experimental hypertext fiction that comes with a user's guide: "How to Read the Programmed Book."

playful, regimented and insane" in order to effect a "ludic subversion of technocratic ideology" (289).

Alongside the literary experimentation of writers such as Borges, Cortázar, Johnson, and Sladek, clear forerunners of the gamebook can be found in texts written for the mass market. Norman A. Crowder's *The Arithmetic of Computers* (1958), the first volume of Doubleday's long-running TutorText series (1958–1972), provides what is perhaps the first example of the form in practice. The book, an introduction to mathematics for computers that offers a reading experience akin to a multiple-choice examination, is significant for the way in which it tests the limits of the technology of the book as an interactive device.[3] E. W. Hildick's children's story *Lucky Les: The Adventures of a Cat of Five Tales* (1967) is perhaps the earliest example of interactive fiction written for the mass market. Hildick's book, which charts the life of "the world's luckiest cat" (1), is structured around a forking path narrative, with five of its fifteen chapters concluding with the refrain, "READER, PLEASE YOURSELF" (5) and two possible directions in which to take the story. Hildick's book offers five discrete endings (which Hildick calls "tales") and a total of ten distinct reading paths. Here, though, the effect of the narrative, which is given in the third rather than the second person, is one of engagement rather than the immersion, or better still reader-character identification, associated with gamebooks proper.

The gamebook reached the mass market with the publication of Edward Packard's *Sugarcane Island* in 1976, the first of the Adventures of You series. Packard and Bell would later launch the better-known Choose Your Own Adventure series, the first volume of which was Packard's *The Cave of Time* (1979), and between 1979 and 1998, Bantam would release 184 books in a series that was published in thirty-eight languages and would reach "an in-print tally of more than 250 million copies" (Lodge), placing them in the top five best-selling book series of all time. In the UK, the genre was established by Steve Jackson and Ian Livingstone's Fighting Fantasy series (1982–1996), which ran to fifty-nine books with titles translated into twenty-two languages and selling an estimated seventeen million copies worldwide. In Jackson and Livingstone's series, the forking path structure and second-person address employed by the Choose Your Own Adventure books was married with a basic game mechanic that required readers to randomly generate their character's key attributes (Luck, Stamina, and Skill) and to refer to these values throughout their reading of the text (largely in managing dice-based combat with the storyworld's other inhabitants). More significant, perhaps, the Fighting Fantasy books included what might be termed "victory conditions" by which success-

---

3. Read in its now-digitized form, this element of the reading experience is lost.

ful reading might be judged.[4] In this respect, the series represents a key phase in the evolution of the gamebook, establishing the move from interactive fiction to a blend of storytelling and goal-oriented gameplay. Properly speaking, then, the books of the Fighting Fantasy series, which were conceived as an introduction to role-playing games such as Gary Gygax's *Dungeons & Dragons* (Green, *YOU* 15), are "adventure gamebooks," a term that identifies them as a subgenre of gamebook, indicating their deployment of more complex game mechanics and a correspondingly greater emphasis on reader-character identification.

While the gamebook has its antecedents in both experimental and mass-market literature, the genre must also be located in the history of digital narrative and video games whose development was near contemporaneous and far longer lived. For Anastasia Salter, the gamebook belongs to the "predigital roots of interactive narrative" (11), a claim that helpfully indicates the gamebook's connection to print media, if perhaps oversimplifying what might be better seen as a parallel development of two forms in which influence was exerted in both directions. Notably, Will Crowther and Don Wood's *Adventure* (a text-based computer game set in a "colossal cave") appeared in 1975–76, one year earlier than *Sugarcane Island,* and seven years earlier than Jackson and Livingstone's first "dungeon crawl" gamebook, *The Warlock of Firetop Mountain* (1982). Ultimately, the demise of the print gamebook can be connected to the limitations of the print "platform," which, as the analysis that follows suggests, required an "unnatural" reconfiguration of the technology of the book. The current revival of gamebooks in digital formats perhaps goes some way to confirming the popular assumption that gamebooks were somehow out of step with their print technology while revealing those elements that cannot be readily translated to the digital medium.[5] As Matt Youngmark tells his reader in the preface to the eBook edition of his *Time Travel Dinosaur* (2015): "If you discover you've made a terrible mistake, you can use your device's 'back' button to retrace your steps. . . . Is this considered cheating? Well, If you were reading the paperback version we assume you'd have your finger stuck in the last page anyway" (Location 16 of 3680).

---

4. Victory conditions in gamebooks may be explicit—for example, in *The Warlock of Firetop Mountain,* the "perilous quest" (Jackson and Livingstone 20) is to locate the warlock's treasure—but in many cases, they rely on the reader's own interpretation of what constitutes a successful reading. In Carole Carreck's *Star Rider* (1985), for example, the reader is informed, "You yourself will be the judge of the winning solution" (5).

5. See, for example, Tin Man Games (http://tinmangames.com.au/blog/), which has digitized a number of the original Fighting Fantasy books. The Fighting Fantasy series were reprinted by Scholastic UK in 2017, confirmation, perhaps, of the argument put forward by David Sax in his book *Revenge of Analog: Real Things and Why They Matter* (2016).

Despite the gamebook's massive, if short-lived, popularity (in the UK the Fighting Fantasy books topped the *Sunday Times* best-seller lists), the genre has received relatively little critical attention, with what commentary there is largely taking place in the footnotes of discussions of second-person narrative, hypertext fiction, interactive fiction (IF), children's literature, and digital gaming. Setting aside the suggestion of academic snobbery (Costikyan 8), the genre's relative invisibility within criticism might be attributed to its situation "in between" realist fiction and digital gaming. The gamebook is neither entirely literary nor entirely game, neither experimental nor mimetic literature. Of the numerous gaps into which the gamebook might be said to fall, it is that between the experimental and the mimetic that is my focus, and it is in considering the genre in this way that approaches associated with "unnatural" narratology are most helpful.

THE UNNATURAL GAMEBOOK

The gamebook manifests "unnatural" qualities in all three of the categories set out by Jan Alber, Stefan Iversen, Henrik Skov Nielsen, and Brian Richardson in their seminal article "Unnatural Narratives, Unnatural Narratology: Beyond Mimetic Models" (2010), namely "unnatural storyworlds," "unnatural minds," and "unnatural acts of narration" (116). The brief analysis of Packard's *The Cave of Time* that follows situates the gamebook in relation to these three categories, while indicating what is at stake in a genre that employs an "unnatural" narrative mode in order to generate an identificatory reading experience in which readers identify as characters within the story world.

Unnatural Storyworlds: The Cave of Time

In Packard's *The Cave of Time*, the reader, addressed in the second person, assumes the character of a young boy hiking alone through Snake Canyon in 1982. On entering the eponymous "cave of time," the reader-character is sent on a series of adventures through time and space. As some readers will discover, the cave is "a crack in the universe—a place outside space-time" [89][6] and an entrance to an unnatural story world in which "physical or logical

---

6. References to individual lexia within individual gamebooks, which often do not have page numbers, are given in square brackets.

impossibilities that concern the represented world's temporal or spatial organization" (Alber et al., "Unnatural Narratives" 116) abound.

In the many stories that follow, the reader dies in a world "several billion years in the past," prior to the release of oxygen into the atmosphere [101]; rides a woolly mammoth in the Ice Age [29]; helps build the Great Wall of China [39]; stands on the deck of the *Titanic* on April 15, 1912 [33]; experiences the horrors of the Blitz in 1940s London [86]; and witnesses the dying of the sun in "the year 2,000—plus about four billion years" [80]. While peculiar in many ways, these time- and space-bending narratives are unnatural only at the level of their subject matter. Given the familiarity of time travel in fiction, a genre popularized by H. G. Wells's *The Time Machine* (1895) and arguably one of the most conventional of unnatural narratives, these stories perhaps fall without a definition of the unnatural on the basis of their subject matter alone (see Alber, "Unnatural Narrative"). In fact, as David Wittenberg suggests, "literature itself might be viewed as a subtype of time travel, rather than the other way around, and time traveling might be considered a fundamental condition of storytelling itself, even its very essence" (1).

The "naturalized" status of time travel notwithstanding, there are a number of points at which Packard's narrative poses a more radical challenge to "natural" notions of time. In one of the book's forty endings, the reader-character writes what is presumably the book she is reading: "Years later, though, you write a book about your adventures in the Cave of Time" [81]. This ending, which would be a conventional "self-begetting story" in a first- or third-person narrative, is unsettling when offered as a conclusion to a second-person story in which the reader, identified throughout with the protagonist, is momentarily divided by this impossible proleptic prophesy. Without labeling the narrator "omniscient," an act that would neglect the narrative's vertical address, it is impossible to account for the possession of such knowledge. Such moments of impossible witnessing recall Alber's "Impossible Storyworlds—and What to Do with Them," in which he outlines "a cognitive model that describes ways in which readers can make sense of unnatural scenarios" (79). Among the numerous unnatural scenarios that Alber considers is one, fairly common in first-person literature, in which the reader encounters "a character-narrator who knows significantly more than he could if he were a 'normal' human being" (90). Alber's suggestion is a reading strategy that blends existing frames of knowledge:

> In order to come to terms with this unnatural scenario, readers have to move beyond real-world possibilities and combine their understanding of the real-world limitations of first-person narrators with the knowledge of an

omniscient narrator. As Rüdiger Heinze (2008: 293) suggests, one can then explain this impossible scenario in terms of our wish to transcend ourselves, to be in an authorial position and to know more than we can. ("Impossible" 90–91)

This is of course a practice common to the reading of fictional narrative of all genres, as Jonathan Culler tells us in *Structuralist Poetics*:

> What we speak of as conventions of a genre or an *écriture* are essentially possibilities of meaning, ways of naturalizing the text and giving it a place in the world which our culture defines. To assimilate or interpret something is to bring it within the modes of order which culture makes available, and this is usually done by talking about it in a mode of discourse which a culture takes as natural. (161)

A more profound challenge to the narrative's mimetic properties, one that cannot be naturalized by recourse to generic convention, and that takes on added significance when rendered in the second person, comes in the nine accounts of the reader-character's death included in *The Cave of Time* ([44], [53], [63], [74], [78], [84], [91], [99], [101]). Here the unnaturalness of the relation of reader and character demanded by the specifics of the gamebook's "you" comes into full focus. It is neither "empathetic," that is, "a vicarious, spontaneous *sharing* of affect" (Keen 208; emphasis added) nor immersive, where "the player becomes emotionally as well as intellectually absorbed in the game world" (Mäyrä 109). Rather, it is a relation of one-to-one identification. The most extended, and most obviously unnatural, accounts of the character's death in *The Cave of Time* come during an adventure to the Ice Age in which "you," the reader, ride a woolly mammoth as it is driven over a cliff:

> You hold tightly to tufts of wool, hoping the mammoth will slow down enough so you can safely slide off. But suddenly it pitches forward, making a terrible bellowing. In an instant you realize you are falling through space. You cry out helplessly as you lose your grip, falling faster and faster.
>
> Thousands of years later when Dr. Careleton Frisbee, the famous paleontologist, finds your bones next to those of a wooly mammoth in the Red Creek excavation, he is amazed at how closely you resemble a twentieth-century human being.
>
> **The End** [53]

Any identification with the "you" of the story at this point is radically undermined by a passage that situates the reader in two "presents," divided by "thousands of years." Moreover, the reader is placed in the logically impossible position of witnessing her own death. In this case, as is generally the case in gamebooks, death marks a moment of narrative "failure." In other words, it is "game over" and the player is ejected from the storyworld, inaugurating a return to the book's beginning and, if play is resumed, a further, likely divergent, iteration of the story.

Unnatural Minds: From Zombie Cats to Second-Person People

As Alber et al. observe,

> Unnatural minds appear in many different narratives. The reader is typically cued to evoke a mind, but this process is obstructed, disfigured or in other ways challenged by identifiable and describable features of the narrative. Unnatural minds may appear on the level of the story (in the shape of a character), on the level of the narrative discourse (in the case of a heterodiegetic narrator), or both (in the case of a homodiegetic narrator). ("Unnatural Narratives" 120)

At the level of subject matter, gamebooks frequently, and in some cases very obviously, align their readers with minds that are unnatural. Examples of texts that "radically deconstruct the anthropomorphic narrator" (Alber et al., "Unnatural Narratives" 114)—and there are many—include Packard's *You Are a Shark* (1985), in which the reader occupies the bodies of various animals, including those of a pig, an octopus, and the eponymous shark; Sherwin Tjia's *You Are a Cat in the Zombie Apocalypse!* (2013), in which the reader-protagonist is feline and, in some readings, a zombie; and Jonathan Green's Fighting Fantasy gamebook *Night of the Necromancer* (2010), in which "you" are a vengeful ghost. However, in the majority of cases, the alignment of the reader with a nonhuman character is not, after all, what makes this form of narrative "unnatural." As Alber has remarked, "the speaking animal is an unnatural scenario that has already been naturalized, that is, turned into a cognitive category, presumably because it is frequently used in fables and animated cartoons. Further examples of unnaturalness that have already been naturalized are supernatural entities, omniscient narration, and reflector-mode narratives" ("Impossible" 94 n. 4).

While "nonhuman" minds are a key feature of the gamebook, it is the genre's consistent use of a present-tense second-person address that constructs minds that are more properly "unnatural." As the tag lines of the Choose Your Own Adventure books ("You are the hero of your own adventure") and the Fighting Fantasy books ("YOU are the hero!") indicate, gamebooks rely on a one-to-one correlation between reader and character. This level of identification requires the use of a "you" that is addressed "vertically" (Herman, *Story Logic* 352) to the reader while collapsing, as far as such a thing is possible, that vertical address onto a "horizontal" address to the character within the storyworld. In this the gamebook "you" is close to what Richardson terms the "autotelic," a form of second-person narrative defined by "the direct address to a 'you' that is at times the actual reader of the text and whose story is juxtaposed to and *can merge with* the characters of the fiction" (*Unnatural Voices* 30; emphasis added). While the kinds of autotelic narratives Richardson considers in *Unnatural Voices* take advantage of the disruptive aspect of this form of address—in his analysis, "the ever-shifting referent of the 'you' that is continuously addressed" is the "most compelling feature" (*Unnatural Voices* 31) of autotelic narrative—the gamebook's "you," while reliant on the interaction of actual and storyworlds, is characterized by its attempt to stabilize what is an inherently mobile narrative address. Richardson's "apostrophic address," which connects reader and character, might in the case of the gamebook be better imagined as an "apostrophic invitation," summoning the reader into the storyworld in a (temporary) reconfiguration of the space between reader and character. This form of address is a defining feature of a genre that relies on identification rather than empathy. While empathy, a function of difference ("I" empathize with "you"), might be readily accommodated by the projection of virtual and actual worlds onto horizontal and vertical axes, a narrative of identification requires the flattening of this two-dimensional model. Thus the identity of reader, narratee, and character are (temporarily and fallaciously) aligned in a manner that recalls the triple reference (author, narrator, character) of Philippe Lejeune's autobiographical pact. This, then, might be regarded as a defining "unnatural" feature of the gamebook genre.

Written almost exclusively in the second person, "one of the most 'nonnatural' or contrived types of narrative" (Fludernik, "Introduction" 290), the gamebook's "you" is akin to the "you" of advertising, directing its message to an audience that is multiple while capitalizing on the misrecognition of this address as one that is personal, offering, as Richardson puts it, "the illusion if identification" (*Unnatural Voices* 36). In the gamebook, this illusory identification is enabled through a lack of detail (detail that if included might promote empathy but would reduce the possibility of identification). The "you" of the reader-protagonist is one of many "places of indeterminacy" in which "it is impossible, on the basis of the sentences in the work, to say whether a certain object or objective situation has a certain attribute" (Ingarden 50) makes possible the identification with the "hero." As Irene Kacandes suggests, "the 'emptiness' of 'you' (potentially) allows all who hear it to feel addressed" (151). At the same time, this "emptiness" opens the texts to others; as Herman puts it, "we are eavesdroppers on the discourse that addresses us and beckoned by discourse addressed to others" ("Textual 'You'" 410).

The ambiguity of address introduced by the gamebook's prominent act of readerly interpellation promises one-to-one identification but at the same time indicates a level of chatter that cuts across the (vertical) conversation between the text and reader in the form of an uninvited second-level horizontal address taking place between a text's multiple actual readers. This sense that the "you" of these "thrilling fantasy adventures" is multiple was confirmed by a survey ("WHO ARE YOU?") conducted by *Warlock*, the official magazine of the Fighting Fantasy books. The answer, published in issue 6:

> You're almost all male, for a start. The Warlock gets quite a few letters from girls (maybe it's his charismatic personality!), but it's the fellas who like filling in questionnaires. Only 8 out of over 500 respondents were female.
>
> And nearly all of you are between 9 and 17 years old; although we had a reply from a man of 60, and the letters we receive least [sic] us to believe that we have quite a few readers who are too young to bother with questionnaires. (Jackson and Livingstone, "Fighting Fantasy Feedback" 46)

Gesturing toward a community of readers that is largely young and largely male, the *Warlock* survey makes clear that identification with the "you" of these narratives is not as neutral as the series might promise. While the gamebook "you" is characterized by "emptiness," this emptiness is inscribed with various markers of identity. Usually these markers are implicit (masculine-neutral, as in the examples above) and sometimes explicit, as is the case in *The Cave of Time,* where all readers, male or female, child or adult, are asked to imagine themselves as a young American boy living on the late twentieth century. The problematics of aligning character and reader in this way are clear. In line with second-person narratives more generally, the gamebook "you" involves, as Alber puts it, "impossible mind-reading abilities" (*Unnatural Narrative* 84) that, directed vertically to actual readers, become impossible projections. As one female reader of the Fighting Fantasy series wrote to the editors of *Warlock,* "Although my friend and I think your books are fantastic, we have one major complaint. All your adventurers are male!!!" (Jackson and Livingstone, "The Warlock's Quill" 14).[7]

Unnatural Acts of Narration: The Ergodic Book

This last category, which bears on narrative structure, directs attention to what is perhaps the gamebook's most immediately evident "unnatural" feature: namely, the "ergodic" (Aarseth 1) gamelike demands that they make of their readers.

At the most obvious level, gamebooks demand input from their readers in the form of the selection from a predetermined set of lexia. The reader of *The Cave of Time*, for example, must choose the best course of action when riding a startled mammoth: "*If you jump down on the wooly mammoth, turn to page 29. If you continue on foot, turn to page 30*" [19]. The effect of this process of selection is to generate a single reading path from a wide number of possibilities.[8] In this, gamebooks clearly diverge from the structure of conventional narrative, which "typically has a fairly straightforward story of a certain magnitude that follows an easily recognisable trajectory" (Richardson, "Unnatural Stories" 16). This said, these narratives differ from the kinds of experimental literature that are typically associated with the unnatural, of which Robert Coover's "The Babysitter" (1969) is a particularly helpful example (see Alber, *Unnatural Narrative*; Richardson, "Unnatural Stories"), in facilitating rather than "challenging" (Richardson, "Unnatural Stories" 16) the reader in the construction of story. In fact, the key significance of the choice in these texts lies in their function in aligning reader and character. Gamebook "life" is existential in the sense that existence, in the form of actions, precedes essence, albeit under radically circumscribed conditions of possibility. In this, choice, far more than the generation of numerical characteristics that precede the more complex of adventure gamebooks, plays the central role in the generation of an owned identity.

While the sense of ownership generated by choice contributes to the immersive properties of the gamebooks, it is a mechanism that clearly "violate[s] the conventions of natural narrative and, in particular, the model of narrative communication" (Alber et al., "Unnatural Narratives" 124). In

---

7. Puffin Books' six-book series Starlight Adventures (1985) was published under the same banner ("Adventure Gamebooks") as their Fighting Fantasy series but targeted a female readership. The first volume, Carole Carreck's *Star Rider*, a story of horse riding, promised "ambition, mystery and romance," beginning: "You, the reader, are the heroine of this story" (5).

8. There have been a numerous attempts to map the number of paths through interactive fictions. Mark Sample's website (www.samplereality.com) features a history of the many "Choose Your Own Adventure Visualisations" and a schematic of Packard's book: "*The Cave of Time* Choose Your Own Adventure Narrative Map."

their requirement that readers engage with roles traditionally attributed to the author (namely, determining plot), gamebooks situate their readers in multiple and mobile positions within classical narratology's usually static triumvirate of author-text-reader. This is an inevitable outcome of the gamebook's hybrid form as story and game, and while I would wish to resist Greg Costikyan's suggestion that games and stories "are, in a sense, opposites" (6), the gamebook, which requires its reader-player to function as both "game executor" and "game player" (Deterding 34), radically undermines familiar models of narrative communication by foregrounding both the construction and interpretation of story. In effect the gamebook, which generally includes a brief user's guide, instructs its reader to adopt a *"Do it yourself"* (Alber, "Unnatural Narratology" 454) strategy in order to naturalize a text that otherwise "violates the principle of non-contradiction" (Alber, "Unnatural Narratology" 454). In this, authors of gamebooks might appear to cede control to the reader, though the reality is that "obedient" readers follow one of many preconceived narratives bound within a single print volume. Ultimately, then, readers of gamebooks assume the function not of authors but of bookbinders faced with poorly paginated manuscripts.

To the injunction to "Do it yourself," gamebooks add, "Do it again": "The best part is that you can keep reading and rereading until you've had not *one*, but *many* incredibly daring experiences!" (Packard, *The Cave of Time* back cover). This "do it again" is further complicated by a rereading practice that is peculiar to its print form, namely the possibility of pursuing multiple reading paths at any one time—as Ian Livingstone remarked in a 2015 interview, "Everyone cheats when they play *Fighting Fantasy*!" (Toh). *The Cave of Time* engages directly with this aspect of interactive fiction when its time-traveling reader-character finds herself in the year 3742, where, in a world where work is a thing of the past, the reader is installed in a fine bedroom:

> Your room contains a computer terminal that enables you to select any movie or other program you desire from over 10,000 possibilities. There are even films where *you* are the main character and *you* can make choices as to what will happen next in the story. Then, if you don't like the way the plot is working out, *you* can go back to an earlier point and make different choices from then on. [57]

As this passage suggests, while the gamebook's forking path narratives dismantle any illusion of narrative transparency, their game mechanics, which depend on the possibility of "failed readings," undermine received notions of narrative temporality by inviting an iterative reading experience in which the texts are read repeatedly in order to reach desired conclusions.

Readers as rereaders experience multiple competing stories in which familiar passages are encountered repeatedly and in new contexts. Responding to Marie-Laure Ryan's suggestion that "contradictory passages in the text are offered to the readers as material for creating their own stories" (671), Alice Bell argues that the application of Possible Worlds Theory to hypertext "ignore[s] the fundamental structure and form of the hypertext by attempting to eradicate its multilinearity" and "assumes that we dismiss our previous experience of a text as we encounter new material" (190). For Bell, "examples of narrative contradiction are therefore housed in a structure that is peculiar, if not unique, to hypertext, and the unnaturalness is facilitated by the structures afforded by the medium" (191). While Bell's and Ryan's readings of hypertext are not incompatible (Ryan's position does not preclude the possibility of a single text generating multiple possible worlds, just as Bell's does not preclude the generation of a single possible world), the emphasis on the medium itself is telling. If, as Bell suggests, simultaneous multiple worlds are characteristic of IF, then a more immediate example of this can be found in the paper-hypertext and gamebooks that precede the digital form, where the print medium precludes any illusion of the single-track text. Put simply, the gamebook's multiple lexia are necessarily bound as a single volume. Sladek's "Alien Territory" provides an extreme example, its thirty-six lexia appearing across a two-page spread, reminding the reader that the weight of the unread is, literally and figuratively, always at hand, capitalizing on the inexorable nature of the reader's progress toward the story's single outcome (located, in keeping with a traditional reading track, in the bottom right corner). In contrast to Sladek's experimental narrative, gamebooks proper make recourse to careful pagination in order to conceal the constrained ("bound") nature of the narrative choices on offer.

CONCLUSION: *CREATURE OF HAVOC*—THE "CONVENTIONALIZED" AND THE "UNNATURAL" UNNATURAL

While a pathology of the gamebook's unnatural symptoms such as the above might be helpful in accounting for its narrative strategies, any attendant diagnosis of the genre as unnatural should be made with caution. Indeed, the genre might be said to complicate decisions about what counts as "unnatural." Such complications arise from the fact that gamebooks, while radically divergent from traditional models of narrative communication, function precisely because of the rapidity by which their demands on the reader become conventionalized. This notwithstanding, as narratives that invite the translation of an apostrophic "you" (directed to the reader) into an identificatory "I" (constructed by the reader), a move demanding rapid conventionalization, as games they rely on their unnatural structures to generate a connection between reader-player and reader-as-character. The level of success and the rapidity of this process of conventionalization, and the seemingly paradoxical retention of the unnatural, is well illustrated by Steve Jackson's *Creature of Havoc* (1986), the twenty-fourth gamebook in the Fighting Fantasy series.

In *Creature of Havoc*, "the most unusual Fighting Fantasy adventure yet" (back cover), the reader takes the part of a violent creature, "a creature of instinct, ruled by hunger and rage. It is unable to speak and the speech of others is incomprehensible. It has a taste for fighting and for the flesh of other creatures" (1). The creature begins the narrative out of control and, in contradistinction to the other books of the series, with no discernible motive. As the reader is informed by the book's prefatory user's guide: "During the course of the adventure, it may be possible for you to begin to control your bestial nature; it may be possible for you to find out more about yourself; it may even be possible for you to learn your destiny and charge your aimless existence with meaning and purpose" (1). What follows is a gamebook in which choice and motive are initially suspended. Playing with the reader's expectations, and as if to underscore the absence of agency, *Creature of Havoc* opens with an apparently standard set of choices:

> The wounded Dwarf you have found is evidently in need of help. Will you:
> Show him you mean no harm? Turn to **93**
> Try to talk to him? Turn to **364**
> Bring your foot down heavily on his neck? Turn to **185** [1]

Regardless of the reader's selection, the result is the same. The dwarf is killed: "Although you wished to help the Dwarf, you have helped him only to an early grave" [93]. At this point, the reader is again offered three options and, again, regardless of the choice made, the creature will rifle the dwarf's body and steal his possessions: "Instead of responding to your wishes, you find that your body has other ideas" [218]. To readers familiar with the genre, the withholding of reader agency, a denial of the gamebook's now-conventionalized mechanism, renders *Creature of Havoc* once again unnatural. The estranging effect is, of course, deliberate: "You are looking down *with mixed feelings* at the lifeless form of the dwarf" [185], "the incident has left you *feeling very strange*" [93], and "your *thoughts are confused*" [364; emphasis added in all three quotes].

In effect, *Creature of Havoc* resembles in its opening passages the traditionally natural form of classic mimetic fiction. This move toward mimetic fiction is clear from the novel's opening section. Where other Fighting Fantasy books set the scene in a single-page "history," *Creature of Havoc* begins with nineteen pages of third-person narrative, the "Tales of Trolltooth Pass." The book then withholds agency from the reader-protagonist for a minimum of thirteen lexia, and it is entirely possible, given the random nature of choice in the book's early sections ("Roll one die. If you roll 1, 2 or 3, turn to **308**. If you roll 4, 5 or 6, turn to **148**" [399]), for the reader to reach one of four possible ("failed") endings without having made a single meaningful decision. With choice removed, *Creature of Havoc* restores narrative control to its "proper" (now improper) location: the author. The emergent tension between reader and author recalls Costikyan's observation that "Divergence from a story's path is likely to make for a less satisfying story; restricting a player's freedom of action is likely to make for a less satisfying game" (6). This is a tension that Jackson exploits, with reader and character "enjoying" a similar lack of control until the accidental discovery of the "vapour of reason." Similarly, the text works to confound the reader's sense of language, replacing direct speech with lines of gibberish—"Jib mar flfbsf defr pmo myorf st" [382]—that are later revealed as a meaningful language system that can be decoded once the creature locates the "vapour of tongues." Thus, briefly, as an animal in *Creature of Havoc*, humans are encountered as "animals that speak like animals" (see Alber, "Impossible" 93–94). Or, more properly, the "unnaturalness" of language itself is encountered in and of itself.

The significance of *Creature of Havoc* lies in part in its confirmation of the conventionalization of the adventure gamebook and in part in its exposure of the processes of familiarization that are always at play in literary narratives. In this, Jackson's gamebook might be seen as an example of the rapid habituation of a genre that became so familiar to readers that after just four years it could sustain such effective formal subversion.

Having established the gamebook's need for the rapid conventionalization, it remains the case that in order to effect a move from immersive reading to a reading of identification, an inherently unnatural relationship, gamebooks continue to rely on the unnaturalness of their autotelic form, a fact that is evident not in the reader's initiation into the storyworld but at the point of their ejection from that world. This is nowhere better seen than in the gamebook's depiction of death, an area already touched on earlier under the heading "Unnatural Storyworlds." For the reader of the gamebook, death, the most unlikely of iterative experiences, is encountered repeatedly and in many forms. The reader of *Creature of Havoc*, for example, is variously guillotined [10] [175], shot [14] [260], speared [36] [99] [413], crushed [47] [179], drowned [60] [68] [71] [83] [94] [418], eaten [286] [336] [439], suffocated [108], starved [109], stabbed [135], poisoned [317], smashed into the side of a cliff [338], roasted [339], harvested for organs [35] [229], and killed by zombies [150] [194] [321], a Blackmouth Floortrap [30] [80] [445], Toadmen [287], a Devil's Locks [345], frenzied legionaries [305], and Tree Spirits [413].

In one of these many ends, to give a single example, the creature is decapitated: "You are too tired and weak to resist as rough hands shove your neck through the nearby guillotine. This foraging expedition has been most successful. The crew of the *Galleykeep* will have a hearty meal tonight" [175]. To witness your own beheading, and to remain alert to the fact that your future is to be eaten, is of course impossible. Death, which Heidegger describes as "*Dasein's ownmost possibility*" (303), as "*the possibility of the impossibility of any existence at all*" (307), cannot be realized within our own experience. As the ejection of the reader at the point of these accounts of the creature's death might suggest, death is "*non-relational*" (Heidegger 303): "The dying of Others is not something which we experience in a genuine sense; at most we are always just 'there alongside'" (Heidegger 282). The gamebook's unnatural narratives of the death thus position the reader in two distinct locations, reasserting the distinction between the world of the reader and that of the story. It is at these points that the reader's identification with narratee and character in the gamebook's storyworld is radically undermined: The unnatural *as unnatural* returns. Death in the gamebook, then, makes visible the conventions by which it achieves the "unnatural" identification of reader, narratee, and character, and, as death confirms the authentic Being of Dasein in Heidegger's writing, it is the collapse of this fragile, always unnatural, identity that ultimately confirms and sustains that identity. Hence my claim that the gamebook, a conventionalized unnatural form, relies at once on the habituation of readers to its unnatural demands while capitalizing on a structure that is well described, in the words of David Herman, as an "ontological interference pattern produced by two or more interacting spatiotemporal frames" (*Story Logic* 345).

WORKS CITED

Aarseth, Espen J. *Cybertext: Perspectives on Ergodic Literature*. Johns Hopkins UP, 1997.

Alber, Jan. "Impossible Storyworlds—and What to Do with Them." *Storyworlds: A Journal of Narrative Studies*, vol. 1, 2009, pp. 79–96.

———. *Unnatural Narrative: Impossible Worlds in Fiction and Drama*. U of Nebraska P, 2016.

———. "Unnatural Narrative." *The Handbook of Narratology: Vol. II*, edited by Peter Hühn et al., De Gruyter, 2014, pp. 887–95.

———. "Unnatural Narratology: The Systematic Study of Anti-Mimeticism." *Literature Compass*, vol. 10, no. 5, 2013, pp. 449–60.

Alber, Jan, et al. "Unnatural Narratives, Unnatural Narratology: Beyond Mimetic Models." *Narrative*, vol. 18, no. 2, 2010, pp. 113–36.

———. "What Is Unnatural about Unnatural Narratology? A Response to Monika Fludernik." *Narrative*, vol. 20, no. 3, 2012, pp. 371–82.

———. "What Really Is Unnatural Narratology?" *Storyworlds*, vol. 5, 2013, pp. 101–18.

Bell, Alice. "Unnatural Narration in Hypertext Fiction." *A Poetics of Unnatural Narrative*, edited by Jan Alber et al., The Ohio State UP, 2013, pp. 185–98.

Bode, Christoph, and Rainer Dietrich. *Future Narratives: Theory, Poetics, and Media-Historical Moment*. De Gruyter, 2013.

Borges, Jorge Luis. *Labyrinths: Selected Stories and Other Writings*. Edited by Donald A. Yates and James E. Irby, Penguin Books, 2000.

Carreck, Carole. *Star Rider*. Puffin Books, 1985.

Cortázar, Julio. *Hopscotch*. Translated by Gregory Rabassa, The Harvill Press, 1998.

Costikyan, Greg. "Games, Storytelling, and Breaking the String." *Second Person: Role-Playing and Story in Games and Playable Media*, edited by Pat Harrigan and Noah Wardrip-Fruin, MIT P, 2007, pp. 5–13.

Crowder, Norman A. *The Arithmetic of Computers*, https://www.arithmeticofcomputers.co.uk/.

Culler, Jonathan. *Structuralist Poetics: Structuralism, Linguistics and the Study of Literature*. Routledge, 2002.

Deterding, Sebastian. "Living Room Wars: Remediation, Boardgames, and the Early History of Video Gaming." *Joystick Soldiers: The Politics of Play in Military Video Games*, edited by Nina B. Huntemann and Matthew Thomas Payne, Routledge, 2010, pp. 21–38.

Fludernik, Monika. "How Natural Is 'Unnatural Narratology'; or, What Is Unnatural about Unnatural Narratology?" *Narrative*, vol. 20, no. 3, 2012, pp. 357–70.

———. "Introduction: Second-Person Narrative and Related Issues." *Style*, vol. 28, no. 3, 1994, pp. 281–311.

Green, Jonathan. *Night of the Necromancer*. Wizard Books, 2010.

———. *YOU ARE THE HERO: A History of Fighting Fantasy Gamebooks*. Snow Books, 2014.

Heidegger, Martin. *Being and Time*. Translated by John Macquarrie and Edward Robinson, Oxford UP, 1962.

Herman, David. *Story Logic: Problems and Possibilities of Narrative*. U of Nebraska P, 2002.

———. "Textual 'You' and Double Deixis in Edna O'Brien's *A Pagan Place*." *Style*, vol. 28, no. 3, 1994, pp. 378–410.

Hildick, E. W. *Lucky Les: The Adventures of a Cat of Five Tales*. Anthony Blond, 1967.

Ingarden, Roman. *The Cognition of the Literary Work of Art*. Translated by Ruth Ann Crowley and Kenneth R. Olson, Northwestern UP, 1973.

Jackson, Steve. *Creature of Havoc*. Puffin Books, 1986.

Jackson, Steve, and Ian Livingstone. "Fighting Fantasy Feedback." *Warlock: The Fighting Fantasy Magazine*, vol. 6, Oct. 1985, p. 46.

———. *The Warlock of Firetop Mountain*. Puffin Books, 1982.

———. "The Warlock's Quill." *Warlock: The Fighting Fantasy Magazine,* vol. 7, Dec. 1985, pp. 14–15.

Johnson, B. S. *The Unfortunates.* Panther Books, 1969.

Kacandes, Irene. *Talk Fiction: Literature and the Talk Explosion.* U of Nebraska P, 2001.

Keen, Suzanne. "A Theory of Narrative Empathy." *Narrative,* vol. 14, no. 3, 2006, pp. 207–236.

Latham, Rob. "Assassination Weapons: The Visual Culture of New Wave Science Fiction." *Cutting Across Media: Appropriation Art, Interventionist Collage, and Copyright,* edited by Kembrew McLeod and Rudolf Kuenzli, Duke UP, 2011, pp. 276–89.

Lejeune, Philippe. *On Autobiography.* U of Minnesota P, 1988.

Lodge, Sally. "Chooseco Embarks on Its Own Adventure." *Publishers Weekly,* 18 Jan. 2007, web.archive.org/web/20071009094529/http://www.publishersweekly.com/article/CA6408126.html?.

Mäyrä, Frans. *An Introduction to Game Studies: Games in Culture.* Sage, 2008.

Packard, Edward. *The Cave of Time.* Bantam, 1979.

———. *You Are a Shark.* Bantam, 1985.

Richardson, Brian. "Unnatural Stories and Sequences." *A Poetics of Unnatural Narrative,* edited by Jan Alber et al., The Ohio State UP, 2013, pp. 16–30.

———. *Unnatural Voices: Extreme Narration in Modern and Contemporary Fiction.* The Ohio State UP, 2006.

Ryan, Marie-Laure. "From Parallel Universes to Possible Worlds: Ontological Pluralism in Physics, Narratology and Narrative." *Poetics Today,* vol. 27, no. 4, 2006, pp. 633–74.

Salter, Anastasia. *What Is Your Quest? From Adventure Games to Interactive Books.* U of Iowa P, 2014.

Sax, David. *The Revenge of Analog Things: Real Things and Why They Matter.* PublicAffairs, 2016.

Sladek, John. *Maps: The Uncollected John Sladek.* Cosmos Books, 2003.

Sample, Mark. "*The Cave of Time* Choose Your Own Adventure Narrative Map." *Samplereality,* 2008, www.samplereality.com/gmu/fall2008/343/wp-content/uploads/2008/09/caveoftime.jpg. Accessed 7 Dec. 2015.

———. "Choose Your Own Adventure Visualisations." *Samplereality,* 2009, www.samplereality.com/2009/11/11/a-history-of-choose-your-own-adventure-visualizations/. Accessed 7 Dec. 2015.

Tjia, Sherwin. *You Are a Cat in the Zombie Apocalypse!* Conundrum Press, 2013.

Toh, Terence. "For Fighting Fantasy Co-Creator Ian Livingstone, Life Is but a Game." *The Star Online,* 6 Jan. 2015, www.thestar.com.my/Lifestyle/Books/News/2015/01/06/For-Fighting-Fantasy-cocreator-Ian-Livingstone-life-is-but-a-game/. Accessed 16 Nov. 2015.

Wittenberg, David. *Time Travel: The Popular Philosophy of Narrative.* Fordham UP, 2013.

Youngmark, Matt. *Time Travel Dinosaur.* Chooseomatic Books, 2015.

AFTERWORD

JAN ALBER AND BRIAN RICHARDSON

MANY READERS will be interested in learning our reactions to the extensions, revisions, and challenges presented in the essays in this anthology, so we will articulate our responses to these points here. We hasten to note that despite any differences we express with the authors of the essays, we strongly believe in the importance of each one to the development and clarification of unnatural narrative theory. We are happy to include even those essays with which one or both of us has certain disagreements to promote continued dialogue and constructive debate. Also, if certain scholars disagree with our responses, we would like to learn more about their critiques and we would be more than happy to continue these discussions in another venue.

The first group of essays concentrates on ideologically charged texts and employs the conceptual resources of feminist, gender, and postcolonial theory. In her chapter, Catherine Romagnolo shows that the use of unnatural narrative parameters lends itself to a feminist agenda. She teases out additional possible connotations of the term *unnatural* and puts them to good use. For Romagnolo, there is no intrinsic connection between narrative strategies and ideological implications: One can always use the same technique to make a different point and a different technique to make the same point. At the same time, however, she argues that there is an element of "fit" between representational strategies that move beyond real-world possibilities and a feminist perspective that is interested in disobedient subjects who break, transcend, or disrupt the boundaries of naturalized gender and sexuality. Romagnolo's careful fusion of unnatural narratology and feminism is exemplary. She shows convincingly that the unnatural in the specific case of Angela Carter's novel *Nights at the Circus* (1984) (i.e., the narration that fuses several different consciousnesses as well as the impossibilities pertaining to time, space, and the characters) comes to represent a sense of freedom from conventional and naturalized ideological structures; the unnatural here denaturalizes historically restrictive notions of female voice and subjectivity. By means of this analysis, Romagnolo takes unnatural narratology an important step further.

Sylvie Patron provides an overview of the various positions within unnatural narratology and draws attention to neglected aspects of the theory. In particular, she provides a crucial qualification and clarification of unnatural narratology through her application of Gregory Currie's concept of "representational correspondence." The distinction Currie makes between aspects that are (normally) intended to be taken as verisimilar reproductions and those that are accepted conventions is an important one. It can help clarify precisely what is and what is not unnatural in specific representations; Richardson employs it in his essay in this volume, and it can be expected to be regularly utilized in the future. Patron also raises the very important question of a text's resistance to naturalizing strategies within the narrative itself. When, at the end of *The Cabinet of Dr. Caligari* (1920), the audience is presented with images that reveal that the events of the film were merely the delusions of an individual in an insane asylum, we may well object that the naturalization is inadequate to encompass the extent of the expressionist storyworld presented up to that point. If Kafka's "Die Verwandlung" (1915) ended with an additional sentence stating, "And then, Gregor woke up and went to work," we would likewise be correct in feeling that the unnaturalness of the storyworld is not entirely explained by or contained within the introjection of the dream scenario frame. Patron astutely raises this most important question and provides an answer that can be further discussed and extended.

In her essay, Patron looks at Wajdi Mouawad's novel *Anima* (2012) from the perspective of Henrik Skov Nielsen's "unnaturalizing" reading strategy. Perhaps, as in the case of Nielsen, more could be said about the question of what specific readerly response an "unnaturalizing" reading strategy entails. For his part, Nielsen argues that such an approach allows the reader to construct impossible situations "as authoritative, reliable or matter-of-fact renderings of the fictional universe." In addition, "an unnaturalizing reading is an interpretational choice that, unlike naturalizing readings, does not assume that real world conditions and limitations have to apply to all fictional narratives when it comes to logic, physics, time, enunciation, framing, etc." (241). One might wonder what else recipients do once they have identified the unnatural in the context of an "unnaturalizing" reading. Alber agrees with Patron's argument that his (i.e. Alber's) own reading strategy "subjectification" (in the context of which readers explain the seemingly unnatural as an internal state) reveals the ostensibly impossible to be something entirely natural, namely nothing but an element of somebody's interiority. But since all his other reading strategies accept the unnatural or impossible as an objective constituent of the represented world, Alber wonders what the difference between his navigational tools and so-called unnaturalizing reading strategies might be.

Dorothee Klein provides a reading of the novel *Benang* (1999) by the indigenous Australian author Kim Scott, a descendant of the Noongar. She urges unnatural narratologists to reflect upon their cultural backgrounds when they apply the term *unnatural*, and goes on to argue that cultural contexts, questions of cultural differences between authors and readers, and precisely what counts as impossible need to be more fully addressed. These issues are important both in their own right and because they provide the opportunity for the clarification of our own conceptions. Regarding interactions with non-Western cultural backgrounds, especially at all levels of interpretation, we follow Susan Stanford Friedman's call for a transnational narratology that leads to an interest in "both commonalities and differences across cultures" (5).

Though we formulate it differently, both of us agree that "physically impossible" means what is impossible in the actual world as established by empirical evidence and basic scientific inquiry. We do not view this as culturally relative. Like the principle of noncontradiction, the force of gravity holds around the globe, whether people know of it or not. A fully grown man cannot float in the air unaided in normal conditions in Southern Germany, or Northern California, or Western Australia. There is no empirical evidence to suggest that it has ever happened and no physical reason to think that it ever could. Though Newtonian and Einsteinian theories of gravity differ, concerning events at normal velocities well below the speed of light near the surface of the earth, there is no great discrepancy that would entail a significant reformulation of what is possible or impossible in the physical world.[1] For Alber, the only presupposition for the identification of the unnatural is that the recipient takes physical laws, logical principles, and standard human limitations of knowledge and ability for granted. He thus admits that he looks at narratives from the perspective of "a contemporary and neurotypical reader who has a rationalist-scientific and empirically minded worldview" (*Unnatural Narrative* 37–38). But Alber would also like to note that he firmly believes that representatives of this (commonsensical) world view exist in all cultures.

---

1. Similarly, recent cosmological hypotheses of multiple universes do not alter the fact that in this world, physical laws do not change and we are unable to access other possible worlds, if they exist (see Richardson, *Unnatural Narrative* 15–16).

We both question the extent of the binary division that Klein posits between Indigenous and non-Indigenous readers and their world views. Her essay suggests that when dealing with the first-person narrator's ability to fly and his telepathic qualities, non-Indigenous readers will experience a sense of defamiliarization, while indigenous readers won't.[2] Such a differentiation would make most sense in the case where a monocultural Western individual encounters traditional Indigenous Australian myths. But in the case of *Benang*, we find a much greater degree of hybridity that gestures outward and calls for a more analytically flexible framework. As Klein herself points out, the narrative and authorial audiences do not fully fit within such a binary formulation. We suspect that the idea of multiple authorial audiences might be helpful in articulating how this novel works. In short, we feel the full force of the unnatural cannot be contained within a simple opposition between Western rationalist and non-Western supernatural thinking.[3] Finally, both Alber and Richardson affirm their decidedly positive understanding of the terms *impossible* and *unnatural*. The unnatural is not deviant or perverse but a very special (and potentially mind-bending) literary phenomenon that calls for a distinctive kind of response. Hence, we fully agree with Klein's idea that "the unnatural is an effective means to incite readers to adopt a reading stance of deference and respect" (p. 64).

The next three essays examine a variety of texts as they explore questions of empathy, emotion, immersion, and reception. Christopher D. Kilgore looks at three graphic memoirs, Art Spiegelman's *Maus* (1986–91), Alison Bechdel's *Fun Home* (2006), and *Are You My Mother?* (2012). He demonstrates convincingly that although these texts are nonfictional narratives, they use unnatural techniques, in Richardson's definition. In addition, these graphic texts engage the full range of readerly participation and cultivate an unusual type of empathy between the reader and the autographic narrator and thereby add to our understanding of empathy in narrative. Kilgore's approach is particularly impressive because he branches out into new areas: The role of the unnatural in nonfictional narratives has hitherto been barely imagined as a possibility, except in a single essay by Stefan Iversen. Kilgore's observations concerning

---

2. To shed more light on this assumption, Alber is planning to carry out an empirical investigation to compare indigenous and non-indigenous readers concerning the question of how they process these two phenomena.

3. In this context, Richardson explores the ways in which Indigenous writers like Leslie Marmon Silko can validate traditional belief systems allegorically without having to commit entirely to the literal truth of their supernatural claims (*Unlikely Stories* 142–43). Salman Rushdie is especially adept at producing supernatural events in *Midnight's Children* (1981) that are subsequently revealed to have naturalistic causes, to be allegorical tropes made literal, or to be parodies of common narrative formulas (see Herman et al. 105–8).

the empathy-evoking potential of the unnatural inverts conventional assumptions even as it confirms Alber's claim that unnatural narratives are not different in kind from other narratives (*Unnatural Narrative* 28).[4] Alber also argues that we can only make sense of the unnatural by using our cognitive architecture and preexisting frames and scripts, that is, the protocols or templates that we also use to make sense of the real world. The unnatural urges us to create new frames (such as that of the speaking coin or the dead narrator) by recombining, extending, or otherwise altering preexisting cognitive parameters. But when we try to interpret the unnatural, we always deal with the question of what it has to say about us and the world we live in. Readers try to connect the unnatural to themselves, that is, to their existence as human beings and their experiences in the actual world. Kilgore's discussion of the reading of unnatural texts is impressive, and while his arguments for the similarities between fictional and nonfictional narrative practices are provocative and compelling, we both retain the belief in the importance of the distinction between the two. Events narrated in a graphic autobiography, as in more conventional works of nonfiction, can be confirmed or falsified by reference to external sources, while those in a novel, graphic or otherwise, can't be.

Dan Punday's essay is in some respects similar to Kilgore's: He also seeks to fuse empathy studies and unnatural narratology. But whereas Kilgore investigates the relationship between the reader and the narrator, Punday addresses the ways in which ontological metalepsis provides the emotional context of a narrative. He challenges the unnatural account of the estranging effects of metaleptic jumps, and illustrates the unlikely ways in which metalepsis can work to deepen our emotional attachment to the story. Along the lines of Kilgore's and Punday's interest in potential connections between empathy and the unnatural, Alber has recently argued that we deal with logical impossibilities in fictional narratives because they touch us emotionally (Alber, "Logical Contradictions"). More specifically, he believes that bodily reactions to logical contradictions serve as a kind of "protointerpretation": It is because logical contradictions elicit emotional responses—they may make us feel uneasy, confused, afraid, fearful, joyful, or pleased—that we build interpretations on the basis of the "experiential feel" (Caracciolo 55) they evoke in us. We both appreciate Punday's demonstration of the immersion that metalepsis can produce in the reader, contrary to what most earlier theorists have suggested.

Roy Sommer examines Walter Abish's novel *Alphabetical Africa* (1974) and argues that readerly reactions to unnatural narratives are not fundamentally

---

4. Alber follows Mark Turner, who points out that "the literary mind is not a separate kind of mind"; rather, "it is our mind" (v).

different from the ways in which readers approach mimetic fiction. Compared to most of the other contributors, Sommer is more critical of the unnatural project. For this reason, we will address his concerns at greater length. Since our responses differ and because he debates one of us by name, we will address his points separately.

Alber disagrees with a number of his claims. First, in contrast to Sommer, he does not think that unnatural narratology is "a theory of non-narrative and antinarrative elements." For Alber, narratives presuppose (1) a *discourse context* in which they represent (2) *worlds* that involve temporal and spatial parameters. These worlds are inhabited by (3) *characters* that undergo experiences that are connected to (4) *event sequences*. In addition, narratives involve (5) *a sense of moving through time,* and (6) the quality of "what it is like" to *experience* changes in the represented world takes center stage (see Alber, "Introduction"). Many unnatural narratives (such as, say, Philip Roth's *The Breast* [1972], Martin Amis's *Time's Arrow* [1991], or Mark Z. Danielewski's *House of Leaves* [2000]) fulfill all these criteria and thus qualify as prototypical narratives. At the same time, it is worth noting that unnatural narratives deconstruct narrative parameters such as the narrator, the character, time, or space. However, they typically only undo one of these parameters at a time, while the others usually remain untouched. This focus on one unnatural parameter at a time seems to suggest that if too many narrative parameters were deconstructed simultaneously, readers might potentially consider the degree of cognitive disorientation to be too high. In contrast to Sommer, Alber defines unnatural narratology as a narratology that systematically addresses the ways in which fictional narratives move beyond real-world frames and that then tries to make sense of these deviations.

Second, Sommer deals with Walter Abish's *Alphabetical Africa* (1974), but Alber does not consider this text to be an example of an unnatural narrative because it does not represent impossibilities. For him, the text rather qualifies as a playful postmodernist language game: Its fifty-two chapters list words that begin with a specific letter (and from his perspective, there is nothing unnatural about this). *Alphabetical Africa* is perhaps rather a minimally narrative text that moves toward the condition of poetry or music (like Samuel Beckett's "Ping" [1966]). Alber argues that it is difficult to make larger claims about unnatural narratology on the basis of such a text. Third, Sommer writes that readerly reactions to unnatural narratives are not fundamentally different from the ways in which readers approach mimetic fiction. In this context, Alber would highlight that unnatural narratives at least urge us to conduct seemingly impossible mapping operations to orient ourselves within storyworlds that refuse to be organized through real-world parameters only. In such cases, we are invited to blend preexisting frames and create what Mark Turner calls "impossible blend[s]" (60) to adequately reconstruct the unnatural elements of the storyworld. In this respect, the unnatural calls for a special kind of readerly response that differs from the ways in which we react to, say, novels like *Robinson Crusoe*.

Richardson admires both Sommer's work in general and his chapter in this volume; his reading of Abish's novel is a perspicacious one. He draws attention to the ways in which unnatural narratives can test the very boundaries of narrative and calls for an investigation into the act of reading such narratives. Concerning the question of what constitutes a narrative, Richardson affirms that the definition of *narrative* and the establishment of the degrees of narrativity are logically distinct and should not be conflated. Even though a philosophical novel like Proust's *Recherche* has a much lower degree of narrativity than does a thriller, it is no less a narrative. Most significantly, the status of a work's narrativity does not address the question of works that test the boundaries of narrative, like those of Beckett, Robbe-Grillet, Calvino, and many others: Such texts require a definition of narrative to determine just what they challenge and how far their challenge extends (see Richardson, *A Poetics of Plot* 13–36). It will not do to say that narratives that have low narrativity need not be taken into consideration since they are too far from the central narrative paradigm. Such a stance must look like an attempt to undergird past narratology's mimetic prejudice by removing unnatural narratives because they defy mimetic orders. But what then do we do with difficult texts? It is obviously the case that not all literary experiments are narratives, and Sommer may well have found one just on (or perhaps beyond) this boundary. Since the criteria of its degree of narrativity (which we all agree on) is logically irrelevant to its status as a narrative (which we agree is subject to dispute), we need to ask how this can be resolved.

In his analysis, Sommer provides some helpful hints as to how this might be done. He discusses the nonmimetic nature of the narrator, but this would seem to be a red herring: Theorists from Roland Barthes to Marie-Laure Ryan have shown that a narrator need not resemble a person (see Richardson, *Unnatural Narrative* 33–36). He is on much more solid ground when he discusses the fragmentary nature of the fictional world(s) and the limited and contradictory nature of the events. If the world is utterly inchoate, then we may not have a narrative. How do we determine that boundary? Definitions take this question on. Richardson has argued that narrative is a representation of causally related events; Gerald Prince, for his part, insists that "an object is a narrative if it is taken to be the logically consistent representation of at least two asynchronous events that do not presuppose or imply each other"

(19). By Richardson's definition, *Alphabetical Africa* is a narrative (albeit a very strange one); for Prince it is not. Investigating this point further would clarify other issues, such as how much deliberate internal contradiction a narrative can contain. We can easily discern a slippery slope coming into view: No one (I think) would deny that, despite its denarrated ending, John Fowles's *The French Lieutenant's Woman* (1969) is a narrative—and one with a high degree of narrativity at that. Many might pause before assenting to the narrative status of Robbe-Grillet's *Jealousy* (1957). Where would Sommer draw his line? At a larger level, how would he respond to the charge that he is not providing a theory of narrative, but merely a theory of mimetic narratives? Richardson remains genuinely puzzled as to what a non-narrative novel could possibly be, especially since this formulation seems to have to reject the standard definition of a novel as an extended fictional narrative in prose. Perhaps he shuns these definitions as well, and sticks instead to ideas of "prototypical novels"? In any case, Richardson and Alber both look forward to continued discussions and debates on these subjects in the future.

The next three essays bring unnatural narratology to new kinds of texts, narrative forms, and compositional strategies. Richardson's essay has several goals. It attempts to move deeper into literary history as it excavates significant unnatural works from different centuries and millennia. It also brings together unnatural works from a range of genres, high and low, as it examines antimimetic effects in characterization from films to cartoons to advertisements. It attempts to identify how specific authors move beyond conventional nonmimetic characters to create truly antimimetic figures. This essay also engages in a defense of important earlier work in character theory that was able to comprehend antimimetic figures. Finally, it attempts to open up the new field of performance to unnatural studies, discussing cases of antimimetic visual representations, including cases in which the verbal text is entirely mimetic though its performance is utterly unnatural. As always, Alber is impressed with the scope and richness of Richardson's work. The only possible catch is that he feels that Richardson might invoke too many categories in this chapter. Alber would limit his own analysis or discussion of unnatural characters to storyworld participants that display physical, logical, or human impossibilities (for examples, see Alber, *Unnatural Narrative* 104–48).

Raphaël Baroni helps clarify some of the conventions of the unnatural in comics and graphic novels. He argues that a variable *sjuzhet* should be considered as a natural quality of the medium because of the nonlinear organization of story elements, which are spread on a page and meant to be read in different orders. On the level of the *fabula*, he shows that many examples of time travel that we find in European comics until the 1980s are a mere extension of the motif of the "extraordinary journey," and therefore they do not engender time paradoxes, nor do they appear as completely unnatural to their readers. As Baroni points out, comics have always been designed in such a way that a strictly linear reading of a set of panels is neither desirable nor always possible. Various forms of metalepsis, frame breaking, and narrative progressions that would be impossible in nonfiction are also presented here, giving us a clearer sense of both narrative sequencing and some distinctive forms of the antimimetic in comics. The question of convention recurs in Baroni's discussion of time travel narratives in comics. We both appreciate Baroni's analyses of the historical progression of time travel in comics, but at some points we prefer to disagree. Richardson would affirm that insofar as time travel is presented as realistically possible, as it is in Wells's *The Time Machine* (1895), it is not unnatural. It is not antimimetic since it still attempts to mimetically justify the extraordinary events it recounts, and the laws of the world of our experience are not discernably transgressed. In this regard, traditional science fiction obeys a realistic canon of probability—unlike distinctively postmodern (and thereby unnatural) varieties. Alber disagrees with Baroni's argument that Shklovsky's defamiliarization should remain the decisive criterion of unnaturalness simply because the defamiliarizing effects described by Shklovsky cannot be upheld forever. From his perspective, time travel qualifies as a conventionalized instance of the unnatural (because in the real world, we cannot travel into the future or the past), while he is more skeptical regarding the unnaturalness of unfixed *sjuzhets*. We both differ with Baroni concerning the assessment of the compelling polytemporal progression performed by Dr. Manhattan in *Watchmen* (1986–87). Though it does not involve temporal contradictions, it seems quite unnatural to both of us. For Alber, it violates human possibility; for Richardson, a synoptic view of time is clearly antimimetic. Nevertheless, Baroni is very effective in demonstrating that the elements that constitute the unnatural vary from genre to genre, and that some sequences may not in fact be as unnatural as they seem.

Paul Wake's essay traces the many unnatural elements of the interactive gamebook, and persuasively suggests that the genre itself is inherently unnatural. His chapter follows two goals: First, he argues that the addition of the gamebook to the unnatural canon brings attention to an important genre that has to date been the subject of little critical discussion. Second, Wake challenges the stability of the "unnatural" as a category by defining the gamebook as a form of writing that is predicated on the dynamic relation between "natural" and "unnatural" forms of writing. We are convinced by his many examples and very interested by his speculations on the unnatural nature of the gamebook player. We are, like Wake, intrigued by what it means for a genre to have unnatural conventions. This puts the question of the conventional into stark relief. However, it may well be that the genre's unnatural features depend on the player/reader's awareness of the impossibility of such sequences in a traditional realistic verbal story: You cannot die several times, shift around from century to century, and replay the events of your life in a mimetic narrative. Insofar as these constraints are on our minds, the unnatural will also produce its effects in gamebooks. While Baroni teaches us to respect the differences between genres, Wake is showing us how interdependent they may be.

Many of these essays develop, extend, and modify the theory of unnatural narrative in a number of ways. Taken together, they considerably extend the scope and parameters of unnatural narrative theory by bringing it into hitherto unexplored arenas. This anthology presents new methodologies by fusing unnatural narratology with other approaches engaging with a number of different critical discourses. It also adds several new bodies of work to the corpus of unnatural narratives. The essays demonstrate the continuing utility of the unnatural paradigm, open up new areas of research, argue for extensions and revisions of the unnatural model, and frequently make important contributions to narrative theory itself.

WORKS CITED

Alber, Jan. "Introduction: The Ideological Ramifications of Narrative Strategies." *Storyworlds*, vol. 9, no. 1–2, 2017, pp. 3–25.

———. "Logical Contradictions, Possible-Worlds Theory, and the Embodied Mind." *Possible-Worlds Theory and Contemporary Narratology*, edited by Alice Bell and Marie-Laure Ryan, U of Nebraska P, forthcoming.

———. *Unnatural Narrative: Impossible Worlds in Fiction and Drama*. U of Nebraska P, 2016.

Caracciolo, Marco. *The Experientiality of Narrative: An Enactivist Approach*. De Gruyter, 2014.

Friedman, Susan Stanford. "Towards a Transnational Turn in Narrative Theory: Literary Narratives, Traveling Tropes, and the Case of Virginia Woolf and the Tagores." *Narrative*, vol. 19, no. 1, 2011, pp. 1–32.

Herman, David, et al. *Narrative Theory: Core Concepts and Critical Debates*. The Ohio State UP, 2012.

Iversen, Stefan. "'In Flaming Flames': Crises of Experientiality in Non-Fictional Narratives." *Unnatural Narratives, Unnatural Narratology*, edited by Jan Alber and Rüdiger Heinze, De Gruyter, 2011, pp. 89–103.

Nielsen, Henrik Skov. "The Unnatural in E. A. Poe's 'The Oval Portrait.'" *Beyond Classical Narration: Transmedial and Unnatural Challenges*, edited by Jan Alber and Per Krogh Hansen, De Gruyter, 2014, pp. 239–60.

Prince, Gerald. "Narrativehood, Narrativeness, Narrativity, Narratibility." *Theorizing Narrativity*, eds. John Pier and José Ángel García Landa. De Gruyter, 2008, 19–28.

Richardson, Brian. *A Poetics of Plot for the Twenty-First Century: Theorizing Unruly Narratives.* The Ohio State UP, 2019.

———. *Unlikely Stories: Causality and the Nature of Modern Narrative.* U of Delaware P, 1997.

———. *Unnatural Narrative: History, Theory, Practice.* The Ohio State UP, 2016.

Turner, Mark. *The Literary Mind.* Oxford UP, 1996.

LIST OF CONTRIBUTORS

JAN ALBER is a professor of English literature and cognitive studies and the head of the Department of English at RWTH Aachen University (Germany) as well as past president of the International Society for the Study of Narrative (ISSN). Alber is the author of *Narrating the Prison* (Cambria P, 2007) and *Unnatural Narrative: Impossible Worlds in Fiction and Drama* (U of Nebraska P, 2016). He received fellowships and research grants from the British Academy, the German Research Foundation, and the Humboldt Foundation. In 2013, the German Association of University Teachers of English awarded him the prize for the best *Habilitation* written between 2011 and 2013. From 2014 to 2016, Alber worked as a COFUND (Marie-Curie) Fellow at the Aarhus Institute of Advanced Studies (Denmark).

RAPHAËL BARONI is an associate professor at the University of Lausanne (Switzerland). He is the author of *La tension narrative* (Seuil, 2007), *L'oeuvre du temps* (Seuil, 2009), and *Les rouages de l'intrigue* (Slatkine, 2017). He has co-edited several collective books or journal issues, among them *Narrative Sequence in Contemporary Narratology* (The Ohio State UP, 2016). He is a member of the Group for the Study of Comics (GrEBD, http://wp.unil.ch/grebd/) and co-founder of the recently founded Network of French-Speaking Narratologists (RéNaF, https://wp.unil.ch/narratologie/). He is currently co-directing, in partnership with the EPFL, a research program funded by the Swiss National Science Foundation, which is called "Reconfiguring Comics in our Digital Era" (CRSII5_180359).

CHRISTOPHER D. KILGORE is the special programs coordinator for Teaching and Learning Innovation at the University of Tennessee. He has published on narrative theory, graphic narrative, and interdisciplinary writing instruction and support and has served as a service learning faculty fellow and sustainability faculty fellow at UTA. In his spare time, he runs an online serial fantasy narrative, *The Adasir Project* (www.adasir.com).

DOROTHEE KLEIN is a research assistant in the English Department at the University of Stuttgart (Germany). She studied English and history at the Universities of Freiburg and Melbourne and recently completed her PhD thesis, *The Poetics and Politics of Relationality in Contemporary Australian Aboriginal Fiction*. Her research interests include Aboriginal Australian literatures, Australian cultural studies, postcolonial theory, and narratology. She has published articles on Australian Aboriginal fiction and life writing in venues such as *Interventions: International Journal of Postcolonial Studies*.

SYLVIE PATRON is a lecturer and research supervisor (*maître de conférences habilitée à diriger des recherches*) at the Université Paris Diderot / Université de Paris and the vice-president of the International Society for the Study of Narrative. A specialist in the history and epistemology of literary theory, she is the author of three books in French and English and editor or co-editor of three volumes on narrative theory, including *Le narrateur. Introduction à la théorie narrative* (Armand Colin, 2009), reprinted as *Le narrateur: Un problème de théorie narrative* (Lambert-Lucas, 2016), *La mort du narrateur et autres essais* (Lambert-Lucas, 2015), translated as *The Death of the Narrator and Other Essays* (WVT, 2019), and the anthologies *Théorie, analyse, interprétation des récits / Theory, analysis, interpretation of narratives* (Lang, 2011) and *Introduction à la narratologie postclassique: Les nouvelles directions de la recherche sur le récit* (Presses universitaires du Septentrion, 2018).

DANIEL PUNDAY is a professor and the head of the Department of English at Mississippi State University. He is also past president of the International Society for the Study of Narrative (ISSN). He is the author of five books, the most recent of which is *Computing as Writing* (U of Minnesota P, 2015). His next book will be due out in the Theory and Interpretation of Narrative series at The Ohio State UP, called *Playing at Narratology: Digital Media as Narrative Theory*.

BRIAN RICHARDSON is a professor in the English Department of the University of Maryland, where he teaches modern and postmodern literature and narrative theory. He is the author or co-author of five books and editor of nine volumes on narrative theory, including *Unnatural Voices: Extreme Narration in Modern and Contemporary Fiction* (The Ohio State UP, 2006), *Unnatural Narrative: Theory, History, and Practice* (The Ohio State UP, 2015), *A Poetics of Plot for the Twenty-First Century: Theorizing Unruly Narratives* (The Ohio State UP, 2019), and the anthologies *Narrative Beginnings: Theories and Practices* (U of Nebraska P, 2009) and *A Poetics of Unnatural Narrative* (The Ohio State UP, 2013, co-edited with Jan Alber and Henrik Skov Nielsen). He has published articles on many aspects of narrative theory, including story, time, narration, character theory, and reader response theory. His website is www.english.umd.edu/englfac/BRichardson/index.html.

CATHERINE ROMAGNOLO is a professor of English and the chair of the Department of English at Lebanon Valley College. She is the author of *Opening Acts: Narrative Beginnings in Twentieth Century Feminist Fiction* (U of Nebraska P, 2015). Romagnolo has published multiple articles on narrative form and identity, including "Naturally Flawed?: Gender, Race, and the Unnatural in The Color Purple" (*Storyworlds*, 2016) and "Toward a Critical Race Narratology: Narrative Beginnings in Toni Morrison's Song of Solomon" in *Narrative, Race, and Ethnicity in the United States* (The Ohio State UP, 2017).

ROY SOMMER is a professor of English and the director of the Center for Graduate Studies at the University of Wuppertal (Germany). He is co-founder of the university's Center for Narrative Research and co-editor of DIEGESIS, an open access journal dedicated to cross-disciplinary narrative research. Sommer was awarded the prize for the best PhD dissertation submitted in 2001 at the University of Giessen (*Fictions of Migration*, WVT, 2001) and completed his postdoctoral thesis (*Habilitation*) there in 2005. He has received scholarships and research grants from the German Science Foundation, the Federal Ministry of Education and Research, and the Volkswagen Foundation. His research interests include fictional and factual storytelling, narrative theory, and the study of reading.

PAUL WAKE is a reader in English literature at Manchester Metropolitan University and a co-director of the Manchester Game Study Network. He is the author of *Conrad's Marlow: Narrative and Death in "Youth," Heart of Darkness, Lord Jim and Chance* (Manchester UP, 2007) and co-editor of *The Routledge Companion to Critical and Cultural Theory* (Routledge, 2013). He is one of the general editors of the Irwell Edition of the Works of Anthony Burgess and editor of Burgess's science fiction novel *Puma* (Manchester UP, 2018). His essays have appeared in *Archival Science, The Conradian, JNT: Journal of Narrative Theory, The Lion and the Unicorn, Narrative, Research in Learning Technology, Rethinking History,* and *Textual Practice*.

INDEX

300 (Miller), 43

Aarseth, Espen, 200
Abbott, H. Porter, 136n4
Aboriginal: audience, 59–60; culture, 54, 56, 62–63; dreaming stories, 56; fiction, 53, 60; life-writing, 62n9; storytelling, 55–56, 60
accuracy, 73, 74, 74n2, 75, 83, 91
Acker, Kathy, *Empire of the Senseless,* 93
addressee, 37, 44; virtual addressee, 44
adequacy, inadequacy, 76, 78, 79, 79n9, 92, 93
aesthetic experience, 117, 127
agency, 17
Alber, Jan, 1–11, 31n1, 31n2, 32, 32n4, 33, 33n5, 33n6, 34, 34n6, 34n7, 35, 35n8, 38n12, 38n13, 40n14, 40n15, 41n16, 42n20, 44, 48, 48n24, 49, 49n26, 50–54, 58, 61, 69–72, 80, 99, 101, 136n4, 140n6, 141, 165, 184, 190, 194–95, 197, 199, 201, 209–18
Alber et al., 14–18, 16n3, 21, 26
Alexander, Jacqui, 13
Alfau, Felipe, 138, 146, 150, 158
Ali, Muhammad, 155
"Alien Territory" (Sladek), 191, 202
"All You Zombies" (Heinlein), 143
Allbritton, David W., 136
Alphabetical Africa (Abish), 104–6, 110, 113, 115–33, 213–15
ambiguity, 69–71, 86, 89, 91, 94
ambivalence, 70, 88, 91, 93

Andreas, 175
Angels in America, Part One (Kushner), 141, 154n15
Anima (Mouawad), 31, 31n1, 33, 34, 35, 36n10, 37, 38, 39, 41, 43, 48n24, 49, 49n26, 51
animal narrators, 36n10, 42, 43, 44, 47, 48
animals, 33, 34, 46; social animals, 39
antimimetic form, 17, 26
antimimetic narrative elements, 6, 32, 72, 115, 116, 123, 128, 131. *See also* nonmimetic narrative elements
antinarrative, 116, 131
Antony and Cleopatra (Shakespeare), 152–53
Apple, 86
Aristophanes, 135, 152
Aristotle, 7–8, 135
Arithemetic of Computers (Crowder), 192, 194–96, 199–201
Artist, The (Hazanavicius), 43
As You Like It (Shakespeare), 152
Attempts on Her Life (Crimp), 139–41
"August 15, 1983" (Borges), 143
author, 49, 119, 120, 121, 125; author function, 119; authorship, 120; fictional, 45
authorial audiences, multiple, 212
authority, 21–23, 25–27
autobiography, 80, 81
autographic, autography, 69, 72–75, 77–80, 82, 85, 92, 94
autotelic narrative, 198, 204
avatar, 74n5, 75, 77, 78, 86

225

"Babysitter, The" (Coover), 112, 160
Badiou-Monferran, Claire, 31n1, 50
Baetens, Jan, 172, 184
Barjavel, René, 175
Baroni, Raphael, 166, 169, 178, 216
Barthes, Roland, 135
Basement, The (Pinter), 160
Bazin, André, 181
Bechdel, Alison, *Are You My Mother?*, 69, 80, 85–95; *Dykes to Watch Out for*, 87; *Fun Home*, 69, 80–85, 86, 87, 91, 93
Beckett, Samuel, 32, 79n9, 138, 141
Bell, Alice, 99, 101, 202
Benang (Scott), 53n2, 54, 56–60, 61, 62–64
Benhabib, Seyla, 13
Berlatsky, Eric, 156
Bernaerts, Lars, 33n5, 50
Bertens, Hans, 109
biography, 75
blending, 73n4
Boehm, Beth, 14, 18, 21, 26n8
Boillat, Alain, 169, 178
Bolter, Jay David, 184
Booth, Stephen, 155
Bortolussi, Maria, 158–59
Boule, Pierre, 177
braiding, 94, 166–74, 179–83
Bray, Joe, 50
Brecht, Bertolt, 152
Brooks, Peter, 111
Buchholz, Laura, 55
Bundgaard, Peer F., 50
Burroughs, William, 109
Butler, Judith, 70; *Giving an Account of Oneself*, 93

Camus, Albert, 81, 151
Carpentaria (Wright), 53n2, 56, 60
Carter, Angela, 13, 16–28
cartoons, 73, 75, 76, 77, 79n9, 87, 90, 151
Cave of Time (Packard), 190
Cavell, Stanley, 184
Cet obscur objet du désire (Buñuel), 154
character, 116–22, 124–26, 128, 129, 135–60; actor vs., 152–56; antimimetic (*see also* character, unnatural), 135–60; cognitive theories of, 136, 158–59; contradictory, 138–42; doubling (theatrical), 155–56; fabricated entities, 144–46; imperfectly human, 137–42; insufficient traits for, 137–38; metacharacters, 146–51; mimetic, 124; multiple versions of same, 142–43; nonmimetic, 135; parodic, 143–44; performative aspects of, 151–58; synthetic, 119, 125; theories of, 135–36, 158–60; unnatural, 136–58
"Character, A" (Alfau), 146, 158
character narration, 125, 128
Chatman, Seymour, 70
Choose Your Own Adventure, 189, 192, 197, 200n8
Christin, Pierre, 175, 178
Churchill, Caryl, 154, 156
Clash of the Titans (Leterrier), 43
cliffhanger, 169
Cloud Nine (Churchill), 154
Cohn, Dorrit, 38, 50, 100
Comforters, The (Spark), 149
comics, 72, 72n3, 75, 80, 81, 83. See also graphic narrative
communal narration, 26
confabulation, 83
convention, conventionalization, 8–9, 32, 33, 190, 195, 200, 202–5, 217–18. See also habituation
conventional narrative, 13
coofying, 87
Coover, Robert, 112–13
counterfactual, 82, 84
counterhegemonic, 15, 15n2, 26
Create a Person, 157
Creature of Havoc (Jackson), 190, 202–5
Culler, Jonathan, 195
cultural discrepancies, 53, 54, 65
cultural relativism, 9–10, 211–12. See also cultural discrepancies
"culturalization": as reading strategy, 61
Currie, Gregory, 43, 50, 151, 210

d'Hoker, Elke, 51
Damasio, Antonio, 107n4, 108
defamiliarization, 32, 33, 36, 55–59, 64, 117, 165, 168–69, 184–85, 217. See also Russian Formalists
denarration, 41, 42n18

denaturalization, 15, 18, 27
Denooz, Laurence, 31n1, 50
Derrida, Jacques, 72, 81n10
dialogue, 40, 44, 45, 48. *See also* direct speech
Dictionary of Unnatural Narratology (Alber et al.), 14
diegetic level, 77. *See also* narrative level
différend, 93–94
direct speech, 45
disclosure functions, 45, 49
disnarration, 82
Dixon, Peter, 158–59
Docherty, Thomas, 138
Duchan, Judith F., 51
"Duck Amuck" (Jones), 157–58
Dungeons & Dragons (Gygax), 193

editor, fictional, 44
Eisner, Will, 167
emotion in narrative, 103–13; appraisal theory, 107; cognitive vs. affective responses, 107
empathy, 69, 79, 80, 94, 118, 212–14; authorial, 85; empathetic connection, 93; "false," 80; "fast tracks," 69, 94; "the long way 'round" 79, 80, 85, 87, 92–94; situational, 85
encyclopedia: cultural, 55; Doležel's notions of, 55n5; fusion of different, 57–59
epistemic consistency, 35, 38, 41
epistemology, 71, 79
essentialism, 15, 15n2, 21
ethos attribution, 120
experiential triggers, 108; and constraints, 111–13; in postmodern fiction, 109–10
experientiality, 5, 37, 42, 71, 130, 214; animal experientiality, 37
experimental fiction, 115, 116, 127
Extremely Loud and Incredibly Close (Foer), 103
"Eyes Have It, The" (Dick), 70

fabula, 165–68, 174–82, 216–17
faction, 44
fairy tale, 18
familiarization, 35, 49. *See also* defamiliarization; naturalization
Felski, Rita, 17n5
female voice, 18

feminism, 13–15, 209–10
Fernihough, Anne, 20
fiction, 73, 83, 91, 94, 95
fictional present, 38
fictional worlds, 10, 117. *See also* storyworlds
fictionality, 34, 35, 119, 127, 132
Fielding, Henry, 4
Fighting Fantasy, 157, 189, 190, 192–93, 197, 199, 201, 203
Fludernik, Monika, 7, 16, 32n3, 50, 51, 101, 102–3
Fokkema, Aleid, 138, 141
Forest, Jean-Claude, 177
Franklin, Aretha, 154
French Lieutenant's Woman, The (Fowles), 5, 71n2, 159, 216
Fresnault-Deruelle, Pierre, 167
Freud, Sigmund, 86; Freudian narrative, 87
Friedman, Susan Stanford, 211
Frow, John, 159

Gaboriau, Linda, 31n1
Galbraith, Mary, 45, 46, 51
Gallagher, Catherine, 159
gamebook, 189; a history of, 190–94; and conventionalization, 202–5; as unnatural, 194–202
"Garden of Forking Paths" (Borges), 191
Garuba, Harry, 62
gender, 14–17, 17n5, 21, 23, 25–27
gender impersonation, failed, 152–53
gendered subjectivity, 17
Genette, Gérard, 38n13, 51, 100, 101
genre, 86, 115, 116, 121, 131, 217–18
Gerrig, Richard J., 107, 136
Gibbons, Alison, 50
Gillon, Paul, 177
graphic narrative, 69, 72, 79, 80, 93, 94, 151, 156
Groensteen, Thierry, 72, 81, 94, 167–68, 172–73, 178, 182
Grusin, Richard, 184

habituation, 190, 204–5. *See also* conventionalization
Haldeman, Joe, 177
Handke, Peter, "Publikumsbeschimpfung" 138

Hansen, Per Krogh, 32n4, 33n5, 38n12, 38n13, 40n15, 50, 51, 52
Hawkes, John, 33; *Sweet William: A Memoir of Old Horse*, 33
Hazanavicius, Michel, 43; *The Artist*, 43
Heartbreaking Work of Staggering Genius, A (Eggers), 103, 110
hegemonic, 13, 14, 15n2, 17
Heinlein, Robert, 175
Heinze, Rüdiger, 31n2, 32n4, 33, 33n5, 34n6, 34n7, 38n13, 40n15, 41n16, 44n23, 50, 51, 52, 166
Helms, Lorraine, 153n14
Hergé, 169, 169 fig. 8.2, 182
Herman, David, 10, 32n4, 42n18, 51, 136, 198, 205
Herrmann, Anne, 153n14
heteronormative, 81, 87
Hirsch, Marianne, 17
historiographic metafiction, 95
Hite, Molly, 15n2
Hochman, Baruch, 136
Hogan, Patrick Colm, 107–8
Holocaust, 71, 73
Homans, Margaret, 15, 17
House of Leaves (Danielewski), 104–6, 109, 110
Hühn, Peter, 50
Hutcheon, Linda, 14

iconic solidarity, 72
identification (reader-character), 192–93, 196–99, 204–5
"Identity" (Alfau), 138
ideologically unnatural, 15
ideology, ideological concerns, 14–17, 20, 25, 27, 209–12
immersion, 118
implausibly knowledgeable narration, 38n13
implied author, 77n8, 121
implied reader, 59–60. *See also* authorial audiences
Importance of Being Ernest, The (Wilde), 144
impossible scenarios, 9–10, 32, 33, 34, 42, 53; division between possible and, 55–56, 58, 65; function of, 53–54, 62–64; humanly impossible, 32; impossible knowledge, 57–58, 61; logically impossible, 32, 33;

mind, 58–59, 63; physically impossible, 32, 56; impossible storyworld, 10, 49. *See also* unnatural
Improvisation, or The Shepherd's Chameleon (Ionesco), 155
inadequacy. *See* adequacy
Indigenous. *See* Aboriginal
interior monologue, 37, 41, 48
interpretation, 32, 48, 69, 70, 71, 73, 75, 77, 80, 85, 88, 93, 94. *See also* interpretational strategies; naturalizing reading strategies; unnaturalizing reading strategies
interpretational strategies, 32, 33, 34. *See also* naturalizing reading strategies; unnaturalizing reading strategies
intersectional feminism, 14
iterative, 75, 77, 78, 80, 84, 86, 92; iteration, 74, 83, 90, 92
Iversen, Stefan, 34n7, 51, 145, 190, 194, 212

Jackson, Steve, 189, 190, 192, 193, 199–200, 203–4
Jacobs, Edgar P., 176–77
James, Henry, 4
Jealousy (Robbe-Grillet), 216
Jousselin, Pascal, 167–68, 168 fig. 8.1, 182
Joyce, James, 93, 144. *See also Ulysses*

Keen, Suzanne, 69, 79, 80, 85, 94
"Kholstomer" (Tolstoy), 33, 37
Kilgore, Christopher J., 156, 212–13
Kim, Sue, 14, 17
Klauk, Tobias, 7, 32n4, 42n21, 49n25, 51
Klein, Dorothee, 211–12
Köppe, Tillman, 7, 32n4, 42n21, 49n25, 51
Kott, Jan, 143–44
"Kugelmas Episode, The" (Allen), 101–2, 105, 150
Kukkonen, Karin, 151

Leki, Ilona, 139
Leterrier, Louis, 43
linear narrative, 15, 17
linguistic constraints, 118, 122, 123, 127, 128; linguistic restrictions, 123
literary fiction, 116, 118, 131
Livingstone, Ian, 189, 192, 193, 199, 201
"Lost in the Funhouse" (Barth), 104–6, 109, 110

Love's Last Shift (Cibber), 160n21
Lucky Les (Hildick), 192
Lyotard, Jean-François, 70, 93, 94

Macbeth (Shakespeare), 5, 155–56
Madman and the Nun, The (Witkiewicz), 142
magical realism, 60–61
Maison de rendez-vous, La (Robbe-Grillet), 138–39
Mäkelä, Maria, 6, 70–71
Margolin, Uri, 141
Marker, Chris, 175
Martens, Gunther, 51
Mathieu, Marc-Antoine, 166, 173–74, 174 fig. 8.4, 185
Maus (Spiegelman), 69, 72, 73–80, 81, 83, 85, 87, 91, 95
McCay, Winsor, 170–72, 171 fig. 8.3, 182, 185
McCloud, Scott, 72, 74, 167, 172
McHale, Brian, 50, 102–3, 149
McLuhan, Marshall, 184
McMahon, Melissa, 31, 31n1
memoir, 72, 80, 85, 86, 92, 93
Mercier, Louis-Sébastien, 176
meta-mimetic, 116, 126, 129; meta-mimetic mode of representation, 126; metanarrative, 94
metafiction, 14, 18, 123, 124, 129
metalepsis, 75, 77, 99–106, 109–13, 123, 213; in story vs. discourse, 100, 102; narrational vs. lectorial, 101; rhetorical vs. ontological, 100–101, 102, 103; vertical vs. horizontal, 101
metareferentiality, 116
Metzengerstein (Vadim), 153
Meursault, contre-enquête (Daoud), 151, 159
Mézières, Jean Claude, 175, 178
Midnight's Children (Rushdie), 212n3
Miller, Alice, 86, 92
Miller, Frank, 43; *300*, 43
mimesis, 6, 7–8. 94, 95, 119
mimetic effect, 125
mimetic elements, 35, 126
mimetic form, 15, 15n2, 17, 21
mimetic model of narrative, 115, 128
mimetic narratives, 3–4, 69, 71, 72, 116
mimetic novel, 129

Mohanty, Chandra, 13
Moll, Andrea, 55
Montgomery, R. A., 189
Morrison, Toni, 70n1
Mouawad, Wajdi, 31, 34, 35, 36n10, 44n22, 49, 51; *Anima*, 31, 31n1, 33, 34, 35, 36n10, 37, 38, 39, 43, 44n22, 48n24, 49, 49n26, 51
Murphet, Julian, 159

Nabokov, Vladimir, 149
narratee, 121, 122; position of, 59–60
narration and narrators, 13, 18, 21–26, 34, 35, 36, 37, 39, 40, 40n15, 41, 41n17, 42, 42n20, 43, 45, 48; 69, 71–73, 75, 77, 78, 79–83, 85–95, 119–28, 130, 131; authorial, 120; autodiegetic, 119–21, 125, 130; covert, 125; disembodied voice, 125, 126; framing/embedded, 73; functions, 45, 49; heterodiegetic, 21, 26, 119–21; homodiegetic/first-person, 116, 119–20, 124–26, 128; nonmimetic, 215; omniscient, 1, 42, 42n20; overt, 125; reliability, 121, 124, 128, 130–31; second person, 189, 192, 193, 194, 195–99; technique, 69, 93, 94; theory, 70, 94; unreliable, 42n19, 116, 121, 128, 130. *See also* animal narrators; voice
narrative, definition of, 4, 214–16; basic elements of, 32; levels/layers of, 74–77, 77n8, 78 fig. 4.4
narrative discourse, 116, 118, 120, 124–28, 130
narrative form, 13–15, 15n2, 17
narrative situation, 35, 37, 44
narrative techniques, 42, 49
narrative theory, 14–15
narrative voice, 25
narratives, women's experimental, 14–16, 27
narrativity, 116, 117, 119, 122, 123, 127, 215
narratology, 128, 130, 131; classical, 32, 42, 42n21, 116; natural, 42; postclassical, 32, 42, 42n21, 115; rhetorical, 42, 121; structuralist, 130; transmedial, 166–67, 181–85; unnatural, 1–11, 115–16, 131
"natural," 16, 20–22, 24–25
natural elements, 35. *See also* mimetic elements
natural narratives, 10, 32
natural narratology, 42
natural response, 115, 116, 126, 131

230 • INDEX

naturalizing, naturalization, 15–17, 16n3, 27, 31, 33, 34, 35, 39, 42n19, 43, 44, 45, 47, 48, 49, 70–72, 75–77, 115, 126–30, 210
naturalizing reading strategies, 32n2, 33, 33n6, 34n6, 45, 46, 47, 48, 49, 49n26
"Nature Morte" (Sonenberg), 141–42
Neuville, Alphone de, 177–78
Niebla (Unamuno), 150
Nielsen, Henrik Skov, 1, 6, 31n2, 32, 34, 35, 35n8, 38n12, 38n13, 40n14, 40n15, 41n17, 42, 47, 48, 48n24, 49, 51, 210–11
Night of the Necromancer (Green), 197
"Night Sea Journey" (Barth), 145
Nights at the Circus (Carter), 16–18, 20–27
nonfiction, 69, 70, 70n1, 71, 81, 91, 94, 95, 212–13; unnatural, 70, 71, 212
nonmimetic narratives, 3, 32. See also antimimetic narratives
non-narrative, 116, 117, 131
nouveau roman, characterization in, 138–39, 141, 147
novel, 129; definition of, 216
now, narrative position of, 88, 89, 92
Nutshell (McEwan), 145

omnimentality, 42n20
ontology, ontological, 71, 75, 76, 77, 79
Orchids in the Moonlight (Fuentes), 153
oscillation, 76
Othello (Shakespeare), 43, 151

Pale Fire (Nabokov), 71n2, 77
Palmer, Alan, 63
panel, 72, 76 fig. 4.2, 81–83, 86, 87, 90, 91
paralepsis, 38n13, 44n23, 58–59; illusory paralepsis, 44n23
passepartout, 72
patriarchal, patriarchy, 87
Patron, Sylvie, 31, 42n21, 51, 210–11
Peeters, Benoît, 170, 172
Pentzell, Raymond J., 153
perspective, 13, 16, 21, 22–23, 26
Pettersson, Bo, 7
Pfister, Manfred, 138
Phelan, James, 5, 38n13, 42, 45, 51, 141n7, 160
Plato, 7–8
postcolonial, 54–55, 54n3, 54n4

postmodernism, 8, 13–15, 27, 70, 73, 81, 94, 95, 117, 118; feminist critique of, 13–14, 27; postmodern fiction, 116, 118, 126, 127, 130
present-tense narratives/narration, 42, 43
Prince, Gerald, 215–16
"Prisoner on the Hell Planet" (Spiegelman), 75, 156
Punday, Dan, 213
Purple Rose of Cairo, The (Allen), 110n5

"Quad" (Beckett), 138

Rabinowitz, Peter, 175
Rayuela (Cortázar), 191
reading process/practice/methods, 5–6, 31, 49, 58–61, 70, 71, 74, 75, 80, 85, 94, 115, 116, 123, 126, 131, 210–11, 212, 213, 214–15; first reading, 45; second reading, 35, 45, 47, 48, 49, 49n26; reading stance: in *Benang*, 54, 60, 64. See also naturalizing reading strategies; unnaturalizing reading strategies
realism, 4–6, 32, 69, 71, 81, 121, 130; psychological realism, 33. See also mimesis; mimetic
Reconstruction (Boe), 103–4
recursive, recursion, 81, 85, 87, 90, 92, 93
Reed, Ishmael, 70n1
Relapse, The (Vanbrugh), 160n21
relevance, 48
reliability, 34, 46–47, 48. See also unreliable narration
representational correspondence, 42, 43, 49, 210; limitation of, 43, 151
Restoration drama, casting of, 153
Revaz, Françoise, 169
rhyming, visual, 81, 83, 85, 86
Richardson, Brian, 1–11, 14–15, 24, 31n1, 32, 32n4, 33n5, 34n7, 35, 38n12, 38n13, 39, 40n15, 41n16, 42n18, 42n20, 51, 52, 54n4, 61n8, 69–71, 72, 80, 81, 99, 141, 156n17, 160n20, 166–68, 175, 184, 190, 194, 198, 200, 209–18
Ricoeur, Paul, 94, 183
Riou, Edouard, 177–78
River of Fire (Hyder), 142–43
Robbe-Grillet, Alain, 147
Robinson, Marc, 137–38
Romagnolo, Catherine, 209–10

romance, 18
romantic conventions, 18
Rosset, François, 176
Russian Formalists, 36
Ryan, Marie-Laure, 10, 202

Saint-Ogan, Alain, 176–77
Satanic Verses, The (Rushdie), 141
Sayre, Henry M., 155
Schaeffer, Jean-Marie, 8
Scott, Kim, 53n2, 54, 60. See also *Benang*
second person, 189, 192, 193, 194, 195–99
self-reflexivity, 69, 73, 75n6, 89, 94
Shakespeare, William, 152–53, 160. See also *Antony and Cleopatra*; *As You Like It*; *Macbeth*; *Othello*
Shklovsky, Viktor, 184–85, 217
Silko, Leslie Marmon, 212n3
Six Characters in Search of an Author (Pirandello), 146, 150
sjuzhet, 70–75, 80, 81, 83, 85, 88, 89, 94, 95, 172–73, 217; in comics, 166–74, 179–83; variable, 165–67
Skalin, Lars-Åke, 42n21, 52
Skriker, The (Churchill), 145
Smith, Will, 155
Snickers commercials, 154–55
Solaris (Lem), 145–46
Sommer, Roy, 104n3, 213–16
Sontag, Susan, 109–10
Stafford, Jeff, 153
Stein, Gertrude, "What Happened," 137–38
storyworld, 10, 18–19, 21, 24, 42, 49, 70, 71, 72, 74, 77, 81, 85, 86, 94, 95; impossible storyworld, 10, 49
Stranger Than Fiction (Forster), 103, 112, 148–50
subjectivities, 13, 17–18, 22, 26
Sugarcane Island (Packard), 192–93
supernatural elements, 212
Sweet William: A Memoir of Old Horse (Hawkes), 33
symbol, symbolic, 83
sympathy, 93–94

tellability, 119
temporality. *See* time, narrative

Terlaak Poot, Luke, 169
textual interpretation, 69
Thesmophoriazusae (Aristophanes), 152
Thon, Jan-Noël, 43, 52, 167
time, narrative, 7, 15, 24, 73, 74, 81, 86, 87, 88, 92, 179–81, 217; time of the narration, 38, 44. *See also* narrative situation, now
Time Machine, The (Wells), 195
time travel, 165–66, 174–84, 194–95, 216–17
Time Travel Dinosaur (Youngmark), 193
Tolstoy, Leo, 33
Tomashevsky, Boris, 167
Tomorrow Stories, 151
trait, 72
transnational feminism, 14–15
Travesties (Stoppard), 144
tressage, 94. *See also* braiding
Trollope, Anthony, 4
Trondheim, Lewis, *Bludzee*, 172
Turner, Mark, 5, 215
Tzara, Tristan, 144; "Le Coeur à gas," 138

Ulysses (Joyce), 93, 141, 144
undecidability, 71, 90
Unfortunates, The (Johnson), 191
Unnamable, The (Beckett), 141, 159
unnatural discourse features, 70, 72, 75, 77, 80, 84, 88, 95
unnatural elements and techniques, 8, 17, 33, 35, 40, 42, 44, 45, 49, 71–73, 80, 81, 86, 93–95; and non-Western texts, 55; function of, 54, 64–65
unnatural media, 166–67, 181–85
unnatural narration and narrators, 7, 58–59, 72, 73, 79, 81, 85, 91. *See also* unnaturalization
unnatural narrative: definitions of, 2–3, 8, 14–15, 53–55, 214; name, 10, 14–18, 27, 209–10, 212; poetics of, 69–70, 86, 93
unnatural narratives, 27, 31, 32, 33, 34, 49n25, 99, 115, 116, 130; and conventionalization, 190, 195, 200, 202–5; and gamebooks, 194–205
unnatural narratologists, 35, 40, 42, 42n21
unnatural narratology, 15–17, 27, 31, 33, 33n5, 34, 49, 95, 115, 116, 130, 131; history and development of, 1–2; paradigm, 6
unnatural nonfiction, 70, 71, 212

unnatural response, 126, 131
unnaturalization, 70
unnaturalizing reading strategies, 32n2, 34, 35, 45, 47, 48, 49, 49n26, 210–11

"Vampires in the Lemon Grove" (Russell), 145
Van Looy, Jan, 184
Verne, Jules, 176–78
"Verwandlung, Die" (Kafka), 145, 159
video games, 157
Vidocq, Eugêge François, 147
voice, 18, 19, 21–27, 35
Voice in the Closet, A (Federman), 111
Voice of the River, The (Thon), 145
Vol de Icare, Le (Queneau), 146–48, 150
Vultur, Ioana, 8

Wag the Dog (Levinson), 106–7, 109
Wagner, Frank, 147
Wake, Paul, 157, 217–18
Walton, Kendall L., 8, 43, 52

Ware, Chris, 168
Warhol, Robyn, 15, 106–7, 109
Warlock of Firetop Mountain, The (Jackson and Livingstone), 192n4, 193
Watchmen (Gibbons and Moore), 166, 179–81, 180 fig. 8.4, 183, 185, 217
Water Hen, The (Witkiewicz), 143
Weinsheimer, Joel, 159
Wells, H. G., 176
"What is Unnatural About Unnatural Narratology?," 15–16
Willie Masters' Lonesome Wife (Gass), 109
Winnicott, Donald, 86, 92
world making, 115, 118, 127, 129
Wolf, Werner, 99–100, 110n5
Woolf, Virginia, 86, 87, 92
Wright, Alexis, 53n2, 56, 60

You are a Cat in the Zombie Apocalypse (Tija), 197
You are a Shark (Packard), 197

THEORY AND INTERPRETATION OF NARRATIVE

JAMES PHELAN, PETER J. RABINOWITZ, AND KATRA BYRAM, SERIES EDITORS

Because the series editors believe that the most significant work in narrative studies today contributes both to our knowledge of specific narratives and to our understanding of narrative in general, studies in the series typically offer interpretations of individual narratives and address significant theoretical issues underlying those interpretations. The series does not privilege one critical perspective but is open to work from any strong theoretical position.

Unnatural Narratology: Extensions, Revisions, and Challenges edited by Jan Alber and Brian Richardson

A Poetics of Plot for the Twenty-First Century: Theorizing Unruly Narratives by Brian Richardson

Playing at Narratology: Digital Media as Narrative Theory by Daniel Punday

Making Conversation in Modernist Fiction by Elizabeth Alsop

Narratology and Ideology: Negotiating Context, Form, and Theory in Postcolonial Narratives edited by Divya Dwivedi, Henrik Skov Nielsen, and Richard Walsh

Novelization: From Film to Novel by Jan Baetens

Reading Conrad by J. Hillis Miller, edited by John G. Peters and Jakob Lothe

Narrative, Race, and Ethnicity in the United States edited by James J. Donahue, Jennifer Ann Ho, and Shaun Morgan

Somebody Telling Somebody Else: A Rhetorical Poetics of Narrative by James Phelan

Media of Serial Narrative edited by Frank Kelleter

Suture and Narrative: Deep Intersubjectivity in Fiction and Film by George Butte

The Writer in the Well: On Misreading and Rewriting Literature by Gary Weissman

Narrating Space / Spatializing Narrative: Where Narrative Theory and Geography Meet by Marie-Laure Ryan, Kenneth Foote, and Maoz Azaryahu

Narrative Sequence in Contemporary Narratology edited by Raphaël Baroni and Françoise Revaz

The Submerged Plot and the Mother's Pleasure from Jane Austen to Arundhati Roy by Kelly A. Marsh

Narrative Theory Unbound: Queer and Feminist Interventions edited by Robyn Warhol and Susan S. Lanser

Unnatural Narrative: Theory, History, and Practice by Brian Richardson

Ethics and the Dynamic Observer Narrator: Reckoning with Past and Present in German Literature by Katra A. Byram

Narrative Paths: African Travel in Modern Fiction and Nonfiction by Kai Mikkonen

The Reader as Peeping Tom: Nonreciprocal Gazing in Narrative Fiction and Film by Jeremy Hawthorn

Thomas Hardy's Brains: Psychology, Neurology, and Hardy's Imagination by Suzanne Keen

The Return of the Omniscient Narrator: Authorship and Authority in Twenty-First Century Fiction by Paul Dawson

Feminist Narrative Ethics: Tacit Persuasion in Modernist Form by Katherine Saunders Nash

Real Mysteries: Narrative and the Unknowable by H. Porter Abbott

A Poetics of Unnatural Narrative edited by Jan Alber, Henrik Skov Nielsen, and Brian Richardson

Narrative Discourse: Authors and Narrators in Literature, Film, and Art by Patrick Colm Hogan

An Aesthetics of Narrative Performance: Transnational Theater, Literature, and Film in Contemporary Germany by Claudia Breger

Literary Identification from Charlotte Brontë to Tsitsi Dangarembga by Laura Green

Narrative Theory: Core Concepts and Critical Debates by David Herman, James Phelan and Peter J. Rabinowitz, Brian Richardson, and Robyn Warhol

After Testimony: The Ethics and Aesthetics of Holocaust Narrative for the Future edited by Jakob Lothe, Susan Rubin Suleiman, and James Phelan

The Vitality of Allegory: Figural Narrative in Modern and Contemporary Fiction by Gary Johnson

Narrative Middles: Navigating the Nineteenth-Century British Novel edited by Caroline Levine and Mario Ortiz-Robles

Fact, Fiction, and Form: Selected Essays by Ralph W. Rader. Edited by James Phelan and David H. Richter.

The Real, the True, and the Told: Postmodern Historical Narrative and the Ethics of Representation by Eric L. Berlatsky

Franz Kafka: Narration, Rhetoric, and Reading edited by Jakob Lothe, Beatrice Sandberg, and Ronald Speirs

Social Minds in the Novel by Alan Palmer

Narrative Structures and the Language of the Self by Matthew Clark

Imagining Minds: The Neuro-Aesthetics of Austen, Eliot, and Hardy by Kay Young

Postclassical Narratology: Approaches and Analyses edited by Jan Alber and Monika Fludernik

Techniques for Living: Fiction and Theory in the Work of Christine Brooke-Rose by Karen R. Lawrence

Towards the Ethics of Form in Fiction: Narratives of Cultural Remission by Leona Toker

Tabloid, Inc.: Crimes, Newspapers, Narratives by V. Penelope Pelizzon and Nancy M. West

Narrative Means, Lyric Ends: Temporality in the Nineteenth-Century British Long Poem by Monique R. Morgan

Understanding Nationalism: On Narrative, Cognitive Science, and Identity by Patrick Colm Hogan

Joseph Conrad: Voice, Sequence, History, Genre edited by Jakob Lothe, Jeremy Hawthorn, James Phelan

The Rhetoric of Fictionality: Narrative Theory and the Idea of Fiction by Richard Walsh

Experiencing Fiction: Judgments, Progressions, and the Rhetorical Theory of Narrative by James Phelan

Unnatural Voices: Extreme Narration in Modern and Contemporary Fiction by Brian Richardson

Narrative Causalities by Emma Kafalenos

Why We Read Fiction: Theory of Mind and the Novel by Lisa Zunshine

I Know That You Know That I Know: Narrating Subjects from Moll Flanders *to* Marnie by George Butte

Bloodscripts: Writing the Violent Subject by Elana Gomel

Surprised by Shame: Dostoevsky's Liars and Narrative Exposure by Deborah A. Martinsen

Having a Good Cry: Effeminate Feelings and Pop-Culture Forms by Robyn R. Warhol

Politics, Persuasion, and Pragmatism: A Rhetoric of Feminist Utopian Fiction by Ellen Peel

Telling Tales: Gender and Narrative Form in Victorian Literature and Culture by Elizabeth Langland

Narrative Dynamics: Essays on Time, Plot, Closure, and Frames edited by Brian Richardson

Breaking the Frame: Metalepsis and the Construction of the Subject by Debra Malina

Invisible Author: Last Essays by Christine Brooke-Rose

Ordinary Pleasures: Couples, Conversation, and Comedy by Kay Young

Narratologies: New Perspectives on Narrative Analysis edited by David Herman

Before Reading: Narrative Conventions and the Politics of Interpretation by Peter J. Rabinowitz

Matters of Fact: Reading Nonfiction over the Edge by Daniel W. Lehman

The Progress of Romance: Literary Historiography and the Gothic Novel by David H. Richter

A Glance Beyond Doubt: Narration, Representation, Subjectivity by Shlomith Rimmon-Kenan

Narrative as Rhetoric: Technique, Audiences, Ethics, Ideology by James Phelan

Misreading Jane Eyre: *A Postformalist Paradigm* by Jerome Beaty

Psychological Politics of the American Dream: The Commodification of Subjectivity in Twentieth-Century American Literature by Lois Tyson

Understanding Narrative edited by James Phelan and Peter J. Rabinowitz

Framing Anna Karenina: Tolstoy, the Woman Question, and the Victorian Novel by Amy Mandelker

Gendered Interventions: Narrative Discourse in the Victorian Novel by Robyn R. Warhol

Reading People, Reading Plots: Character, Progression, and the Interpretation of Narrative by James Phelan

www.ingramcontent.com/pod-product-compliance
Lightning Source LLC
Chambersburg PA
CBHW020331240426
43665CB00043B/372